Blue Smoke

BLUE SMOKE

The Recorded Journey
of Big Bill Broonzy

ROGER HOUSE

LOUISIANA STATE
UNIVERSITY PRESS
BATON ROUGE

Published by Louisiana State University Press
Copyright © 2010 by Louisiana State University Press
All rights reserved
Manufactured in the United States of America
LSU Press Paperback Original
First printing

FRONTISPIECE: Big Bill Broonzy, 1930s booking agent publicity photo.
GAB Archive, Redferns Collection, Getty Images.

DESIGNER: Michelle A. Neustrom
TYPEFACES: Whitman, text; Chinese Rocks, display
PRINTER AND BINDER: McNaughton & Gunn, Inc.

LIBRARY OF CONGRESS CATALOGING-IN-PUBLICATION DATA
House, Roger, 1957–
    Blue smoke : the recorded journey of Big Bill Broonzy / Roger House.
        p. cm.
    Includes bibliographical references and index.
    ISBN 978-0-8071-3720-8 (pbk. : alk. paper)
    1. Broonzy, Big Bill, 1893–1958. 2. Blues musicians—United
States—Biography. I. Title.
    ML420.B78H68 2010
    782.421643092—dc22
    [B]
                                                    2010019179

For Mom and the family

When the Negro musician or dancer swings the blues, he is fulfilling the same fundamental existential requirement that determines the mission of the poet, the priest, and the medicine man. He is making an affirmative and hence exemplary and heroic response to that which Andre Malraux describes as *la condition humaine.*

—ALBERT MURRAY, *OmniAmericans*

Big Bill Broonzy's Martin & Co. guitar used during his late career as a folksinger.

CONTENTS

ACKNOWLEDGMENTS

THIS BOOK BEGAN MANY YEARS AGO AS PART OF MY DOCTORAL RESEARCH in the American and New England Studies Program at Boston University. I was introduced to the potential for popular songs to articulate social experience in the cultural anthropology class of Professor Anthony Barrand. My interest in art as a means of documenting the human condition in the Great Depression was awakened in the art history class of Professor Patricia Hills. This interest sharpened when I was hired as a researcher for a Public Broadcasting System documentary series on the Great Depression produced by filmmaker Henry Hampton. During the dissertation process, my research was guided to completion by Professors William Vance and Marilyn Halter, both of whom lent their expertise in literature and history, respectively, to the development of the project.

The pathway from dissertation to the present book was a long and often confusing process that benefited from the support of cultural institutions. Special aspects of this study were pursued under grants from the National Endowment for the Humanities, the Illinois Humanities Council, and most especially, David Tebaldi and the Massachusetts Foundation for the Humanities. The financial support of such institutions enabled the production of oral history programs for National Public Radio and subsequently some of the materials used for the book. Professor Henry Louis Gates and the W.E.B. Du Bois Institute for African and African American Research at Harvard University brought me in as a fellow and provided resource support in the early phase of the project. It also was helpful to talk out various aspects of my research as lectures at the Cambridge Center for Adult Education and the Lowell National Historic Park in Massachusetts, and as a guest speaker at numerous colleges in the United States, and in Japan as a J. William Fulbright scholar.

While the institutional resources were invaluable, the book would have stalled completely without the support of a community of scholars and friends. My colleagues at Emerson College, Jerry Lanson and Mike Brown, were essential advisers and cheerleaders throughout the development of the work. In a similar vein, my late friend and mentor Gerald Gill of Tufts University provided substantive suggestions and criticism. Historian James Green was a mentor and friend throughout the transformation of the work. My good buddy Preston Smith of Mount Holyoke College was a guide to key figures—and blues lounges—of Chicago. Professor Mark Sanders of Emory University illustrated the way in which the blues of folk culture was converted to the poetry of high culture in the imagination of capable writers. My friends Jon Millman, David Hebden, Jimi Yuma, and Kenneth Graham offered thoughtful suggestions and constant encouragement over the many years.

Finally, Jim O'Brien was critical in turning the mound of papers into a readable book, and Rand Dotson of LSU Press was key to bringing the work in from third base to home plate. This project relied on the special studies of blues culture to tell the story. As such, I cannot acknowledge enough the debt to which I owe the musicians and scholars of the many works on American cultural history that went into this book.

Blue Smoke

Big Bill Broonzy performing as a folksinger in a Brussels cellar club in the documentary film *Low Lights, Blue Smoke*. The film was produced by Belgian filmmaker Jean Delire in 1956. Although his black fans knew Broonzy as a sophisticated urban musician, he had to cultivate the image of the country folk singer for white audiences.

INTRODUCTION

THE SONGS AND STORIES OF THE BLUES SINGER WILLIAM "BIG BILL"
Broonzy (1893–1958) chronicle many aspects of black urban folklife in modern America. Raised on Mississippi and Arkansas cotton plantations, Broonzy
was positioned to take up the life of a sharecropper, the lot of many rural
blacks after Reconstruction. This way of life, however, was about to undergo
radical change as the farmworkers of Broonzy's generation were caught up in
the economic and social transformation of the industrializing South.

Broonzy was drafted into the army during the First World War and
shipped to France as part of the American Expeditionary Forces. He returned
to Arkansas with a different outlook on life's possibilities, seeing little opportunity in working as a field hand as farmwork became increasingly mecha-
nized. Broonzy joined the trek of sharecroppers to the smokestack cities of
the North—in his case, Chicago. Over time, he adjusted to urban life as a
laborer and part-time musician, gaining a reputation as a blues singer who
articulated the new outlook of the black working class. Broonzy later had the
opportunity to introduce the blues of the black urban folk to white youths in
the United States and Europe.

This book presents Bill Broonzy as both an important blues artist and an
archetype of the working-class black man. It places what was known about
his life in the context of the transformation of African American life that
took place over a seventy-year period of economic and social change that constituted an "Age of Blues." The lack of information about Broonzy's life has
made telling his story a challenge—much of what is known about him came
from Broonzy himself. A key source of my information was his often frustrat-
ingly whimsical autobiography, *Big Bill Blues*. Other sources included press reports, written accounts, oral testimony, films, and photographs. Constructing

Broonzy's story required peering through the haze of facts, statements, pictures, and songs to construct a larger mosaic of his life. I chose the title *Blue Smoke* to emphasize the challenge of telling the obscure story of an urban migrant. Yet, despite the gaps in the account, the portrait Broonzy rendered of his life and times provides one of the more substantial bodies of information left behind by a prewar blues singer.

Most of all, I sifted through the oral/aural statements captured on Broonzy's voluminous body of recorded music. Between 1927 and 1957, he released 997 sides of songs, stories, and music. In these works, Broonzy introduced social topics with a cast of characters from the world of ordinary folk. He spoke about sharecroppers, mule drivers, train conductors, prostitutes, barmen, policemen, shopkeepers, soldiers, and lovers in the changing locales of the plantations, towns, railroads, and ghettos. His recordings explored the themes of farming, poverty, unemployment, migration, gambling, drinking, and dancing. As a result, his recordings constituted a valuable resource for recovering the lost voice of an observer of a generation. My approach to Broonzy's blues songs follows that of the cultural historian Angela Davis, who argues that blues lyrics and themes "constitute a patchwork social history of black Americans during the decades following emancipation."[1]

My interest in Broonzy dates from the time I was studying the social effects of the Great Depression on ordinary people. I wanted to learn about the qualitative responses of black sharecroppers and urban migrants to the economic crisis. Influenced by Lawrence Levine's use of black oral culture in exploring the consciousness of the folk, I hoped to use recorded blues music to uncover sentiments that revealed critical thought. My research began in the blues collections of Boston-area libraries. One day, as I combed through the record bins of the Cambridge Public Library, I stumbled upon *Big Bill Broonzy Sings Folk Songs*, an old Folkways album with a cover photo depicting a thoughtful, middle-aged man. The photo—so different from those used on most blues albums—attracted my attention. I took the album home to see what this earnest-looking man had to say. Impressed by the confident voice and ragtime guitar picking, I decided to look further into the career of Big Bill.

I later came to see that his legacy was more complicated than the folkie image on the album might suggest. Broonzy was a key figure in the evolution of black popular music from the traditional folk songs to urban blues. He was part of a class of musicians who created a vital new blues for rural migrant audiences in the streets, tenement rent parties, taverns, nightclubs, dance halls, and recording studios of New York and Chicago. His music achieved unprecedented penetration in the black community through the mass distribution of records via direct sale, jukeboxes, and radio. Well known in the Chicago studios as a singer, guitarist, band leader, songwriter, and talent scout, Broonzy was one of most successful urban blues recording artists of the Depression era. I came to see in him the embodiment of the black American transition from rural folk to urban working class.

His standing in the black community, however, was at odds with the traditional image of his late career. I learned that Broonzy transitioned to a solo singer of rustic folk songs in the 1950s, a period when he was surpassed by innovative young blues artists. He opted to restart his career with a new following among young white audiences interested in Negro folk music. When exploring his musical transition, I noted other moments in his life when he felt stretched between the demands of black fans and white fans. At times, some white enthusiasts choose to overlook his role as an urban blues performer and to promote him as an icon of an antimodern black culture. Nonetheless, Broonzy used the opportunity to entertain white audiences to promote ideals of racial equality. He raised the consciousness of young white fans around the world in the critical early years of the civil rights movement.

My approach in this study has been influenced by the work of the cultural historians Paul Oliver, Lawrence Levine, Angela Davis, LeRoi Jones, William Kenney, Burton Peretti, William Barlow, Donald Spivey, and Guido van Rijn, scholars who generally hold that the lives, the songs, and the venues of blues and jazz artists are valuable sources for understanding the black urban folk experience. Oliver observed that the blues had "realized its greatest potential during the 1930s when the movement of thousands of migrants, the loss of jobs and the fruitless seeking for new work provided subjects for scores of recordings." William Barlow concluded: "As the collective voice of the black masses, the blues reaffirmed their historic quest for equality, prosperity, and freedom in the United States." He added, in regard to Broonzy, that Big Bill "was unique as a blues composer in that he wrote from the many vantage points he had experienced in his own rural-to-urban migration."[2]

This work puts Broonzy's story in the context of African American social and cultural history during the first half of the twentieth century. Chapter 1, "Born in the 'Age of Blues,'" reconstructs the story of the Broonzy family as they eked out a living as sharecroppers in the rapidly industrializing South. Chapter 2, "Makin' My Get Away," examines the impact of World War I on

Broonzy's life—his induction into the army and service overseas, and his out-look after returning to the plantation. Chapter 3, "House Rent Stomp," explores his participation in the postwar urban migration as depicted in song, story, and history.

Chapter 4, "Stuff They Call Money," examines Broonzy's urban blues recordings for commentary on the social impact of the Great Depression. Chapter 5, "Done Got Wise," presents his role as a leading figure in the urban blues of the 1930s, and the role of the blues in expressing a modern outlook. At the same time, the chapter describes Broonzy's debut as a crossover artist with white audiences. Chapter 6, "Blacks, Whites, and Blues," evaluates Broonzy's contributions to rhythm-and-blues music in the post–World War II period, and his new career as a singer of traditional Negro songs for young white admirers at home and abroad. Chapter 7, "Final Days," chronicles the end of his life and the outpouring of respect and love he received from fans around the world.

With this work, I seek to offer a comprehensive account of an important, but undervalued, prewar bluesman. I hope the reader gains an appreciation for Broonzy's contributions to the lives of ordinary people, to the entertainment industry, and to the white fans who turned to African American culture for insights, and who looked up to him as an ambassador of the blues.

1

BORN IN THE "AGE OF BLUES"

WILLIAM LEE CONLEY BROONZY TOLD STORIES ABOUT HIS PARENTS AND grandparents that placed them in the context of emancipation from slavery. His narratives were drawn from memory, folk song, and, no doubt, some measure of speculation. What was important, however, was that he chose to construct a personal history that expressed the themes of resilience, renewal, and optimism. The stories he told about his parents and grandparents were illustrations of the saga of black people stepping into the dawn of freedom.

The struggles of his parents and grandparents were part of a larger effort of black people to recover from nearly 250 years of slavery in North America. The descendents of Africans had endured a life sentence of labor; whites viewed them as beasts of burden to be exploited for maximum profit. Blacks cleared the land, planted the crops, developed the roads, seaports, and railroads, constructed the streets and buildings, tended the farm animals, nursed the children of the landlord, and bore their own children to be sold at auction. They were the human capital that created the wealth of the nation.

It took the Civil War to bring about their liberation. But freedmen began their new lives in the chaotic aftermath of war without assets or education, and among a hostile white majority with the education, resources, and military experience to thwart the blacks' efforts to achieve political power and economic self-reliance. These challenges for blacks formed the backdrop of Broonzy's family story.

Broonzy claimed that his parents, Frank Broonzy and Mittie Belcher, knew each other when enslaved as children on a cotton plantation near Baton Rouge, Louisiana. His father came from a family of four brothers and one sister with a tragic legacy of sexual oppression. His paternal grandmother was the illegitimate child of rape by a white man, perhaps the slaveholder, and

5

worked in the plantation house. Although it is not possible to confirm this allegation, Broonzy told the story often and, in doing so, highlighted the issues of race, power, and identity that were interwoven with his personal history. For example, he asserted that some family members had gained a sense of status from his grandmother's mixed racial heritage, to the point where she was punished for having a relationship with a dark-skinned man, his grandfather: "Her family throwed her out when she married my grandfather, because he was real black."[1] Nevertheless, she went on to have a family of six children with him, one girl and five boys.

This story raises a number of intriguing questions that cannot be answered based on available evidence: for example, what type of marriage was possible for his grandmother as a slave? Might this "marriage" have been in the custom of equating a pregnancy with matrimony? Would this explain why she was "thrown out," since as a house servant she is likely to have lived with the family of the planter? It also should be noted that Broonzy offered conflicting accounts about the size of his father's family. He once said that his father came from a household of seven boys and one girl.[2] Still, his stories consistently touched on issues such as the large size of the family, the preponderance of boys, and the importance some family members attached to having light skin.

Broonzy said he recalled his father's stories of the days of slavery. His father worked in the cotton fields, and it was in the fields that he met the dark-skinned slave girl Mittie, who came to his attention when she was punished for failing to pick cotton quickly enough: "He said they had to pick so much cotton a day and she didn't get her task done and he'd seen her get a lashing, after that he said he would pick cotton fast to get his task done and crawl through the grass and weed and help her, and he did that every day." Mittie came from a family of ten sisters and one brother, according to Broonzy. She worked in the cotton fields from a young age and decided early on to marry Frank because of the risks he took to help her during their childhood in bondage.[3]

Many men and women tested out their new liberties with caution, leaving the plantations with trepidation, unsure of what freedom meant and whether they would be punished for leaving; others remained on the plantations with family and friends, waiting out the postwar chaos until they could learn the fate of those who left.[4] Booker T. Washington recalled his mother's tears of joy upon learning of emancipation and a period of widespread rejoicing, followed by a sense of dread: "The great responsibility of being free, of having charge of themselves, of having to think and plan for themselves and their children, seemed to take possession of them. . . . In a few hours the great questions with which the Anglo-Saxon race had been grappling for centuries had been thrown upon these people to be solved."[5]

The families of Frank and Mittie joined the first mass movement of black people from the plantations to the towns and river cities of the South. While most did not know what this new freedom held for them, they were prepared to learn, to take risks and to explore new places in search of better opportunities. The joy of this moment gave a new secular meaning to the spiritual "Oh, Freedom":

> An' befo' I'd be a slave,
> I'll be buried in my grave,
> An' go home to my Lord an' be free.[6]

Although legally freed from slavery, blacks in Louisiana floundered in their first steps toward taking control of their lives. Many entered into coercive labor contracts designed by planters loyal to the Union. The planters found allies in the military, which sought to keep the plantations running by controlling black workers. Soldiers resorted to arresting men and women on the charge of vagrancy and forcing them back to work in the fields. Yet even in the midst of such obstacles, the new social and political advances of blacks often were too much for white southerners to accept. So-called "vigilance committees" began brutal campaigns to eliminate black leaders, organizations, and allies—in short, to reinstitute the reign of white supremacy. The postwar years were marked by acts of racial terrorism such as beatings, rapes, mutilations, and murders for the slightest offense real or imagined by a white southerner. In 1866, a group of black laborers rallying at a constitutional convention to demand equal suffrage were set upon by a white mob—48 men were killed and 166 wounded.[7]

In this climate, the families of Frank and Mittie began their new lives. It was at about this time that black families decided on their surnames. The process of selecting names represented a positive step toward self-definition, enabling people once considered property to establish a legal identity. Some dropped the first names given them in slavery, although others kept them; many had secretly taken surnames in bondage as a means of tracking lost loved ones, but few had official surnames because this was seen by masters as showing a slave too much respect.[8] In the case of Booker Washington, for example, selecting his surname was an act of privilege and self-determination. He devised his surname in a schoolroom when the teacher was taking attendance. Realizing that other children had surnames, and some had middle names as well, he found himself in a state of confusion over his own identity and sought to make himself the equal of all. When the teacher asked his name, he calmly stated, "Booker Washington"; he always would remember this act as one of dignity.[9]

After Broonzy's grandparents had selected the surnames Broonzy and Belcher, his parents eventually took another step in asserting their rights as human beings—they legally married. Broonzy's description of his parents' eagerness to marry supports the findings of recent scholars regarding the desire of blacks to form families with the protection of law. Thousands of freedmen and freedwomen took the marriage vows, sometimes in mass weddings involving as many as seventy couples.[10] Emancipation expanded blacks' matrimonial choices, but most often they chose a formal recognition of the commitments they had formed during slavery.[11] Broonzy's parents lived in an "extended household" near Baton Rouge, sharing a cabin with Frank's mother and others, an economically expedient living arrangement in freedom.

The arrangement, however, may have put some strain on his parents' marriage. Slavery had created tensions over the issue of beauty, status, and complexion for some people. It appears that Broonzy's light-skinned grandmother had problems with her daughter-in-law because of her dark complexion. Broonzy remembered hearing about his grandmother's "bitter tongue" and her insulting reference to his mother as "Black Mittie."[12] The stories reveal the complex psychology related to skin color in his family, at least in regard to this grandmother, who, as noted, once found herself embroiled in family conflict over her choice of a darker-skinned husband.

The preference among blacks for a lighter complexion was one of the legacies of slavery and segregation, highlighting a way in which white supremacy shackled not only the bodies of black people, but also their minds. Indeed, not only African Americans, but nonwhite peoples enslaved and colonized by European nations around the world have often internalized a standard of beauty that valorizes fair skin. Blues recordings document this issue of status based on complexion. Broonzy, for example, offers a protagonist who reveals insecurity over his complexion in the 1935 recording "I'm Just a Bum":

Yeah, sometime I wonder why my dad give poor me away (2×)
Lord, because I was dark in complexion, mmm, and, lord, they all
    throwed me away.[13]

Conversely, he created a persona who comments on the stereotypical connection of dark-skinned women and violent temperament in the 1935 release
"Evil Woman Blues":

I've got a real dark woman, just as sweet as she can be (2×)
Yeah, sometimes she get evil and talks on killing me.[14]

And, in the 1939 recording "Dreamy Eyed Baby," the character speaks about
the possibility for a woman of light complexion to pass as a white woman in
another country:

I bet you was a beautiful baby, lord, had them big black curls in your
    hair,
Gal, if you was over in England, I believe you would pass over there.[15]

Frank and Mittie Broonzy left Louisiana about 1870, at a time when the
state was rocked by political upheaval as white reactionaries attempted to
overthrow the racially integrated government. The Broonzys made a risky
decision to follow the Mississippi River in search of economic opportunity
and civil rights. In doing so, they joined a mass movement of blacks trekking
to the rich farmlands of the Mississippi Delta, in Mississippi and Arkansas especially. Many came in response to enthusiastic reports from family, friends,
and labor agents working for planters. Even the overthrow of the Mississippi
Reconstruction government in 1875 could not stem the flow of new residents
to the Delta.[16]

The Broonzy family found work on plantations in the Mississippi Delta.
Over many years, they would work hard as tenant farmers to make a good
life for their family. Most likely their living conditions resembled those of
many field hands: one-room cabins overcrowded with family and sometimes
friends; meals of fat pork and cornmeal bought at inflated prices from the
plantation commissary. While some farmworkers planted vegetables to supplement their diet, most opted to use the land for growing cash crops.[17] Over-
work and poor diet and sanitary conditions led to the common problems of
malnutrition and high rates of infant death, including in the Broonzy family.

According to Broonzy, his family had twenty-one children, of whom only sixteen survived to adulthood. He recalled his mother's stories about the stillborn deaths of three siblings and the infant deaths of two others. She attributed the losses to the rigors of plantation work during pregnancy.[18]

The infant survival rate of the Broonzy family, however, may have exceeded that of the average family in the region. For example, in Issaquena County, Mississippi, not far from where the Broonzy family lived, nearly one in two children died in infancy.[19] Broonzy mentions the names of several siblings—brothers Frank Jr., Jim, and Jerry, and sisters Gustaree, Desteria (an accurate spelling is not available), and Laney. All of the children pitched in on the plantation, but only two, Frank Jr. and Desteria, were encouraged to attend school. The family relied on them to write, read, and interpret official documents. Broonzy remembered how strange it seemed to watch his brother speak from writing on a page.[20] The story demonstrated the coordination of efforts that enabled the family to carry on. It showed that Frank and Mittie recognized both the necessity of hard work and the importance of education for boys and girls.

With the story of his birth, Broonzy evoked the theme of resilience in the face of adversity. He was born on a cotton plantation near Scott, Mississippi, during a time of change in the American economic system. His parents struggled to overcome tough times in the cotton fields. At the time of Broonzy's birth, they reportedly lived on a plantation in Bolivar County on the edge of the Mississippi River, a base of the Delta and Pine Lands Company, which managed the big plantations in the county.[21] A day before Broonzy was born, his father decided to ask the plantation commissary for food on credit, a sign that they were in dire need since borrowing meant sinking deeper in debt. As he left home, he asked an elderly midwife known as Auntie Lizer Thompson to stay with the pregnant Mittie. When he returned, Thompson met him at the door smiling broadly.

> "You done a good job this time," she said.
> "What do you mean?"
> "You shot both barrels this time," she said. "You got twins, a girl and a boy."
> Mittie kissed him and said, "Ain't you lucky?"
> But at that moment Frank, feeling more desperate than fortunate, said, "Like hell I'm lucky."[22]

Broonzy believed his date of birth to be June 26, 1893; however, his twin sister had birth papers showing a date of June 26, 1898.[23] While the actual year of birth may have been in question, the scenario he offered about his family revealed a larger truth about the conditions of poverty and hunger on the plantations. The year that Broonzy gave as his birth date, 1893, marked the worst year of a devastating economic recession. It was a time when the economy was so unstable that even oil barons like John D. Rockefeller worried about financial ruin, and the business periodical *Bradstreet* trumpeted the historic dimension of the collapse: "The business year 1893 promises to go into history with heavier net losses in financial, commercial, and industrial circles throughout the United States than in the more severe panic periods in the past eighty years."[24]

The 1890s saw the rise of industrial capitalism transform American life with the development of complex corporate organization in transportation, communications, utilities, natural resources, and agriculture. This web of interlocking economic activity incorporated the urban markets of the North and Midwest foremost, but also affected the cities, towns, and isolated farm districts of the South. In this decade, business managers assumed the leadership of industrial corporations. With their managerial expertise, they erected powerful and complex business organizations. At the center was a financial network of thousands of investors providing the funds for corporate expansion. New ventures in capital industries like steel and coal led to profound socioeconomic changes, from the growth of business institutions to the modernization of agriculture to the interconnection of global markets. The competition between corporations in the United States and those of other industrial nations fostered a search for markets around the world and influenced American leaders to connect the continent, embark on imperial adventures in the Caribbean, Latin America, and Asia, and send hundreds of thousands of young men like Broonzy into the Great War.

Corporate expansion brought rural areas into the national economy. In the rural Midwest and Northeast, whites responded to the creation of industrial jobs by abandoning farms and moving to the cities. Between 1860 and 1920, the mass movement of population transformed white America to an urban society and—along with immigration—created vast pools of labor for the steel mills, railroads, factories, and meatpacking houses. In 1865, for example, only fourteen U.S. cities had populations of more than 100,000; by 1929, the number had climbed to ninety-three.[25]

The South produced the raw material for the northern textile industry. As such, the Cotton Belt states made the most important commercial crop in America, for which it relied on a reserve of cheap black labor controlled through tenancy. In the 1890s, cotton agriculture began to undergo a dramatic change in response to the larger impact of monopoly capital. Over the next forty years, the transformation in plantation farming would set in motion the "Age of Blues" with profound consequences of social dislocation for black tenant farmers.[26]

This was the national economic framework in which Bill Broonzy's parents raised their family in rural Mississippi. The region was changing in ways they could not foresee and for which they could not prepare their children. Nevertheless, they taught their children the skills of survival such as mutual assistance, personal dignity, and spiritual integrity. Moreover, they taught them how to use music to foster group solidarity and cultural identity.

In addition to the economic change, Broonzy recalled that tenants had to endure periodic floods in the region. In fact, his parents may have used a flood to calculate his birth year, which he acknowledges in the song "Blues in 1890," an adaptation of the traditional Joe Turner ballad. As he tells the story, the year was 1892, and the sharecroppers had scrambled to survive a flood, watching the waters carry away the crops and leaving them to starve.[27]

Broonzy reinvented the ballad to express the turmoil encountered by his parents and community, and to illustrate the benefits of racial cooperation and mutual assistance. He framed the chorus with a spoken-word rendition of the legend of Joe Turner—whom he described as a composite of two men, a white shopkeeper named Turner and his black assistant, Joe.[28] Broonzy describes the surprise of hungry tenants when they return home after a day of hunting "rabbits, 'coons, 'possums, anything they could catch to eat." People were overwhelmed by the generosity of the mysterious patron who donated a bag of staple goods: "Then they would come home, look in their kitchens. They would find flour, meat and molasses that Joe Turner had left there for them."[29]

The family crossed the Mississippi River to work on plantations in Arkansas, where Broonzy grew to adulthood. He was unclear about the location or locations of the plantations that his family farmed but suggested that they lived on several farms over the years. For example, he spoke about the regions near the towns of Dumas and Lonsdale (which Lomax apparently misheard as Langdale). He later noted that his mother lived in Little Rock.[30] As a boy,

Broonzy recalled the close relationship with his twin sister, Laney, born about thirty minutes ahead of him. His father joked, "You came into this world behind a woman and you'll always be behind them."[31]

The two siblings spent most of their time together when growing up. However, he remembered starkly the time they were separated: they were hunting crawfish in a pond when he noticed blood in the water. He asked Laney if she had cut herself and guided her to land. They searched her feet and legs and found blood, but could not find the wound. Broonzy carried her home to their mother, who took charge. From that point onward, Bill and Laney were separated into the societies of men and women. Both had come of age—Laney through puberty and Bill, no doubt on the verge of physical puberty himself, by witnessing her maturation. Their innocence gone, Broonzy recalled, they could no longer share living spaces as before. Frank Broonzy took his son away, telling Laney that he was taking Bill to buy dewberry pie, and left him with an older sister. When he next saw Laney—he estimated it was eight months later—he felt that she had made the transition to womanhood. As Broonzy described the event, the separation was a type of coming-of-age ritual performed by his parents to help the children transition to adulthood.[32]

As a boy, Broonzy willingly turned his hand to whatever jobs were required of him. His narrative presents the image of a hustling young man who kept busy working on the farm, at various jobs, and in public performances. He remembered joining the ranks of the sharecroppers at about age ten, helping the family cultivate the land. He first learned to use a small plow that opened the earth for planting chickpeas. Over time, he would progress to an assortment of mule-drawn plows of increasing difficulty with such names as "Prairie Harry" and "Middle-Buster" that could tear apart thick grass and vegetation, cut deep grooves in the earth, and turn over soil for cultivation: "Of course I wasn't big enough at that time to handle the big plow, but the small ones such as double-shovels, single plows and things like that I could handle them. . . . After I got to be about 12 years old, I could handle all the plows then. We called them, down there, middle-busters—that was a man's job. When you got big enough to handle one of them, that's what they call a man's job. And I got so I could handle them kind of plows."[33]

His eagerness to master the craft of plowing marked a new phase in his development from a dependent boy to a productive man. This transition to adult contributor to the household income came with the reward of gaining the attention of young women. Broonzy noted with pride the interest girls showed in his development in a comment that, like a blues lyric, could be interpreted several ways: "I knew that all the girls like a big boy who could handle a middle-buster, so every year I tried to handle it and when I got fifteen years old I could handle all the plows on a farm."[34]

Cotton agriculture was subject to the whims of market forces, the commodity prices rising and falling in response to industrial demand. By 1910, about the time Broonzy learned to handle the plow, the prospects for young farmers had rebounded somewhat from the recession of the 1890s. While most blacks were sharecroppers, there also existed a class of more than 200,000 black landowners, including 124,000 in the southeastern cotton states. However, the larger economic transformation was making itself felt as plantations once owned by families fell under the control of insurance companies, banks, and corporations.[35]

Increasingly, the evolution of plantation agriculture left tenant farmers with little to show for their labor. As a result, Broonzy worked in a wide variety of menial positions available to blacks in the regional economy. Many were commonly known as "Negro jobs" such as caring for the children of a white family, collecting garbage, and cleaning streets. Other work included constructing levees and lining railroad track, working in semi-industrial fields such as coal mining and logging, and producing fertilizer and turpentine. While Broonzy's community was a stable agricultural district, as a young man he traveled to other areas such as the Arkansas Delta and Tennessee to find work. In one story, Broonzy migrated with a brother to work in a mine in Tennessee, where they earned a dollar a day plus meals and a bunk. Broonzy recalled the shift beginning at five and breaking for an hour at noon. Broonzy said he would return to his bunk at the end of the day and fall into it too tired to undress.[36] At one point, he was assigned to mine coal in a pit some twenty feet deeper than the other miners. He comments on the experience in a persona created for the 1940 recording "Looking up at Down":

> The men in the mine, baby, they all looking down on me.
> Gal, I'm down so low, baby, I'm low as I can be.[37]

However, while men found mine work hard and dirty, some women considered a black miner to be a good catch—a man with a steady job. Merline Johnson sang the praises of such men in the 1937 recording "Got a Man in the 'Bama Mine":

> I've got a ma-a-an in the 'Bama Mine,
> I can spend his dollars, like I can his dimes.[38]

The young Broonzy appeared willing to do every kind of job around. He described, for example, working in a levee camp, perhaps in the flood-prone Arkansas Delta, where he discovered that the overseers, like plantation bosses, would use tactics of intimidation and debt to keep workers under heel: "The only thing that is different between a levee camp and a prison farm is that a levee camp you can go from one levee camp to another when you get ready, you could run off."[39] In the 1939 recording of "Levee Camp Blues," Broonzy backs up Washboard Sam for a song that criticizes the rigor and injustice of levee work:

> We slept just like dogs; eat beans both night and day (2×)
> But I never did know just when we drew our pay.[40]

In Arkansas, Broonzy built roads in working conditions he described as awful. They worked under the hot sun, lived in tents, and ate miserable food. He said that a cook once prepared a bland soup of spoiled beans and collard greens from a camp garden, joking that the gruel was called "La-la-lu—if I don't like it, he do." The camps also could be lawless places that exposed young men to the brutality of hustlers and toughs. Generally crimes other than capital offenses were dealt with on-site with justice exacted by the whip or gun.[41] One could argue that such experiences helped to prepare Broonzy for the work culture of the industrial centers. In the mines, for example, he learned the regimentation of working by the clock, which fostered work habits suitable for the urban job market.

In his rural community, the young Bill Broonzy absorbed the ambience of rustic sounds, from the calls of animals to the rhythms of sawmills and train whistles. In this musical setting, he was taught the songs and stories that had fortified blacks through the experience of slavery to freedom—the spirituals, field hollers, ballads, minstrel tunes, ring dances, and string band performances constituted the panorama of music that would tutor the singers of the blues. Black musical culture was a force that galvanized group solidarity and articulated group responses to social conditions. The musician was highly regarded by some people in the community, at times singing songs and telling stories that addressed the same existential concerns as the preacher and teacher.

Broonzy demonstrated an early appreciation for this culture and a drive to express his feelings through music. He tried to imitate the sound of a fiddle by scratching out tunes on a makeshift instrument crafted from cornstalks: "That was my cornstalk fiddle. I rubbed it hard when I wanted a loud tone and I rubbed it easy when I wanted to play soft."[42] His story evoked the type of rural imagery that inspired poetry such as "The Corn-Stalk Fiddle" by Paul Laurence Dunbar, which describes the plantation festivities that took place after the harvest, the preparation of the instrument, and the joy with which men and women danced to the music:

> And you take a stalk that is straight and long,
> With an expert eye to its worthy points,
> And you think of the bubbling strains of song
> That are bound between its pithy joints—
> Then you cut out strings, with a bridge in the middle,
> With a corn-stalk bow for a corn-stalk fiddle.[43]

On his fiddle, Broonzy practiced his version of tunes heard around the plantation. He remembered calling out the lyrics as he played, while the children clapped and danced to the scratchy rhythms of "Turkey in the Straw" and "John Henry." While the version of "John Henry" he performed in boyhood was lost to time, the version he would record in the 1950s was a popular ballad of the "big man" legend. John Henry was a major heroic figure in U.S. working-class folklore, a renowned steel-driving man in the era of transcontinental railroad expansion in the mid-nineteenth century. His feat was to single-handedly defeat a steam-powered jackhammer in a contest to save the jobs of his section gang. Henry beat the machine but died as a result and became a martyr to the cause of the worker. Because he died from the strain of the contest, Henry's deed illustrated the vulnerability of workers trying to preserve their skills and jobs against replacement by the machine. Scholars of the legend offer different theories on its origin: Henry has been described as a slave in Missouri who competed with the Chesapeake and Ohio Railroad (C&O) in Talcott, West Virginia, in the 1840s; as a convict in Virginia leased to the C&O in the 1870s; and as a former slave who competed with the Columbus and Western Railway in Leeds, Alabama, in 1887. Broonzy's rendition presented an affirmative tale of working-class courage, sexual confidence, and self-assertion.

His most important boyhood mentor was Uncle Jerry Belcher, a blacksmith and local "songster" whom he mentioned frequently over the decades.

Belcher played a five-string banjo and innovated musically with a number of percussive farm tools. Broonzy remembered Belcher's workshop as a treasure trove of implements that he could turn into instruments that chimed, squealed, squeaked, hummed, and popped. As a singer, Belcher pulled from an encyclopedic memory of songs that spanned nineteenth-century African American folk music. Belcher entertained the community with a type of "juba" music created through the interplay of banjo, percussive accompaniment, and engaging songs and stories, often with the assistance of choral group singing: "They would sing and pat their hands, and to get different sounds some would pat their hands hard and some of them would rub their hands together. When they sang, there would be a woman between every two men. They would put a young man with an old man and that was their bass and tenor, and an old woman and a young girl together for their alto and soprano."[44]

Belcher created rich harmonies by tapping the points of plow blades like a xylophone, beating a washtub with sticks, and rubbing a broomstick between a tabletop and his wet hands. He had learned to create musical tones from plow blades when sharpening them. He would suspend the blades from wires and arrange them in order of ascending tones, selecting them so that the various tones matched his voice. He played drums on an old washtub, discovering one day when repairing the tub that he could make appealing music with it. And he mastered the broomstick as an instrument by rubbing the handle against his wet hand and fingers.[45] Belcher formed a duo with a friend named Stonewall Jackson, with Belcher playing the washtub and broom handle while Jackson chimed in on the plow blades. Broonzy's stories reflect a broad tradition of instrumental innovation and craftsmanship at the time, including the use of jugs, washboards, quills, harmonicas, fiddles, mandolins, and kazoos to make music.[46]

Belcher was part of a folk music tradition common in African American rural communities. Such troubadours served an important role as community entertainers, using music, song, and story to amuse and affirm, and sometimes to comment on daily life. These musicians served an important purpose in folk culture, even if they were sometimes criticized for living the fast life. Broonzy said that his uncle cared little for church, liked to drink, and enjoyed teasing churchgoers by playing music that would begin as a spiritual but evolve into the blues.

He credited Belcher with teaching him spirituals, ballads, and reels such as "Crawdad Blues," "Frankie and Johnnie," "Mindin' My Own Business," "Alberta," "This Train," and "John Henry."[47] Belcher passed on the beloved narrative ballads of the community, sharing with his nephew some of the most compelling folk songs in American culture, and a means of using song to express popular values that Broonzy later drew upon in the urban folk forums of the rent party, tavern, and studio. An example of a traditional folk song carried over to audiences in his late career was the 1956 recording "Mule Riding–Talking Blues." The protagonist encounters animals and people during a slow ride on a country road to town. (Broonzy apparently confused the location of the animals during the recording session.):

> One day I was riding along, riding my old mule
> Minding my own business, wasn't bothering a soul
> And I see the possum, and see the raccoon
> The possum was up in the 'simmon tree
> And the raccoon was on the ground
> The possum holler up to the raccoon
> Says, "Hey, Bub, throw me some simmons down."[48]

The song goes on to describe a conversation with a rabbit, an argument overheard between a rooster and a hen over the rooster's infidelity, a plan being hatched between a black cat and a yellow cat to party in town, an invitation by a man in a Cadillac to a pretty woman to ride with him, and a passing chat with a man in a whorehouse. The "Talking Blues" borrowed from a traditional fiddle tune dating back to the days of slavery called "Bile Them Cabbage Down." The square-dance "reel" refers to the relationship of a raccoon and a possum primarily, but also introduces the characters of the jaybird and sparrow. The following is one of the stanzas that Broonzy adapted to his song:

> Possum up a 'simmon tree,
> Raccoon on the ground,
> Raccoon say to the possum,
> "Won't you shake them 'simmons down?"[49]

Another example of a folk song taught by his uncle was "Crawdad Blues." His uncle told him that the song was used as a lullaby during slavery to send children to sleep. Broonzy recalled that just as the women had settled the children down, the men would return home and disturb them with their rowdy behavior. The men would get drunk on a concoction called "ruckus juice"—a type of firewater drawn from the grain fluids that settled at the bottom of the silo. The delightful recording tells about the misfortunes of a man who spent the day catching crawdads only to lose them when his bag rips open:

Man fell down and he broke that sack, now honey (3×)
You might have seen them old crawdads going back, now honey, baby
   mine.[50]

Broonzy once claimed that his uncle lived to be 107 years old. He told this tale to a folk music producer, no doubt for the purpose of homespun entertainment. Broonzy described his uncle as a courageous plantation singer and entertainer, and in doing so turned him into a folk hero in his own right.

Broonzy gave a similar depiction of a riverboat fiddler named See See Rider, a songster who captured the hearts—and money—of people in the plantation community. Rider was an itinerant musician, spreading folk songs, ballads, and primitive blues throughout the countryside. His real identity was unknown, but Broonzy remembered him as a short man of about 140 pounds, said to be a former slave, who played a one-string fiddle; but most of all he remembered him as one of the first singers of what would later be called the blues. "We didn't call it the blues, that was after years later," Broonzy said. "We called it Negro reels, a square dance."[51]

Rider apparently was part of the songster tradition, popular entertainers who performed songs and music to street audiences. The songsters were "a class of black American musicians of the post-Reconstruction era [who] performed a wide variety of ballads, dance tunes, reels, minstrel, coon and ragtime songs, a repertory that overlapped with that of white rural singers. In many areas, these popular bards were called 'songsters' if they sang well, 'musicianers' if they played fiddle or banjo well, and 'music physicianers' if they both sang and played well."[52]

Broonzy listened in awe to the music of See See Rider and witnessed his cool way of dealing with the public: "See See Rider came through when I was about 9 or 10. He sang a tune, 'See See Rider,' but he played it slow. . . He didn't have to pay no train fare, just get on the train and ride, got free meals, free place to stay. He didn't have to work. He'd go in any restaurant, they'd give him food and he'd sing a couple of songs. He's the first guy I seed had a one-string fiddle. . . . I'd never seen a fiddle like that."[53]

See See Rider associated himself with the popular character of a blues song recorded by Ma Rainey in 1924 (but by Broonzy's estimate in vogue some twenty years earlier). In one version of the song, Rider was the object of affection of a woman tragically enthralled with the fly-by-night lover. She blamed him for leading her astray, unwilling to accept that he was a philanderer by nature.

In his 1934 recording of "C. C. Rider," Broonzy lent a double meaning to the name, both as the protagonist and as a reference to making love—C. C. Rider, for example, set out to give all his loving to his "Rider." By comparison, in a 1957 recording, Broonzy mixed aspects of the traditional song with memories from his youth and political commentary. The later C.C. Rider was a stevedore living on the riverboats and dreading the prospect of working as a sharecropper. While in the 1934 recording the protagonist laments that "My Rider done got so that she treats me like a dog," in the 1957 recording the character makes the open-ended proclamation that he would rather be dead than exploited:

> My home is on the water; I don't like no land at all (2×)
> I'd rather be dead than stay and be your dog.[54]

Broonzy recalled See See Rider working as a riverboat "roustabout." These were men who loaded goods such as cotton, potatoes, and corn in Mississippi and Arkansas and delivered them to New Orleans, Memphis, and St. Louis. Their travels to other cities, and interactions with different types of people, gave them a worldliness respected by the country folk. The recollections of Piano Red Williams, who worked as a "rousta" when a teenager, offer some insight into the life of a stevedore: "How it would be, you would stop at some landing, you'd have to pick up five hundred bags of cottonseed. And you'd have one or two families to move. Then you would have to worry with some mules. But three or four men get a poor mule, he wasn't more than a little puppy. The baddest thing you could handle was a crate of chicken 'cause they be flopping and going this side and that side in that crate."[55]

In time it appeared that Rider left the riverboats to make his way as a wandering bard. He allegedly found that he could curry favors of meals, train rides, and petty cash in exchange for songs. He was well known for his one-string cigar-box fiddle, an instrument reminiscent of the halam, a traditional West African instrument akin to an early type of banjo. A banjo player named "Fast Black" accompanied him.[56]

As a boy, Broonzy trailed behind Rider in fascination, hungry to learn more about his instruments, playing technique, and songs. Besides the fiddle, Rider also played a homemade guitar and bass, and taught Broonzy to construct his own fiddle and guitar. In this way, Rider mentored the ten-year-old in the traditions of folk music. Under Rider's tutorship Broonzy constructed his first instrument—a cigar-box fiddle to replace his cornstalk fiddle:

> Then I went to the commissary and they give me a cigar box and a big wooden box, and me and my buddy name Louis made a guitar out of the big box and I made a fiddle out of the cigar box. Then I went to the woods and cut a hickory limb and I stole thread from my mama to make a bow. Way we got strings, me an Louis would go to the picnics and barrelhouses and wait for See-See Rider to break a string. We would tie them broken strings together and put them on our homemade instruments. And when See-See Rider seed I knew how to play, he holp me fix the strings and showed me some few tunes, so Louis and me could play "Shortnin' Bread" and "Old Hen Cackle" and "Uncle Bud."[57]

It was a common practice for musicians to make their own instruments, and "nearly every blues guitarist has a story to tell of his 'diddley bow.'" The fiddle instruments included every musical contraption from a wire nailed to a fence to a cigar box with a broomstick for guitar or fiddle; but the totality of instruments ranged far wider, including jugs, "metallophones" made from plows, kazoos, and washtub bass.[58] Bluesman Furry Lewis, for example, recalled making his first instrument: "Well, I guess I was 'bout twelve, thirteen years old, something like that, when I first started playing guitar. I didn't have none so I got a cigar box, I cut a hole in the top, put a board and nail it on there. And I taken four nails, put wire on 'em from a screen door for strings. I couldn't play it, but I rapped the sides, hootin' and hollerin'."[59]

Through the influence of Rider and other such men, Broonzy began his apprenticeship as a "songster." Beyond the music, however, these men also helped Broonzy to shape an outlook on life as a black man. They showed him ways of living with dignity in the midst of social and financial constraints, and how to use music to satisfy the emotional needs of the community.

Many of the songsters were men like Belcher who lived in the community where they entertained and primarily worked as sharecroppers and blacksmiths; others, less fortunate due to blindness or infirmity, sang in the streets for coins. Songsters performed at fairs, racetracks, cookouts, plantation balls, and barn dances, demonstrating proficiency on banjos, guitars, fiddles, mandolins, flutes, jugs, spoons, washboards, and tambourines. In addition, the professional songsters traveled with minstrel troupes, circuses, and medicine shows (helping to hype various cure-all elixirs). These shows originated in southern cities and passed through rural communities across the South. Broonzy most likely would have been exposed to songsters from outside his community from the traveling shows and itinerant musicians of Little Rock, Memphis, New Orleans, and St. Louis. Such performers were steeped in the latest tunes of minstrelsy, ballads, blues, and dance rags, and in the emerging music of blues. In a roundabout fashion, songsters took the folk music of the plantation and adapted it for urban performances, and then returned to the plantations with both new material and modified standards.

As a teenager, Broonzy distinguished himself as a fiddler of dance music on his one-string fiddle. He played rag dances, a syncopated swing music spawned in the frontier culture of black territory communities. (He would demonstrate his fiddle playing in "Mountain Girl Blues" and other early recordings.) Dance rags were performed by banjo players as well as by bands comprised of such instruments as fiddles, fifes, triangles, and quills. The music, which drew from folk tunes, spirituals, and dance music, may have earned its name from the practice of women dancing while waving handkerchiefs called rags or from its ragged-sounding syncopated beat.[60]

Throughout his recording career, Broonzy's music displayed the influence of ragtime syncopation. For example, the lively rhythm was evident in the 1927 version of "House Rent Stomp," when he teamed up with fellow guitarist John Thomas to create a slick, upbeat dance tune. There was a sense of optimism and joy in this music that was absent from the work of contemporary Delta blues recording artists. Even when Broonzy was playing the blues, in fact, the undercurrent of ragtime syncopation at times could be heard, distinguishing Broonzy's sound from that of Chicago bluesmen and leading some scholars to claim that Broonzy was a difficult artist to categorize. One reviewer noted that "hard blues" is played in the key of E, but that Broonzy tended to rely on the "key of C with its heavy ragtime accent."[61] The reality, of course, is that black popular music—particularly before the standardizing influence of recording studios—had drawn from a variety of folk and religious musical influences. The "blues" genre was a creation of song publishers and music producers as a means to market what were then called "race records," an inoffensive way of categorizing the recordings of black music.

In examining Broonzy's musical influences, it is important to consider the music culture of the Delta towns and the city of Memphis. The Age of Blues evolved in the context of an emerging industrial capitalism and its effects on plantation agriculture. From the 1890s, sharecroppers made redundant on the plantations began moving to Delta cities and towns like Clarksdale and Cleveland, Mississippi; Helena, Arkansas; and Memphis. These places were cultural crossroads where the taverns became musical laboratories for singers from the fields of Tennessee, Mississippi, and Arkansas. In these sites, the musicians began adapting songs and music to reflect changing circumstances; in doing so, they sparked the evolution of the modern blues.

In the first decade of the twentieth century, William Christopher Handy—the academically trained composer and leader of "respectable and conventional bands" known as W. C. Handy—took notice of the new music he was beginning to hear in the railroad depots and dance halls of the Delta towns. Handy first heard the blues in 1903, when he was directing the Knights of Pythias band in Clarksdale. An itinerant songster sang it on one occasion, a ragtag trio on another. Recognizing the vitality of this music, Handy codified the sound through the publication of popular compositions like "Memphis Blues" in 1913. His contribution was to standardize the new music that would become known simply as "the blues."[62]

It is not by coincidence that Handy named his hit song after the city of Memphis. The taverns, nightclubs, restaurants, dance halls, and theaters of the red-light district of Beale Street in Memphis were a magnet for musicians. In the early decades of the twentieth century, the city was one of the hotbeds of jazz and blues, rivaling New Orleans and St. Louis. By 1900, Memphis had an estimated population of 100,000, about 50 percent black, with an emergent working class. But along with the legitimate entertainment spots of Beale Street came the gambling dens and whorehouses. Corruption was rife in the police department and the administration of Mayor Edward H. Crump. By 1920, the rate of violence and vice had soared on Beale Street, victimizing blacks most of all, and leading to several efforts to crack down on crime. At the same time, Beale Street offered a variety of musical entertainment catering to the tastes of both black and white patrons. It was this combination of excitement and notoriety, opportunity and poverty, private clubs and public concerts that drew so many regional musicians to the notorious Beale Street.[63]

Broonzy may have heard the music of Memphis from minstrel troupes and vaudeville revues sponsored by the Theater Owners Booking Association (TOBA). Founded in Memphis in 1907, the TOBA attempted to create a chain of theaters in the South for black vaudevillians. The TOBA provided valuable exposure for entertainers such as Bert Williams, Bill "Bojangles" Robinson, Eubie Blake, Ethel Waters, Bessie Smith, and Ma Rainey. The stage shows drew large crowds to theaters across the South. The shows became the premier cultural activity in urban communities, and no doubt spread into the rural areas as well.[64] Broonzy may have been exposed to songs from sheet music distribution, piano rolls, and early cylinder and disc recordings. Although he never mentioned listening to such music, these were common ways of disseminating popular songs, making it quite possible that Broonzy heard the tinny sound of early recordings in rural Arkansas.

Broonzy claimed that he had to defy his parents to pursue his interest in secular music, going so far as to hide his instrument and perform in secret. Because of the powerful influence of the church and its stark depiction of the struggle between heaven and hell, many people equated secular music with Satan. Broonzy, for example, remembered his parents' disdain for such music: "My mother was a Christian, my dad was a Christian an' all the—the whole family was all Baptists an' they didn' think it was right that I should go an' play a fiddle, play the blues an' barn dance songs and thing like that. But anyway we went on through with it."[65] Broonzy's recollections on this issue were not without contradictions, however: he also said that people in the community admired the musical talent displayed by his uncle Jerry Belcher, by See See Rider, and, later, by him.

As a boy, Broonzy navigated the politics of crossing over to white audiences. He was about ten years old the first time he was invited to perform for the plantation boss. Broonzy and a friend named Louis Carter decided to host a dance party for the other children. They supposedly broke into the family chicken shack to steal three birds, which they killed and roasted. As the birds cooked, Broonzy said they played a dance tune that they called the "The Chicken Reel." He sported his one-string cigar box fiddle. His story evoked the kind of folksy image that had inspired such literary characters as Edgar Lee Masters's delightful Fiddler Jones—"And if the people find you can fiddle / Why, fiddle you must, for all your life."[66]—or the meticulous Jim the fiddler in Paul Laurence Dunbar's poem "The Party":

> Jim, de fiddlah, chuned his fiddle, put some rosum on his bow,
> Set a pine box on de table, mounted it an' let huh go!
> He's a fiddlah, now I tell you, an' he made dat fiddle ring.
> Twell de ol'est an' de lamest had to give deir feet a fling.[67]

The festivities were interrupted by the appearance of the white plantation boss, named "Mr. Mack." He questioned them about the chickens and then told them to carry on. Mr. Mack was so impressed with the performance that he brought the boys home to play for his family. He later asked Mittie Broonzy for permission to have Bill play on occasions, and she apparently agreed.[68] Mittie's willingness to let Bill perform seems at odds with other statements regarding her low opinion of secular music. Perhaps she gave her permission because it was an opportunity for Bill to win favor with the boss, or perhaps she did not feel free to turn down the request of a planter. The larger implication of the story is that, faced with a conflict between her Christian values and the interests of a powerful white figure, Broonzy's mother thought it best to yield to the wishes of the planter. (And, of course, Broonzy's own preference apparently was not taken into consideration at all.) This story provides a glimpse into Broonzy's early awareness of the power that a white promoter could exercise over his talent.

Mr. Mack "hired" the boys shortly thereafter. Broonzy and Carter played for parties, fish fries, and events known as "two-way picnics," where the sponsor set up two stages—one for the black band and one for the white. Payment to the young musicians was made in the form of secondhand clothes and party food. Broonzy practiced all the harder when he was not helping his family in the field. He became known as a wizard on the homemade fiddle, earning the admiration of both blacks and whites in the community. At some point, Mr. Mack acknowledged Broonzy's and Carter's talent by providing them with a new fiddle and guitar from the famous Sears, Roebuck and Company in Chicago: "I practiced for a long time till my brother-in-law showed me how to tune the fiddle. He could tune it, but he couldn't play it, and I could play it but not tune it. So they used to pay him to tune and me to play."[69]

Broonzy told this anecdote to Alan Lomax, but he also told the folklorist another version of the incident. In the alternate version, he claimed to be at work behind the plow when Mr. Mack approached him and said: "Well, here's a note. Go down to town and tell the man to give you a fiddle." Broonzy asked if he could play with his friend Louis, and the man said to buy Louis a guitar as well. Broonzy picked up his friend on the way: "We went to town an' we got the fiddle an' the guitar an' things—come back out on the plantation we started playin."[70]

Some years later, Broonzy quit performing and committed himself to living the life of a devout family man. He married his church sweetheart Gertrude Embrie and took up preaching. One afternoon as he worked in the field, he took a break to drink water brought by his wife. They were approached by Mr. Mack, who asked Broonzy to play at a picnic and offered him fifty dollars and a new fiddle—which, if true, was tremendous pay for a struggling field hand. Broonzy declined, saying that he was committed to preaching and no longer interested in performing. When Mr. Mack insisted, his wife took the money and promised that Broonzy would show up.[71] Whether or not this incident actually occurred, the story again implies a tension over the ability of a white patron to influence the course of his music and life.

As a crossover entertainer, Broonzy also dealt with conflict over the type of music his white supporters thought appropriate for him to play. For example, most whites tended to look down on the folk music popular with black audiences. As Broonzy recalled, whites preferred simpler standard waltzes and folk songs like "Over the Waves," "Missouri Waltz," and "On the Road to Texas," and they asked him to change his repertoire. In a foreshadowing of the demands placed on him later in his career, Broonzy adapted his music to suit the tastes of the new audience.[72]

Broonzy was not alone in discovering the conflict inherent in being a crossover artist. For example, Arthur "Big Boy" Crudup recalled the pressures placed on musicians selected to play for white audiences: "A colored person couldn't play for a white person if he couldn't play instrumental music and love songs and waltzes and all of that. He couldn't play for white people because white people did not fancy the blues."[73] Such comments shed light on the larger phenomenon of the racial boundaries imposed on black musicians. During this era, black musicians often were limited to performing spirituals, minstrel tunes, and other music that white audiences considered quaint or comedic. Benjamin Filene argued that white folklorists typically were reluctant to grant black music the respect afforded to the "authentic" folk music of immigrants from the British Isles and Europe.[74]

Over time, Broonzy's popularity with whites led to a sense of estrangement from his people. In the tradition of racial segregation, whatever whites enjoyed had to be restricted from blacks. Thus, as an entertainer, Broonzy found himself disconnected from blacks, a far different result from what he had expected as a songster. It meant that he had to abandon his cultural context to enjoy the perks of playing for whites. At one point, he expressed exasperation over the limitation, saying: "Why didn't I play for Negro dances? Well, you see the way the white man is in the South is this. Anything's good, they think it's too good for the Negro."[75]

Until the time he left Arkansas, however, he used his relationship with white patrons to his advantage. He stopped playing for handouts and began to ask for cash payments. His reputation as a top fiddler enabled him to travel around Arkansas, Mississippi, and Texas to perform. The parties allowed him to supplement the family income and perhaps build up enough of a down payment to either rent or buy land.[76] Ultimately, Broonzy's experience as a crossover artist helped him to develop the composure to appeal to larger audiences. Thus Broonzy emerged from the apprenticeship in folk culture with the skills that would allow him to evolve as an urban blues singer. His mentors showed him how to carry himself with dignity and create songs and stories that articulated the experience of the folk. Little did he realize the way that international events would reach into the plantations and transform the lives of ordinary people.

2

"MAKIN' MY GET AWAY"

WILLIAM BROONZY CAME TO MATURITY IN A POOR BUT STABLE PLANTA-
tion community in Arkansas. He was prepared to live a modest life much like
that of his parents, but circumstances intervened to alter his future dramatically. At the same time that industrial changes in cotton agriculture made
tenant field labor increasingly obsolete, the United States mobilized for engagement in the Great War. Broonzy was among the hundreds of thousands of
young men drafted to serve in the army, and his military experience changed
his outlook on life. From that point on, he considered alternatives to tenancy
and explored the possibility of leaving the plantation for the urban ghettos.
This chapter examines Broonzy's stories and songs in the context of black
reactions to agricultural change, industrial expansion, and military intervention during the World War I era.

For black sharecroppers, the transformative period led to a time of mass
dislocation and insecurity that would constitute an "Age of Blues." The recorded songs of Broonzy and other singers express popular responses to the
profound socioeconomic changes of the time. These recordings tell stories
that validated black tenant farmers' sense of loss and disorientation during a
time when the social networks of church and family were falling into disar-
ray. Moreover, the recordings pose a counterpoint to the minstrel depictions
of blacks found in popular programs such as the *Amos 'n' Andy* radio show and
in advertisements and vaudeville theaters.

As the engines of industrial power, the major U.S. corporations strength-
ened their influence by expanding to overseas markets. American foreign
policy supported such growth by encouraging the control of markets and
resources in the Caribbean, Latin America, and China. In 1912, President
William Howard Taft designated the use of military power in support of cor-

porate interests as "dollar diplomacy." In similar fashion, the competing industrial nations of Germany, Britain, and France advanced their economic interests by imposing colonialism in Asia and Africa. The colonies became more valuable to the ruling countries during times of recession, when monopolistic corporations more keenly felt international competition. This was the case in the United States on the eve of World War I.

The Great War involved numerous issues, but foremost was international tension over trade and colonial markets. Initially the United States sought to remain neutral as its industrial competitors Britain and Germany vied for allies: in the Triple Alliance were Germany, Austria-Hungary, and Italy (and later Turkey). The Triple Entente consisted of Britain, France, and Russia (and later Japan). It soon became apparent, however, that American economic interests would be better served by supporting Britain and France. Germany viewed the supply of goods to Britain and France as an act of non-neutrality and sought to blockade shipping lanes. German U-boats sank untold numbers of British cargo ships in the Atlantic Ocean, the most-publicized such attack being the sinking of the passenger ship *Lusitania* in 1915. The British liner had carried 1,200 passengers along with food and armaments—including 4.2 million rounds of bullets for Remington rifles. A U-boat torpedoed the *Lusitania* off the coast of Ireland, resulting in the loss of 1,198 people, including 128 Americans. The catastrophe paved the way for America to enter the war as public opinion turned in support of Britain and France.

Broonzy was drafted into the army in 1917. His conscription was part of the resolution of a national controversy over the mobilization of black troops. Some military officials—and many whites across the country—objected to the drafting of blacks in the belief that they were genetically unsuited for the rigors of military service. This opinion held sway despite the successful use of African and Indian troops by the armies of Allied nations. Yet, whether these foreign troops performed well or poorly, many white Americans viewed them as inferior to their European counterparts. In the South, furthermore, many plantation owners opposed the conscription of blacks out of fear of losing control over their source of labor. Even with the growing efficiencies of technological innovations, cotton landlords were concerned about the combined impact of conscription and northern competition for black labor. Whites objected to the mass assembly of blacks at army transfer depots and worried about the attitudes of black veterans returning from the war.[1]

In the final analysis, however, the nation's need for soldiers took prece-

dence, and the army drafted blacks and whites for service in racially segregated infantry, cavalry, and National Guard units. On May 17, 1917, the federal
government passed the Selective Service Act requiring mandatory registration. The law was passed in response to the historically slow rate of volun-
teers, a sign-up rate slower than for the Civil War and Spanish-American War.
The law required men to begin enlisting on June 5. By the end of the war, 26
million men would register for the draft—including 2.3 million black men—
out of a total male population of 54 million. Of this number, 2.5 million
whites and 368,000 blacks would serve in the army. At first, black political
leaders pushed for inclusion in the military, but they later expressed alarm at
blacks' higher rate of conscription, contending that Selective Service officials
were denying exemption requests without review. In fact, discrimination in
the process grew so blatant that, in one case, President Wilson had to remove
the draft board in Fulton County, Georgia.[2] The practice of conscripting more
blacks than whites would seem to undermine the efforts of landlords to maintain their black labor force, but it would encourage them to rely more on la-
borsaving devices.

Broonzy recalled knowing little about the war, paying attention to it only
when learning that the draft board had summoned him. He said that the
plantation boss met him in the field one day and told him to report for induction. He accepted the news reluctantly and asked the boss if he could make
arrangements to keep him out of the army. The boss promised to do what he
could; but, regardless of any effort the boss might have put forth, Broonzy
reported to Camp Pike in Little Rock, Arkansas in 1917.[3] Broonzy later commented on the draft in "That Number of Mine" in 1940, and "In the Army
Now" in 1941, calling on his military experience to relate to a new generation
facing the prospect of a draft for World War II. He alludes to the anxiety of
being drafted in "That Number of Mine":

> Everywhere I go, I see that same old one fifty-eight (2×)
> Now, I know I'm billed out, baby, hoo, lord, Uncle Sam said,
> "Bill, don't be late."[4]

Most of the black recruits, coming from the plantations, expected little
more from the army than decent food, clothes, treatment, and pay. While
some earned distinction as combat troops or learned technical skills that
could be used in civilian work, the majority worked as menial laborers, which
was the case for Broonzy.[5] On the day of departure, as he assembled with

other men to wait for the camp train, Broonzy found himself standing at the end of the line and recalled an old superstition: "If you're on the tail end of the line, you're a dead dog's tail." He switched positions with a man named Seburn, who stood next to last in line: "And just about that time the man came along, tagging folks, and when he got down to the end of that line, he didn't have no tag for Seburn. Seburn went back home, see, and I had to go to the Army."[6]

Camp Pike housed both blacks and whites in segregated barracks—blacks on one side of the road, whites on the other. In September 1917, it had 9,600 troops including blacks from Arkansas and Louisiana and whites from Arkansas and western states. By 1919, Arkansas would train 33,000 whites and 18,000 blacks. The camp also served as the site of a federally funded industrial school and reformatory for delinquent females. Camp Pike also was the site of a nasty racial incident involving the opposition of a white officer to the stationing of black and white troops at the camp. Capt. Eugene Rowan, a native of Mississippi, was found guilty of disobeying orders after refusing to follow a superior officer's command to call a formation of black and white units.[7]

While Arkansas accepted black conscripts without major incident, the same could not be said for other southern states. Racial tensions arose around the issue of training camps for blacks, involving the location of the camps, the ratio of black to white inductees, and the transportation of the men to the camps. Some of the problems resulted from the reactions of whites, others from the policies of the War Department. Military policy called for stationing blacks and whites in separate camps, at a ratio of two whites for every black draftee. But many whites, fearful of large numbers of black soldiers in their districts, called on the army to place the men in the North. The *Chicago Defender* supported that idea in the belief that the men would be safer. Meanwhile, many black and some white leaders called on the army to station troops in their home state, but this proposal made it difficult for the army to maintain its "safe" racial balance. Problems also developed from the policy of using segregated trains to transport recruits.[8]

Broonzy described blacks' cool relations with white troops, recalling that, while blacks played games and made friends with whites, it was always with the awareness that black soldiers were expected to stay in their place. The racist practices of superior officers left Broonzy with resentful memories. He bristled over the officers' treatment of black soldiers, the better food given to white soldiers, and the arbitrary way in which black troops were punished and prohibited from going to the white side of camp. Describing a scenario whose accuracy is subject to question, Broonzy claimed that the military had kept some black soldiers in quarantine on the suspicion that they had been exposed to an infectious disease. However, he recalled that white troops were allowed to enter the area at whim. If so, this activity would appear to have defeated the purpose of the quarantine: "And what made us salty was the white boys on the other side of the highway could come over to our camp and shoot craps with us, but we couldn't go over on their side because they had us quarantined. They say they were trying to break up germs—they didn't want the germs to get over amongst the white soldiers, said the germs was over amongst the colored."[9]

Even innocent encounters between black and white soldiers had the potential of igniting racial conflict. One day Broonzy and some friends went to town at the same time as a group of white soldiers. At the edge of town, the black soldiers spotted a cat and, remembering the old superstition about black cats, decided to stop it from crossing their path. After chasing it for some time, they finally caught the cat and carried it back to the side of the street. A group of white soldiers had watched the comic chase, and for days afterward laughed whenever they saw the black soldiers. Not long afterward, as the black soldiers watched the whites conduct exercises, they noticed some of the whites laughing. Thinking the soldiers were making fun of them, the black soldiers complained to a superior officer. The white soldiers were ordered to explain their laughter, and as they described the cat chase, everyone shared in a good laugh.[10]

Broonzy, viewing the army experience from the standpoint of amenities, credited the service with improving his access to basic necessities. He ate better food, practiced better hygiene, wore better clothes, and earned better money. He also received decent medical care and perhaps the first complete physical examination in his life. The soldiers were given purgatives to kill off worms and parasites that they might have carried for years, and received vaccinations against diseases.[11] Broonzy's observations of the benefits of military life mirror the findings of some historians that the war enabled progressive reformers to bring better public health to the rural poor. Most soldiers received better food, clothes, and housing than at home. With forty-two thousand doctors, the army boasted the largest number of physicians in its history. And greater military awareness of the transmission of communicable diseases led to a 300 percent reduction of venereal disease among the troops.[12]

On the other hand, black recruits faced bleak conditions during training. Because blacks were drafted with little regard for their fitness, some camps had higher rates of infectious diseases like chickenpox, smallpox, tuberculosis, pneumonia, and venereal disease, and many men suffered from gum disease and tooth loss. (Conversely, white camps had higher levels of influenza, measles, polio, scarlet fever, diabetes, and skin cancers.) In addition, despite the accessibility of medical care, some men were denied treatment. Moreover, many camps were left to operate in wretched conditions: Young men worked outdoors in the winter without the protection of winter clothes. At Camp Pike, for instance, 2,500 young men reportedly wore overalls and summer underwear in the midst of near-freezing weather. In camps across the country and overseas, black troops complained about poor clothing, tents without floors or stoves for heat, bad food in dilapidated mess halls, and unsanitary conditions due to lack of water.[13]

Nevertheless, Broonzy looked back on his experience in the army as beneficial. For example, he was illiterate going into the service, and, although he never achieved complete literacy, he had the chance to improve his education in the military. Broonzy had long recognized the pitfalls of ignorance and wanted to go to school. As a teenager, he had thoughts about college when he watched white kids he knew go away to college and return to have professional careers. Broonzy believed that a better education would help him succeed in life the way it helped those children. He never had the chance to finish grade school, much less attend college, but in later years he pointed out with amusement that he had a chance to "go to college in 1947"—when he was hired as a janitor at Iowa State College.[14]

The financing of public schools in the South was meager for both blacks and whites, but starkly so for black children. While many families understood the value of education and valiantly supported the segregated schools, the facilities and resources were dismal. Common conditions included shacks for schoolhouses, inadequate funding for teacher salaries and training, low pupil attendance, school terms of three to five months based on the crop season, and low expectations for students. In Mississippi, for example, black teachers received less than half the salary of white teachers, and classes were overcrowded and poorly supplied. Black residents paid taxes that supported schools for white students but saw few resources invested in their schools. Moreover, blacks were excluded from the political process that enabled them to compete for funding. Some evidence of the low priority given to public

education in Arkansas can be seen in the 1910 report of the Southern Education Board (SEB), a philanthropic organization underwritten by the Rockefeller Foundation. The SEB investigated conditions of public schools for
white children in Arkansas and called for a number of reforms. In 1911, the
state responded to the report by creating a board of education and providing
financial assistance to high schools.[15] If these essential changes were required
in the school system for white children, one can only imagine the scale of
improvements needed in the black school system.

In the army, friends taught Broonzy how to write letters. By studying on
his own, he learned to recognize letters and words; he began a daily practice
of building his vocabulary by reading labels on boxes and cans in the stock-
room. As a man in his late twenties, Broonzy gained confidence by achieving
a marginal level of literacy that enabled him to read and write phonetically:
"I learnt to spell out c-a-n-d-y and t-o-m-a-t-o on like that until finally I got so
I could write home to my mother."[16]

Like Broonzy, many young men took advantage of the opportunities the
army offered for advancing education and work skills. They enrolled in night-
school classes taught by educated black instructors, for example, that provided some with the academic preparation that helped them to move beyond
the menial jobs of the South to semi-skilled or skilled work in northern factories after the war.[17] For Broonzy, the army years were a time when he began to
develop a broader sense of the world. His stories convey his awakening to the
possibilities outside of rural Arkansas. He came in contact with men who had
traveled and who told him about life in the North, saw black officers treated
with respect by black and white troops, and witnessed white troops fright-
ened by the horrors of war, which undermined the façade of racial superiority.
Broonzy appreciated the army for providing the chance to be treated like a man.

For the duration of his service, Broonzy was stationed in Brest, France, a port
for deployment on the Continent. He remembered the trip overseas as a swirl
of confusion and wonderment. The speed of events rendered him groggy—
from Little Rock to Newport News, Virginia, to the transatlantic steamship—
as did the enormity of the Atlantic Ocean. He had never seen the Atlantic
before, much less crossed it in a steamship. His reaction to the events, along
with those of other young men from the plantations, ranged from seasickness
to fear to marvel at the adventure.[18]

Broonzy was assigned to a labor battalion where he served with other
men as the stevedores, teamsters, cooks, mess boys, laundrymen, road gangs,

construction workers, and grave diggers of the American fighting machine.[19] The troops distinguished themselves in the "Services of Supply," as the units came to be known. Working at strategic French port cities like Nantes and Brest, they were admired for their speed, stamina, and efficiency: handling mail bags, freight, horses and mules, hay, ice, meat, clothes, gasoline, ammunition, blankets and medicine; transporting goods by car, truck, ox-cart, motorcycle and backpack; building warehouses and telegraph lines; and laying down roads and rail tracks.[20]

Broonzy worked with squads unloading goods and transporting them safely in support of combat operations. His experience no doubt was similar to the port scenes captured in an army photograph of supply troops in Brest that shows work gangs in uniforms and helmets lifting and hauling goods from steamships at a crowded dock. Some operated cranes that lifted vehicles and cargo in nets; many pushed boxed goods in handcarts. Black men comprised nearly all the stevedore units, and they worked like mules—from the moment the ship docked, they hustled in sixteen-hour shifts for a week or more until the job was done. At Brest, a group of men "unloaded 1,200 tons of flour in nine and one-half hours, and then, to break their own record, averaged 2,000 tons a day for five days more."[21]

Stevedore battalions also contributed through construction work, building warehouses, supply dumps, housing, roads, and graveyards. Broonzy recalled going to different areas of France to carry out the mission of "digging up stumps, building barracks, cutting down trees, putting in good roads." He once marched thirty miles in the mud to cut up trees that had blocked a road or to repair a highway. While he and other troops were proud of their "service of supply," Broonzy described how many black troops found it ironic that they would be brought so far to do the same type of manual labor they performed on the plantations. He said that soldiers with ambitions to do more than common labor were informed by officers that they were unqualified for anything but manual labor.[22]

Meanwhile, some of the racism that had afflicted camp life continued overseas, regardless of the need for unity in the face of a common enemy. While black officers—and some white ones—treated black soldiers with dignity and respect in France, many white officers treated them with disdain. Moreover, the army rewarded white troops with the perks of shorter workdays, cleaner assignments, passes to town, and better food rations. Black soldiers who dared to raise the issue of inequity to superiors could face punishment ranging from court-martial to being sent to the front line. Broonzy recalled one such case: "All I know is one time the white and colored boys got together and the colored found out they was getting different rations and well, those boys raised sand at the mess hall and so they shipped um to the front right away. Well, I saw those boys come back later on and they was all kinds of shapes."[23]

Moreover, some white soldiers spread the ideology of white supremacy to the French population by circulating a pamphlet entitled *Secret Information Concerning Black Troops,* which warned of blacks' unnatural propensity to rape white women and called for complete separation of the races. But many French people remained grateful for the contributions of the troops, often treating the black soldiers with respect and, to the chagrin of some white soldiers, mixing with them as equals.[24]

Black troops spent their idle time playing card and dice games, Broonzy recalled, and also praying and singing hymns to ward off fear—especially when they had to don gas masks or put out cigarettes to avoid detection from biplane surveillance.[25] In the 1935 recording of the spiritual "I Ain't No Stranger Now," Broonzy presents a theme of salvation in God. It was a traditional hymn that he might have sung for comfort during the war:

> Lord, I ain't no stranger now,
> Sayin', if I could introduce you to the Father and the Son,
> Lord, I ain't no stranger now.[26]

The end of war brought African American soldiers some accolades for their service in France, but for the most part their deployment ended without fanfare. And for some, it concluded with insult when the army barred them from the Allied victory parade in Paris and excluded them from a war mural that Britain and France created in honor of the contributions of African and Asian soldiers. Yet the black troops still went out of their way to donate 300,000 francs to help French orphans. The army tightened restrictions on black troops to prevent their interacting with French women and leftist intellectuals. Some soldiers reportedly were lynched for dating French women, while others were harassed. Broonzy said, "I saw plenty of French girls and they looked good to me, but I never did get with um like some of the boys did. It was hard to get out." For Broonzy, World War I came to an end without any celebration. One day his battalion was called together for what he thought would be another long march to a hard labor detail, but instead they were marched to the ships heading home. Broonzy was reluctant to believe that the war was over until he arrived in New York and was put on a train back to Little Rock.[27]

The war awakened many veterans to the possibility of living with the full rights and respect of manhood. They returned home with a different outlook on the restricted futures available in the United States. Shortly after returning, Broonzy concluded that he could not achieve the rights that were his due in rural Arkansas. Minutes after he stepped off the train, his old plantation boss met him in the street and ordered him to take off the uniform, don a pair of overalls, and return to the fields, saying, "No nigger gonna walk around here with no Uncle Sam's uniform on, see, up and down these streets." The landlord claimed that Broonzy still owed money for clothes he had bought on credit before leaving. Broonzy protested that he had paid for the clothes before he left for the army. He added that the uniform was the only clothes he had and that he had given the overalls to his brother. The boss brushed aside his explanation, saying that Broonzy should get rid of the uniform and he would supply Broonzy with overalls for fieldwork.[28]

His memory of the incident highlights another episode of conflict over the way he saw himself (as a proud veteran and patriot) and the way a white man saw him (as an "uppity nigger" sharecropper who needed to be brought down a peg). After helping to fight for democracy overseas, he felt that all that awaited him at home were the chains of peonage. Broonzy picked up his new overalls and went back to the field, no doubt harboring a great deal of resentment. He recalled: "In the army I had been used to being a man irregardless. I had got used to being clean all the time—having plenty clean, good clothes and a place to bathe and fix myself up. At home I had been just dumb to the fact. I thought that was the right way to be treated, and when I found out it was the wrong way, I just couldn't take it no more."[29] He would later integrate this sentiment in the lyrics of "When Will I Be Called a Man":

> I helped build the country
> And I fought for it too
> Now I guess you can see
> What a black man has to do.[30]

Soon after returning from France, Broonzy realized that his family and friends were incapable of understanding what he had been through in the military. He quickly developed marital problems with his wife. Broonzy had married at the age of twenty-one through an arrangement between his father and the family of Gertrude Embrie, a seventeen-year-old member of his church. The circumstances behind the marriage were unclear, but his family seemed to have pushed the issue, presenting the marriage as an initiation to manhood. However, his father's encouragement may have been self-serving—he may have been attempting to prevent his son from visiting a particular prostitute. Broonzy recalled his father encouraging the marriage after he began visiting the woman, saying he wanted to save his son before he was ruined. According to Broonzy's story, the prostitute was named Mary Crow, an older woman whom he met one day when his mother gave him three dollars in appreciation of his hard farmwork, telling him to buy whatever he wanted in town.

Broonzy visited Mary on two different Saturdays, and one day told his father that he wanted to marry her. Frank Broonzy condemned the idea and shortly thereafter ordered him to marry Gertrude Embrie.[31] Broonzy heeded his father's instructions, but only after seeing Mary one last time. He was in her room, he said, when he heard a knock on the door. A man asked to see Mary, but the madam told him to wait until Mary finished with another client. The man asked who Mary was entertaining, and the madam said coyly, "The best plough hand on your farm." Broonzy recognized the voice of his father.

Broonzy and Embrie were married on November 11, 1914. Her background and the nature of her relationship to Broonzy are unknown; however, his recollections leave the impression of a hardworking, practical woman who tended to be bossy. They probably had a daughter named Catherine, possibly the real reason for their marriage. Gertrude may have been pregnant, with marriage offering an honorable way for the families to handle the situation: "We was church members together and we was always around different places together. I liked her and she liked me, so she said. Fact of the business, she proved it because she started a family. We had chicken and cake and ice cream at our wedding."[32]

As a married man, Broonzy tried to be an upstanding head of the family, working as a sharecropper and "jackleg" preacher. His stint as a preacher was an extension of his desire to offer spiritual expression to the black folk. Broonzy had a sense of mission, a desire to articulate words of joy and redemption to everyday people, whether in the church, the nightclub, or the recording studio. He apparently preached for four years with his friend Louis Carter, now a deacon in his "church," but the calling cooled when his sermons failed to attract a followings. He blamed his failure on his lack of education, saying that it undermined his ability to study the Bible and deliver the Good News.[33]

Broonzy's writings reveal little about his family life. In one letter, though, he recalled telling bedtime stories to his seven-year-old girl, Catherine. One of her favorites was Little Red Riding Hood; another was his rendition of a grisly tall-tale about two characters, One-Eyed Abraham and Black Saddy. Black Saddy has a fight with her husband, One-Eyed Abraham, and vows to seek revenge. One day as he sits playing cards with friends, she sneaks up on his blind side and cuts off his head with a razor. But the blade is so sharp that One-Eyed Abraham doesn't realize he's been decapitated until his friends convince him. At their urging, he shakes his head and it tumbles to the floor. He realizes at that point that he is dead.[34]

The story was so far-fetched that he recalled Catherine chastising him for "telling lies," a common term among the folk for spinning outrageous tales to entertain family and friends. Other than this brief glimpse into their early relationship, however, Broonzy offered scant information about his daughter. Perhaps his memory of these years faded with time, perhaps interviewers never asked about them, or possibly these were matters too personal to discuss. Broonzy appears to have spent little time with Catherine. When he lived with his family, he hustled to make money in the fields and at performances, and then, when Broonzy was drafted into the army, they were separated for two years.

How the family maintained itself when he was in France is unclear. One can assume that Broonzy's army salary, combined with his wife's earnings from jobs and family assistance, enabled them to make ends meet. But when he came back, Gertrude began pressuring him to find better-paying work on the railroads. Broonzy felt that she bossed him around far too much, saying, "My wife was telling me what I should do about money matters." (Since Broonzy had no problem hustling up jobs, it seems surprising that this would have been an issue.) Nevertheless, his inability to find (or to look for) work better than sharecropping increased feelings of distance from his wife. "Things were different between me and Gertrude," he said. "It was like she didn't sympathize with me no more."[35]

Broonzy was in the position of many returning black veterans. He had outgrown the restrictions of life in the segregated South and resented the economic injustice of debt peonage. He was estranged from his wife and uncomfortable in the marriage. He wanted to restore the sense of renewal and optimism that he had felt when he left the plantation for the military. He began to look for alternative possibilities and became receptive to the prospect of starting a new life in one of the urban industrial centers.

Economic hardship was the major reason for the mass migration of black farmworkers to the urban North, with sharecroppers being especially likely to leave the plantations because of conditions of poverty that had solidified over decades. The system of sharecropping and crop liens made it impossible for most black farmers to make a living. Tenancy had developed during the mid-nineteenth century, when cotton was the principal cash crop of the South. The plantation system was based on controlling a black labor force. It had made U.S. planters the leaders in the world markets but became increasingly obsolete in the face of erratic prices and technological innovations.[36]

Charles Johnson argues that cotton plantation agriculture based on tenancy was moving toward collapse for years before the war. In 1900, an estimated 8 million black people lived in the South, about 6.5 million on plantations and in rural towns. More than 1.1 million black men headed plantation households, comprised of 186,676 full or part owners, 552,000 renters, and 359,000 sharecroppers and field laborers. The price of cotton rose from seven cents per pound between 1890 and 1902 to 10.5 cents per pound between 1903 and 1915. During the war years, the price of cotton doubled to as high as 21.5 cents per pound. After the war, cotton's price fell in response to reduced orders from the military, competition from foreign cotton producers, and tariffs imposed by nations to protect domestic producers; the price would fluctuate throughout the decade. The distinction between a tenant farmer and a sharecropper was often vague. The tenant worked through a rental arrangement, while the cropper worked on a crop-share basis. However, both types of farmers were locked into a system of exploitive credit relations that led to debt peonage to the landlord. In fact, the illiterate tenant often signed off on rental contracts that obliged him to work the land for life.[37] Arkansas sharecropper George Stith describes the limits of tenant farming in the Delta plantations:

> On the plantation there were houses all over the plantation. At least every 40 acres had about two houses and two pair of mules, that's what you used to work 40 acres of land. A four-room house normally would have not less than six and up to 15 [people]. They [the landlord] fur-

nished the mule, they furnished the feed, and they furnished the seed. You worked the crop, you gathered it, your carried it to the gin. He sold it and told you what you got. There was only one bookkeeper and that was the man at the store. You didn't keep books. He would tell you what you owed. He would tell you how much you got for your cotton. He would tell you how much you made, if you made any. If you didn't, he would tell you how much you came out in debt.[38]

Quite a few blues singers, most of whom had some experience as tenant farmers, condemned their powerlessness in both commercial and noncommercial field recordings. For example, one anonymous singer in Tryon, North Carolina, expresses frustration over conditions of poverty in "White Folks Ain't Jesus," captured in the 1920s noncommercial recording of folk song collector Lawrence Gellert:

> White folks ain't Jesus, he just a man
> Taking muffins from a poor man's hand
> How long, baby, how long?[39]

Sharecropper John Handcox comments on the consequences of sharecropper poverty in the 1930s noncommercial field recording of "Raggedy, Raggedy," in which the protagonist speaks out against unfair wages:

> Raggedy, raggedy are we, just as raggedy as raggedy can be,
> We don't get nuthin' for our labor, so raggedy, raggedy are we.[40]

In addition to exploitive economic relations, cotton farmers were hard hit by the invasion of the boll weevil. The tiny cotton-eating insects infested southern crops in the early decades of the twentieth century. The insect moved from the farms of Mexico to the plantations of the United States in 1892, consuming thousands of acres of cotton crops in Mississippi, Alabama, and Georgia by 1915. The infestation caused landowners to reduce cotton acreage, abandon fields, and relocate to farms in Arizona, New Mexico, and California. Many landlords switched from cotton farming exclusively to a mixed plantation of cotton, food crops, and livestock. This meant that the plantations required fewer workers on the whole, and especially sharecroppers untrained to work with animals or food crops.[41] The event is chronicled in the folk song "Boll Weevil Blues" sung by Vera Hall in a 1940 noncommercial field recording:

First time I seen the boll weevil, he's sittin' on the square,
Next time I seen him, he had his family there.

Boll weevil here, boll weevil everywhere,
They done ate up all the cotton and corn, all but that new ground
square.[42]

Sharecropper Sampson Pittman witnessed the boll weevil ravaging cotton harvests in the 1920s and sang "Cotton Farmer Blues" in a 1930 noncommercial field recording to communicate the urgency of the problem:

Farmer went to his merchant, just to get some meat and meal, (2×)
But the merchant told the farmer, you got boll weevil in your field.

You got a good cotton crop, but it's just like shootin' dice, (2×)
Now you gonna work the whole year round, buddy, but the cotton
won't bring no price.[43]

At the same time, sharecroppers experienced threats of nature such as droughts and floods. Southern plantations faced a series of floods in 1915 and 1916 that brought the misfortunes of cotton farming to a head, convincing some planters to reduce investments in future crops and to reduce acreage. For sharecroppers, the result was unexpected displacement and a scramble to find work elsewhere.[44] John Handcox recalls the problem in the Arkansas Delta: "Lots of places was in lowlands and the water would rise and destroy your crop. I had it two years in a row in one place, and one year where my cotton was bloomin', just loaded down, and some of it was openin'. It was the latter part of August. And it (floods) destroyed all the lowland. All I got was the cotton off the rollin' land, off the hill. All my work had went down the drain."[45]

In Broonzy's 1937 recording "Southern Flood Blues," the narrator describes the terror of a flood that consumed his home and family. Broonzy, raised in the region of the Mississippi and Arkansas Delta, was well aware of the catastrophe brought by floods. His story expresses the travails of a man trapped by floodwaters and separated from a loved one. The story renders in dramatic fashion the chaos of swirling winds, torrential rains, and the confusion and panic of a man in danger. The song may have been inspired by his observations of the damage created by the 1927 Mississippi River flood. According to Broonzy, record producer J. Mayo Williams chartered a boat to take singers under his management to the flood zone. In addition to Broonzy,

Williams invited Lonnie Johnson, Kansas Joe McCoy, Springback James, Sippie Wallace, and Bessie Smith. The purpose of the trip was to encourage the artists to write moving songs:[46]

I was hollerin' for mercy and it were no boats around (2×)
Yeah, that looks like, people, I've gotta stay right here and drown.[47]

Tenant farmers confronted unexpected challenges on the cotton plantations such as the degradation of the soil from overfarming, competition from plantations in southwestern states like Oklahoma and Texas with lower costs of production, competition from the creation of synthetic fibers like rayon, and the introduction of tractors to replace the labor of sharecroppers. Planters in the Southwest were the first to use tractors and found that they could cut the cost of production by half while increasing the acreage under cultivation.[48] The end result was a large number of sharecroppers displaced from the plantations. Many sought work on other plantations and in southern towns and cities in the years before the war. One singer expresses the desperation and anger of a field hand made redundant in "Standing on the Streets in Birmingham," a 1920s noncommercial field recording. The protagonist evokes armed robbery as a possible response to destitution:

Do you want me to be bad like Jesse James? (2×)
Gimme two six shooters so I can highway rob and steal.[49]

While economic hardship was a primary cause of the migration, Broonzy and other tenants spoke about freedom and respect as major reasons for leaving as well. After serving in the army overseas, Broonzy said he could no longer stomach living under the restrictions of segregation: "The main reason I left home was because I couldn't stand eating out of the back trough all the time."[50] His sentiments expressed the viewpoint of black veterans of his generation, many of whom had different experiences and more education than their parents and were unwilling to accept the old rules of Jim Crow.[51]

The young generation bumped up against the accumulated constraints and indignities of segregation that had developed over the decades following the overthrow of the Reconstruction governments. Blacks lived with the limitations of Jim Crow laws and customs that bound their lives nearly as effectively as the slave codes. The laws of segregation were sanctioned by the 1896 U.S. Supreme Court ruling in *Plessy v. Ferguson* in support of Jim Crow laws on public transportation. Florette Henri notes that the segregation laws dictated all aspects of life from public services to private interactions. The need to erect such an array of laws bore testimony to the continued push by blacks for full equality. Over time, blacks faced the combined effects of the segregation laws and the denial of voting rights. The methods of disfranchisement included new state constitutions, amendments to existing constitutions, and state laws. Among the means of targeting black men for disfranchisement were the poll tax (which was paid for poor whites in close elections), the grandfather clause (which based eligibility on whether one's father or grandfather voted in 1867 or served in the Confederate or Union armies), and the literacy requirement (which tested ability to write, recite by memory the federal or state constitution, or interpret the constitutions or legal statues).[52]

Some astute journalists anticipated that after the war young blacks would push back against the entrenched racial oppression. The *New Republic* advised southern leaders to restrain whites who used violence and intimidation to oppress blacks, writing: "Is the South willing to admit that white supremacy can not rest on any foundation than fear?"[53] The *Chicago Defender* pronounced that veterans no longer "tamely and meekly submit to a program of lynching, burning, and social ostracism." Black intellectuals heralded the change in outlook as the era of the "New Negro," in which blacks with a cosmopolitan point of view demanded the respect due to them as equals.[54]

In this new social climate, a group of black cotton farmers in Broonzy's home state organized for economic justice. The Arkansas tenants claimed that in 1918 their cotton was seized by landlords and sold without fair compensation. The farmers received some additional payment, but the amount they received was less than the market value of the cotton. In 1919, the sharecroppers formed the Progressive Farmers and Household Union and sued the landlords to prevent them from carrying out another crop seizure.

The actions provoked a violent reaction by white planters, which resulted in the arrest of the union lawyer (a white man) and the sixty-eight farmers who led the movement. The arrest sparked a confrontation between other union members and three law officers who tried to disrupt a union meeting in the town of Elaine. The law officers—a deputy sheriff, sheriff trustee, and railroad agent—shot into a church where the union meeting was being held. Some members returned fire, killing the railroad agent and wounding the deputy. The incident was falsely reported in the newspapers as a plot to kill twenty-one white citizens of the county. This led to armed white vigilantes from Arkansas, Tennessee, and Mississippi descending on Phillips County to terrorize the black community: "Negroes were disarmed and arrested; their arms were given to the whites who rapidly thronged the little town of Helena. Those Negroes who escaped arrest took refuge in the canebrakes near the town where they were hunted down like animals."[55]

The shootout resulted in the deaths of five white men and 250 black men, women, and children. It motivated Arkansas governor Charles Brough to call for five hundred soldiers from Camp Pike to restore order. Brough established a commission of leading white citizens in the county to investigate the cause of the massacre. Unsurprisingly, the commission placed blame on the union organizers, and Governor Brough accepted this version of the event. However, the NAACP conducted an investigation and concluded that the killings were an outgrowth of efforts to destroy the union: "The system, known as 'share-cropping' or 'tenant-farming,' had become so abusive that these farmers felt its continuance meant nothing except peonage."[56] In the aftermath, sixty-five blacks were tried, and twelve were found guilty and sentenced to die. The NAACP challenged the sentences in a celebrated criminal rights case that went to the U.S. Supreme Court. In 1923, the Court ruled in *Moore v. Dempsey* that the union men should be released on the grounds of their not having received a fair trial.[57] While there is no record of Broonzy talking about this case, there can be little doubt that he was aware of it since it involved both his region and his former army outfit.

Some tenants left the plantations to escape mistreatment by the police and courts. Broonzy recognized how the legal establishment conspired with private companies to exploit convicts as a source of slave labor. In an interview with Alan Lomax, he alluded to the evils of the system under which black men were forced to work for companies and state agencies, summing up the harsh treatment with the popular expression: "Kill a nigger, we'll hire another'n. Kill a mule, we'll buy another'n."[58]

Florette Henri describes the exploitation of blacks under the convict lease system in the South. The practice enabled private companies and the state to profit from the free labor of convicts during the course of their prison terms. It created a financial incentive for police and courts to target blacks and mete out exorbitant fines and sentences. Southern states generated substantial revenues from the rentals of able bodies—in 1906, for example, Georgia earned $355,000 from convict leases, the vast majority of whom were black men. As a result, a disproportionate number of blacks were imprisoned, particularly during crop seasons when planters needed pools of cheap labor. During these episodes, when company agents bid for the bonds of the accused, courthouses in the South took on the appearance of the old slave markets.[59] The convicts worked as part of labor squads, often shackled together in chain gangs.

Broonzy remembered seeing one such outfit in Arkansas and described a scene that conjured up images of treatment during slavery. He saw men bound together by a long chain constructing a road; individual prisoners were restrained by either ball and chain or chains staked in the ground—all facing the whip and gun if they failed to keep their work up to speed.[60] In the 1935 recording "Chain Gang Blues," Kokomo Arnold's protagonist is imprisoned for killing his girlfriend. He describes the web of chains that binds him as he works for the state:

> Says I got chains round my body, chains all down round my shoes
> (2×)
> Now that's the reason, Cap'n, hear me singing, Lord, these chain gang
> blues.[61]

Ma Rainey explores the experience of incarceration as it relates to female prisoners in the 1925 recording of "Chain Gang Blues." In her version, the character is sentenced to ninety days' labor on a road after getting arrested over a love-triangle dispute:

> Many days of sorrow, many nights of woe (2×)
> And a ball and chain, everywhere I go.[62]

Many sharecroppers viewed the criminal justice system as an instrument of white supremacy used to control the movement and enforce the subordination of the black population. People were arrested for the slightest violations, and among the most common charges were vagrancy, public drinking, and disorderly conduct. Police sometimes contrived such charges as well. The purpose was to keep blacks in their place and to raise money from fines. Not only were blacks accused of charges that a white person rarely faced, but they received harsher prison sentences. Broonzy described the arbitrary way that a black man fell prey to arrest and imprisonment in the 1935 recording of "Midnight Special":

> If you ever go to Memphis, says you better walk right.
> Don't, the police will arrest you, and they'll carry you down.
> And take you to the station with a gun in his hand.[63]

Barefoot Bill's narrator describes the treatment of his girlfriend by police in the 1929 recording "Big Rock Jail." The narrator describes coming home to discover that the sheriff has arrested his girlfriend. He laments his loneliness in her absence and questions whether her offense merited her arrest at the point of a gun:

> You took your gun, made her raise her hand (2×)
> And you was wrong, 'cause she never harmed a man.[64]

Bessie Smith expresses similar resentment in the 1924 recording "Work House Blues." Her protagonist laments being sent to a prison workhouse for an unknown offense, but blames her fate on "hard luck," a common euphemism for racism:

> Everybody's cryin' the work house blues all day, oh Lord, oh Lord (2×)
> I can't plow, I can't cook, if I'd ran away, wouldn't that be good.[65]

In the 1940 recording "Parchman Farm Blues," Bukka White warns listeners about the travails of receiving an extreme sentence to the notorious Mississippi prison facility. The protagonist does not describe the crime of which he was convicted, but he expresses resignation to the severe prison term. He depicts the long days of working under the sun, cautions other men to avoid his fate, and considers the effect of his absence on his family:

> Judge give me life this mornin' down on Parchman Farm (2×)
> I wouldn't hate it so bad, but I left my wife in mourn.[66]

The lynch mob was the most brutal method used to enforce white supremacy. Henri describes the debate among scholars over the role that fear of lynching played in the decision of tenant farmers to migrate. Some writers consider it to be an important factor—at least in the aftermath of a lynching—while others maintain that economic conditions, injustice generally, and education were leading factors. However, there can be no doubt that the long-standing and widespread practice of lynching starkly illustrated the lack of legal protection for blacks. Any black man who asserted himself in ways offensive to whites could be murdered by the lynch mob. It was a tool of terror used since the overthrow of Reconstruction because of white fears of black competition. After 1900, blacks comprised about 90 percent of the victims of lynching. The usual reason given by accusers was the rape of a white woman.

However, less than 20 percent of blacks murdered by hanging from 1914 to 1919 had been formally accused of rape or attempted rape. In fact, less than 17 percent of black victims of lynching were charged with rape between 1889 and 1941. Most were charged with murder or assault of a white person or inappropriate relations with a white woman, and some were hanged for such seemingly insignificant actions as practicing voodoo and throwing stones.[67]

While the northward migration was partly in reaction to the social and economic problems in the South, tenants also were drawn to the prospect of good jobs in the industrial centers. A sharecropper earned seventy-five cents per day on the plantation, but he could make three to four dollars per ten-hour day working in the mills and factories of the cities. A woman doing domestic service was paid $1.50 to three dollars per week in the South, but she could earn $2.50 per day in the North. Even accounting for the higher living costs of the ghettos, the wage differentials left more money in workers' pockets. Allan Spear provides a breakdown of hourly wages at major companies in Chicago: unskilled laborers averaged fifty cents per hour. The hourly pay rates ranged from forty-two cents in the meatpacking houses to sixty-one cents at International Harvester and Argo Corn Products. Based on the typical workweek of forty-eight to sixty hours, a migrant worker could make twenty-five dollars per week. Women in Chicago earned between twelve and eighteen dollars per week in the factories and more in domestic service, including room and board.[68]

Thus ambitious tenants realized that the South could never offer the occupations and incomes available in the North. Migrants wrote back to their communities describing how thrifty households with several wage-earners could pool resources, amass hundreds of dollars per month in savings, and gradually build wealth. One Cleveland family of five generated $310 per month while paying twelve dollars per month in rent; a Newark, N.J., migrant earned $2.75 per day in a dye plant that provided free transportation and room. He had made less than one dollar per day as a sharecropper. Moreover, urban industrial relations permitted far more daily independence than tenant farming, and a family no longer had to rely on a landlord for its very existence.[69]

The prospect of finding work in the cities was dramatically enhanced by a labor shortage in northern industries. As the Great War simmered in Europe, immigration to the United States plummeted from 1.2 million in 1914 to 110,618 in 1918. During that period, nearly 5 million fewer foreign workers and families came to the United States than in the years before the war. At the same time, U.S. industrial production expanded to manufacture goods and armaments for the war. Northern companies looked to the rural South to supply cheap replacement labor.[70]

By the war, many tenant farmers were ready to take the risk of leaving the plantations. But first they sought out information on what would await them in the cities, and many turned to a variety of informants to answer their questions. Prospective migrants made the decision to leave the South in a deliberate manner, gathering information through networking clubs—which contacted institutions in the North and served as resource centers—as well as through newspapers, traveling railroad workers, and people who had made the trip. They discussed the benefits and drawbacks with family members and in church meetings, recreation halls, and informal gatherings. They turned to church and civic leaders for advice both at home and in the North. In growing numbers, people concluded that their best hope lay in a new life in the industrial centers.[71]

The first people to depart responded to the incentives of labor agents. These representatives of northern companies trekked across the South to recruit young men for the railroad and mining companies. As a result, an estimated one hundred thousand blacks moved to Pennsylvania to work for the Erie and Pennsylvania railroad companies. Some agents charged migrants (and companies) fees of one to three dollars for the service. This practice created an opportunity for unscrupulous individuals to swindle migrants by posing as agents and collect fees. The unsuspecting migrants went to railroad stations to head north only to discover the deception. As more agents fanned into the South, authorities passed laws requiring them to acquire licenses with registration fees ranging from $1,000 to $25,000. The laws served the interest of southern towns in a variety of ways. Foremost, they created a statutory obstacle for labor agents—in addition to the police practice of discouraging agents by imprisoning them on false pretenses. In other ways, the laws enabled towns and counties to generate revenues and single out unregistered agents. Ultimately, however, if the laws had been intended to reduce the flow of the exodus, they failed to stem the flow of the mass relocation.[72]

As more tenants left, they wrote back about opportunities and adventures and encouraged others to follow. Among the common experiences reported in letters were good-paying jobs, respectful treatment by whites, addressing whites by the first name rather than as "Mr. or Miss," sending children to the same schools as white parents, and voting in local and state elections. Amazement at being able to speak to white people on equal terms was an experience so widely shared that it originated a folktale called "Dropping All Titles." The tale was about a tenant named Charley who migrated from Mississippi to Chicago. He swore that he would never again submit to addressing anything as Mister or Miss, even referring to his home state by the abbreviated name of "'Sippi."[73]

Broonzy's description of his decision to leave Arkansas shows that he cautiously prepared for the journey by gathering information from a family informant and the *Chicago Defender*. He recalled that the *Defender* "would open the eyes of a lot of Negroes, tell 'em things that they didn't know." He described how tenants smuggled the newspaper to the rural districts and shared the news with others. He noted that while whites viewed a *Defender* reader as a "bad Negro," blacks saw him as a "Race Man"—a person willing to stand up for the rights of his people. Memphis Slim, for instance, spoke about people secretly reading the paper in a restaurant in Marigold, Mississippi: "They had a restaurant in there and in back they had a peephole. And I thought they were gambling back there or something, and I went back there to see was they gambling. In fact, I was kinda stranded, I want to go back there and shoot a little crap and make me a little stake. And you can imagine what they were doing back there. They were reading the *Chicago Defender*, and they had a man on the door, a lookout man. . . . And if a white man or something came into the restaurant, they'd stick the Defender in the stove, burn it up and start playing checkers."[74]

Many black-owned newspapers supported the urban migrations. For example, the *Richmond Reformer* and *Timmonsville (S.C.) Watchmen* encouraged tenants to leave in defiance of racial oppression. The *Chicago Defender*, however, was the most adamant in calling on black readers to leave the South in a modern version of the biblical exodus. Founded as a local weekly in 1905, the *Defender* was in the tradition of U.S. advocacy and sensationalistic journalism. It gained readers by copying the sensational journalism pioneered by Joseph Pulitzer and William Randolph Hearst: banner headlines, often in red ink, stories of outrageous crimes committed against blacks in the South, promotion of black entertainment, and strongly worded editorials on racial justice. Robert S. Abbott, the editor and publisher, envisioned the newspaper as a tool for the improvement, entertainment, and enlightenment of black America. The newspaper ran both a city edition and a national edition aimed at readers in the South. It reached a national audience through a Chicago-based distribution network of railroad porters, dining-car waiters, and traveling entertainers. They were paid to deliver bundles of copies to distributors along the routes and to hand out copies in towns where the paper was unknown. The *Defender* circulation rose from 300 in 1905 to 283,000 by 1920, with a large segment of its readership in the Mississippi Delta. Abbott encouraged the mass migration with such stunts as declaring May 15, 1917, the official start of "The Great Northern Drive" to the "Promised Land." The *Defender* was believed to have been responsible for more people leaving the South than all of the labor agents combined.[75] One testament to the *Defender*'s influence was the decision of Broonzy to relocate to Chicago.

3

"HOUSE RENT STOMP"

FROM 1910 TO 1920, AN ESTIMATED 300,000 TO 1 MILLION TENANTS relocated from the southern plantations to the industrial cities, with as many as 700,000 leaving during the early years of the Great War. This mass migration of black farm laborers far exceeded the estimated 200,000 people who had left the plantations between 1890 and 1910. The sharecroppers abandoned the depressed rural districts by foot, wagon, truck, car, and train. For people in the coastal Southeast, the steamship often was the most economical means of going to New York City, and many steamed away from Virginia to New York on the Old Dominion Line.[1] In 1920, Broonzy joined the exodus of field hands from Arkansas.

Blues artists highlighted this phenomenon in the many songs that expressed the theme of leaving. The blues of the early migration era commented on people fleeing the plantations and seeking rides with friendly drivers of wagons, cars, and trucks. The songs evoked the images of the road and the rail as symbols of freedom and in doing so created a metaphor perpetuated in the blues songs of later decades.[2]

The railroad, however, was the means of transportation cited most often in blues recordings. The railroad had a long history of commentary in African American folklore, dating back to its connection with deliverance from slavery in the spirituals, where it was a symbol of escape from bondage. The abolitionists created networks of roads and safe houses that constituted the iconic Underground Railroad, with its array of "conductors" and "stations." During the migration, the trains traversed linear roads of steel to the infinite possibilities of the urban centers. In addition, the railroad companies were respected for providing thousands of blacks with decent employment as steam engine firemen, track layers, maids, and porters.[3] The blues recordings expanded on the image of the train in black folklore, depicting the railroads at the height of their power. The songs originated characters and settings that reflected the experience of rural folk caught up in the process of industrial transformation.

Not all travel was one-way from the plantations to the cities. Many people participated in a circular migration as they returned to the plantations to visit family and friends, and many songs expressed nostalgia for home. The character in "I'm a Southern Man" longs to return home. Broonzy's 1936 recording articulates the sense of yearning for the South felt by many migrants as the protagonist declares his allegiance to the region. The narrator considers the prospect of returning home to Memphis as the train passes through the various cities and towns on the route of the IC train:

> I'm on my way to Memphis, I'm gonna catch that I.C. train (2×)
> Yeah, I'm a Southern man and I don't deny my name.[4]

Many of the train lines found their way into the folklore of migrants. The Wabash Cannonball was the famed passenger line of the Wabash Railroad. The route was revised over the years, but the timetable showed it going to Chicago, St. Louis, Kansas City, Omaha, and Detroit. The line entered American folklore in a hobo ballad with many lyrics. Another train line, the Southern, was part of the Southern Railroad incorporated in 1894. By 1916, the Southern had eight thousand miles of track in thirteen states, hauling cotton, tobacco, and other goods. The trains of the Yazoo and Mississippi Valley Railroad Company were known as the Yellow Dog and went through the Delta from Jackson to Memphis. Some believed the "yellow dog" moniker came from the initials for the shortened Yazoo-Delta line; others said it referred to a dog that howled when the train passed by, and some said it was an insulting term used for company track workers. The Southern and the Yellow Dog crossed in Greenwood, Mississippi, and the crossing became an icon of blues folklore.[5] Broonzy picked up on the image in the 1935 recording "The Southern Blues." His character stands at the crossing of the Southern and the Yellow Dog thinking about rejoining his girlfriend. He ponders getting a job with the railroad to earn money to send for her—or perhaps he will follow her to Georgia:

> When I got up this mornin', I heard the old Southern whistle blow
> (2×)
> Says I was thinkin' 'bout my baby, Lord, I sure did want to go.[6]

The wistful nostalgia for the Southland expressed by migrant singers was often more romance than reality. Most people had no intention of returning to their rural homes. The plantation economy was changing, and with the technical innovations and corporate consolidation the South would never again need the mass labor of tenants. Not even the publicity campaigns of southern leaders could entice substantial numbers of migrants to return. Regardless of the rising economic plight in the cities, and the exacting toll migration took on kith and kin, the sharecroppers continued to leave the South. One migrant, responding to a question about a southern campaign to encourage blacks to return, said with disbelief: "Anyone who says conditions now are better than before the war is crazy."[7] Yet many migrants suffered emotionally from the separation from their families.

At the same time, migrants looked forward to the broad array of jobs available in the North. While most had worked as tenants, many also had learned industrial skills in the steel mills, turpentine camps, sawmills, lumber camps, and railroad yards of the South. Others had gained skills as blacksmiths, molders, machinists, brick makers, plumbers, and carpenters. In addition, many came from middle-class backgrounds with training as teachers, merchants, hairdressers, insurance agents, and the like. By 1920, about 40 percent of the black population in the North lived in the ghettos of Chicago, New York, Detroit, Cleveland, Philadelphia, Cincinnati, Columbus, and Pittsburgh. For example, the black population of Chicago increased by 65,500 (148 percent), of Detroit by 36,240 (611 percent), and of New York by 61,400 (66 percent). At the peak of the exodus, black World War I veterans returning from France like Big Bill Broonzy joined the movement. Many, in fact, simply opted to remain in the urban centers when they were demobilized.[8]

During times of migration, depression, and war—when men were pulled away for military service—the family experienced more instability than in normal times. It could be argued, of course, that men had been migrating since the end of slavery. In the years prior to the urban migrations, many traveled within the region to find work in the mines, lumber camps, and turpentine camps. The urban migrations created a new level of insecurity in the lives of tenant couples and families. Men, women, and children grappled with the emotional strain of separation, and the blues recordings conveyed the stories of people contending with the consequences of marital strife and spousal abandonment. E. Franklin Frazier argues that the migrations destabilized social traditions in ways reminiscent of the aftermath of the Civil War.[9]

For example, the longer husbands were separated from their families, the more they risked losing their status as the head of the household. When they were away for work, the wives became de facto heads of the households. In addition, many women had reliable employment as domestic servants and low-wage workers. As a result, some black families experienced a shift in the traditional gender roles, with women becoming the dominant figures, but at the expense of fostering an overall stronger family. Black popular entertainment alluded to resentments and tensions among couples in stories about strong wives and weak husbands. For example, many blues singers admonished characters for becoming a servile "monkey man" who obeyed a domineering woman. The comedy teams of "Stringbeans and Sweetie May" and "Butterbeans and Susie" acted out popular relationship dramas on the vaudeville stage during the migration decades.[10]

In the 1935 recording "You May Need My Help Someday," Broonzy goes as far as to invoke Heaven itself in defense of patriarchy with lines such as, "The Good Lord made men, put 'em on earth to rule / Now and all you women think they all a fool." The narrator gives voice to an embittered man caught up in a struggle for power with his woman in which finances loom large:

Don't mistreat nobody because you got a few dimes,
You're up today, baby, but you won't be up all the time.[11]

Broonzy, in the late-career recording "I Don't Want No Woman," created a folksy persona who uses humor to complain about the bossy nature of his woman:

Now she'll tell you when to go to bed, tell you when to get up,
Tell you where to go, boy, and if you say something she'll tell you to hush.[12]

The migrations created circumstances that fostered large numbers of spousal desertions. Young men left with the intention of sending for wives and children but ended up never returning as the marital ties grew weak and the social consequences distant. Frazier suggested that several external factors played a role in keeping tenant families intact such as the need to cooperate in farming and the opinions and support of family, friends, and neighbors. The migration diminished such factors and made it easier for young people to move on with impunity. Drake noted that over half of the unmarried women in Chicago in the 1930s had been married at some point, and many claimed to be "single" and "widowed," common euphemisms for desertion. Hazel Carby discovered resentment in many songs by blueswomen where the characters were left alone, sometimes feeling trapped or abandoned at home.[13] In the 1931 recording "In the House Blues," Bessie Smith offers a narrative that captures the frustration of a woman left waiting for her man:

> Walking to my window and looking outta my door (2×)
> Wishing that my man would come home once more.[14]

The characters lament loneliness so profound that it leads them to seek the company of other men. The protagonist in Ma Rainey's 1928 recording "Blame It on the Blues" alludes to guilty feelings for cheating on her man. She ponders the reason for her infidelity and concludes that the blame lay in her loneliness. She cannot bear being left in the house alone:

> This house is like a graveyard, when I'm left here by myself (2×)
> Shall I blame it on my lover, blame it on somebody else?[15]

Broonzy, who appears to have deserted his wife and daughter in Arkansas, created characters that left women because of problems with money, respect, and understanding. He also recorded songs that portrayed men deserted by women, such as the 1935 release "She Caught the Train," recorded with the studio band State Street Boys. The protagonist agonizes over a woman who left him for another man. Acknowledging the prowess of his competitor, he says, "Some lowdown man learned my baby how to Cadillac Eight," a luxury sexual experience that captured her imagination. Nevertheless, he vows to win her back. Broonzy captures the protagonist at a moment of pulling into the train depot. The character is uncertain whether she will come back with him, and he tries to convince himself that she will change her heart upon seeing him again:

> I know my baby, she sure gonna jump and shout (2×)
> Say, when that train roll up, mama, and I come walkin' out.[16]

In the 1923 recording "Sam Jones Blues," Bessie Smith offers a story of desertion from the perspective of a wife. In this case, the husband left his wife not for work but for another woman; however, when he returns home he discovers that the tables have turned. She has gotten a divorce, put him out of her mind, and married another man:

Went to his accustomed door and he knocked his knuckles sore,
His wife she came, but to his shame, she knew his face no more.[17]

Such songs constituted a type of public debate over the tensions in male-female relationships during the migrations. In acknowledging the fragile state of couples and marriages, the blues expressed a more realistic attitude than the "stand-by-your-man" narratives offered in country-and-western recordings. By raising such problems in song, the blues artists helped listeners to negotiate the difficult strains that the migrations placed on their love lives.

The families that managed to remain intact contended with issues of distrust, infidelity, and violence. Couples found it difficult to ignore the temptations of urban life after leaving the support systems of kith and kin on the plantations and in the towns and small cities of the South. In the 1939 recording "Baby Don't You Remember?" Broonzy created a scenario that cautions listeners about the way loved ones might change under the influence of the city. The protagonist admonishes his wife for "acting out" in ways that she would not have done back home. He invokes their history back in the South to show her how much she had changed, harking back to their childhood days in Little Rock, Arkansas, when they played games like "hide and switches by the light of the moon." He also describes the way he bought supplies when they lived as sharecroppers on the cotton plantation, and he questions how city life could have changed her so utterly:

When we were schoolmates, nobody could keep us apart.
Now, since you've got to the big city, gal, you done got smart.[18]

In blues songs, the standards for a good spouse focus on basic financial and emotional needs. A good man, for example, works when able, provides financial support for the family, moderates his affairs with other women, and satisfies his woman sexually. A good woman treats her man with respect, shares money, moderates demands for consumer goods, has dinner ready on time, remains loyal to her man during arguments, and is sexually satisfying. She does not put him out of the house or return to her parents' home during bad times. Even more, she does not get involved with, or give their money to, other men.[19] The issue of infidelity was raised in many songs partly because it mirrored reality, and partly because the songs had a proven sales value. Cheating in a marriage was common when young couples were separated for extended periods, or an attractive woman was left alone at home while the man worked long shifts. The new settings of the bustling urban centers provided opportunities for spouses to fool around without fear of detection. Carby explored the sense of rage around this issue in the songs of blueswomen, claiming that many songs taunted lovers, sought revenge, and threatened violence. "I want all the women to listen to me," declares the protagonist in Ma Rainey's 1926 recording "Trust No Man": "Trust no man no further than your eyes can see."[20]

Broonzy, however, addressed the issue of infidelity with the scenario of a woman cheating on her man in the 1935 recording "Tell Me What You Been Doing." The character questions his woman with the attitude of a suspicious parent. He wants to know why she keeps disappearing and seeks confirmation of her infidelity:

> Come here, mama, Tell your daddy what you been doin',
> Aw, your dress is all rumpled and your curls all down,
> Look like, gal, you've been way down town.[21]

It was not uncommon for male figures in the blues to threaten to slap, hit, and beat women to discipline and control them. In daily life, a good man usually avoided hitting his woman too hard but still used violence to keep her in line if necessary. The urban migrations created new tensions that led men and sometimes women to harsh outbursts, and the possibility of violence was heightened in circumstances that involved alcohol or drug use. In the 1941 recording "When I Been Drinking," Broonzy captures the sentiment of a drunken character seeking an obedient woman: "I'm looking for a woman that ain't never been kissed / Maybe we can get along and I won't have to use my fists."[22] He raises the issue of gun violence in the 1936 recording "Low Down Woman Blues." The character resents the infidelity of his woman, presenting her with a list of her offensive actions such as loss of love, lying, drinking, and carousing with disreputable characters. He concludes that violent measures are necessary to put things right:

> I'm gonna buy me a pistol, a shotgun and some shells (2×)
> Yeah, I'm gonna stop these lowdown women, because now I'm gonna
>   start to raisin' hell.[23]

The women characters in the blues made threats of violence as well. Angela Davis suggests that the characters in the 1923 recording "Outside of That" by Bessie Smith and the 1928 release "Sweet Rough Man" by Ma Rainey appear to accept abusive treatment from their men. However, Davis argues that the songs address the problem by raising the awareness of listeners. Carby examines the actions of Ma Rainey's character in "Hustlin' Blues," where a prostitute breaks from her pimp.[24] The character in Ma Rainey's 1925 recording "Cell Bound Blues" tells her story on the way to prison. She describes the fight with her man that led to his murder. She justified the shooting as an act of self-defense:

> I walked in my room the other night,
> My man walked in and begin to fight.
>
> I took my gun in my right hand,
> "Hold him, folks, I don't wanta kill my man."[25]

In January 1920, Broonzy took the Illinois Central train to St. Louis, Missouri, where he stopped and worked for a month to earn money for the next leg of the trip: "I worked aroun' there for a while. Then I got me some money an' I lef' from there an' I come on into Chicago."[26] It was not uncommon for migrants to visit towns and cities en route to their final destination. If possible, they stayed with friends and family while saving money to continue the journey. Broonzy selected Chicago as his destination not only because of the influence of the *Defender* newspaper but because of family connections and employment possibilities. He had a brother living in the city who was willing to help him resettle there. Chicago was the center of industrial capitalism in the Midwest. It offered employment prospects to black migrants in a broad array of occupations in the railroads, steel mills, meatpacking plants, and general service industries.[27] In making the decision to move to Chicago, Broonzy abandoned the dream of generations of tenants to achieve economic independence through land ownership and farming. Like tens of thousands of other tenants, he concluded that the best opportunity to become self-reliant lay in the Windy City.

As Broonzy's IC train entered the environs of Chicago, it sped past fiery smokestacks, labyrinthine rails, and rundown tenement buildings before coming to a stop at Central Station. Broonzy stepped into the confusion of the terminal, no doubt awestruck by the hustle and bustle of travelers, the din of the loudspeaker announcing arrivals and departures, the scooting redcaps carrying suitcases, and the beckoning neon sign of the Travelers Aid Society.[28] Perhaps his brother came to the station to escort him to the South

Side, where he would have found the streets alive with the activity of street-cars, trucks, peddlers, black policemen, and deliverymen laboring against a backdrop of stores, storefront churches, music and letter-writing shops, and tenement buildings.

Broonzy entered a ghetto community struggling to accommodate a five-year wave of mass migration. During the war, the population of the South Side had mushroomed from 44,000 to more than 109,000 people, swelling the narrow strip of land known as the "Black Belt." Within this enclave, black people felt a sense of social comfort and optimism in developing a distinctive community affectionately known as Bronzeville.[29] The black population of Chicago had been expanding since the mid-nineteenth century. The growth was gradual, however, and until the mass migration, most people lived in integrated communities. In 1910, for example, there was no community in Chicago where blacks constituted over 60 percent of the population, and one-third lived in areas less than 10 percent black. By 1920, the migration had created a substantially different demographic—almost 90 percent of blacks lived in areas more than half black.[30]

Shortly after settling in, Broonzy found work with a railroad manufac-turing company: "I had a brother up there and he knowed a friend and he called him up that night. He asked me, 'You wanta go to work?' I told him, 'Yeah.'" So in about four days I got a job at the America Car Foundry and I worked there for about two years."[31] The American Car & Foundry Company (ACF) was founded in 1899 through the consolidation of thirteen railway equipment manufacturers. ACF had shops in St. Louis, Detroit, Chicago, and other areas that built passenger cars, tank cars, subways cars, and auto-motive parts. The Chicago plant was the former Wells, French & Company that made railroad cars and bridges. When Broonzy was hired by ACF, the Chicago plant employed about 1,500 people to build rail loaders, snowplows, and graders.[32] Broonzy and other employed migrants constituted a burgeon-ing consumer market for black-owned enterprises, which some civic leaders hoped would play a vanguard role in the development of Bronzeville. As the ghetto expanded, the stores along Forty-third, Forty-seventh, Fifty-first, and Fifty-seventh streets drew people from across the South. The intersection of Forty-seventh Street and South Parkway was a showcase of commercial and professional activity, featuring retail stores, doctors, lawyers, and dentists, along with theaters, newsstands, and major institutions such as Provident Hospital, the YWCA, the Hotel Grand, and George Cleveland Hall Library.[33]

Migrants occupied the oldest and most rundown housing in Chicago, largely clustered between Twenty-second and Thirty-ninth streets from Wentworth Avenue to State Street, the main commercial thoroughfare. The community spread from its origins in the shacks along the railroad tracks and the red-light district as more affluent blacks and whites moved to better areas. The black community was restricted in its options for housing due to white residential segregation. The policy resulted in severe congestion, with population density levels of about 90,000 people per square mile compared to 20,000 people in white areas. During the first migration, a study of South Side housing availability found 664 applicants for housing and only 50 units available. The shortage of housing led to rent increases by as much as 50 percent. As a consequence, black housing was overpriced and overcrowded and fell into disrepair from landlord neglect. At the same time, Chicago authorities provided inadequate public services such as garbage collection and street cleaning. The combination of factors precipitated the rapid transformation of the South Side into a blighted slum:[34] "In no other part of Chicago, not even in the Ghetto, was there found a whole neighborhood so conspicuously dilapidated as the black belt on the South Side. No other group suffered so much from decaying buildings, leaking roofs, doors without hinges, broken windows, unsanitary plumbing, rotting floors, and a general lack of repairs. In no neighborhood were landlords so obdurate, so unwilling to make necessary improvements or to cancel leases so that tenants might seek better accommodations elsewhere."[35]

The influx of rural migrants sparked concern, and even panic, among both whites and blacks native to the city. In 1910, an estimated 35,000 blacks lived in the city, but a decade later the population would triple with transplants. Most whites—typically economically insecure immigrants or second-generation citizens themselves—were alarmed and threatened by the arrival of black southerners ready to work for cheaper wages and compete for housing and school seats. White residents—especially those who lived near the Black Belt—believed in general that "there is nothing in the make-up of a Negro, physically or mentally, which should induce anyone to welcome him as a neighbor." Civic leaders and homeowners went to great lengths to prevent African Americans from living anywhere except the South Side. White middle-class homeowners of Hyde Park, Kenwood, and Woodlawn, organizing in meetings and rallies, sought to block the efforts of middle-class blacks to move to better neighborhoods with threats to realtors, bombings of homes purchased by blacks, and the creation of racially restrictive covenants. Meanwhile, working-class white immigrants (many of whom did not own homes but feared economic competition) turned increasingly to violence to terrorize migrants who might enter their neighborhoods.[36]

Broonzy came to Chicago a year after one of the bloodiest riots in U.S. urban history. The city was still recovering from a racial explosion that began in July 1919 over a stoning incident at Twenty-ninth Street Beach. A black boy swam into the area recognized as the white section and was chased away by white boys throwing rocks. He drowned as a result of the altercation, and the incident led to fighting between black and white bathers. The event caused tensions that had been simmering for a long time to flare into a devastating six-day race war. White gangs attacked people and property in the South Side, and black gangs retaliated in white areas. The Chicago police lost control of events, and the state militia was called in to quell violence and restore order. Broonzy arrived the same year that the Chicago Commission on Race Relations issued its report on the riot. Among its findings was the total failure of government (police, courts, schools, sanitation) and private institutions (employers, landlords, restaurants, stores) to recognize and address the problem of systemic racism in its handling of black residents.[37]

While migrants could have expected tensions with white residents, they encountered more complex anxieties with native black Chicagoans known as the "Old Settlers." When the migration began, about 44,000 Old Settlers defined the black experience in the city. By the time Broonzy arrived in 1920, the black population was estimated to be 109,000, and the migrant experience defined black Chicago. The two groups often clashed over differences of class and cultural practices. For the Chicago black middle class, status was defined by ideals of public respectability such as good character and conduct, and practices such as cleanliness, thrift, and sobriety. While native blacks stood to benefit from growing black political and consumer power, many believed that the explosive influx undermined the stable race relations established with white Chicagoans. They spoke somewhat disingenuously of an earlier "golden age" where blacks had ample jobs and civic culture. Because blacks had then posed less of a threat to whites, they had faced less overt prejudice.[38]

South Side civic leaders saw the migrants as rough-edged products of the cotton fields that had to be assimilated to the ways of the city. They complained that migrants lacked social graces, ran down property, and complicated race relations, and that migrants had to be taught the proper ways of conducting themselves in public through extraordinary means. They worried whether the traditional institutions of socialization such as the church, family, and community customs were up to the task. Community leaders distributed leaflets and published editorials cautioning migrants to avoid "vile language in public places," "congregating in crowds on the street," "allowing children to beg on the streets," and "acting discourteously to other people." The Urban League, for example, sought to integrate migrants into urban life as quickly as possibly out of a concern that the missteps of migrants would reflect badly on the race in general.[39]

In addition to the Urban League, migrants were aided in the adjustments to urban life by social service agencies, unions, and political parties. The effect of such assistance was to accelerate the pace of assimilation. Migrants changed outlooks and practices as they transitioned from agricultural labor guided by the sun and seasons to the disciplined regimentation of the factory clock. Evidence of the stripping away of rural habits, for example, was seen in the adaptation of clothing, language, diet, and social life better suited to the industrial way of life. As migrants underwent a revolution in cultural practices —such as educational and occupational improvements—many found their former reliance on such institutions as the rural church inadequate for their new lives in the cities. The church, which had been the primary institution in black folklife, had to revise its typical otherworldly approach to ministry to meet the challenges of the new experience. Many migrants sought out churches that could help them cope with the secular challenges of ghetto life.[40]

Frazier argued that gospel music was one outgrowth of the black church responding to the secular needs of migrants. Gospel fused elements of hymns, spirituals, and the blues into a music that reconciled the folk traditions of the church with the modern sentiments of black urban congregations. The music filled a void in the lives of migrants by helping them to believe that God would improve their conditions on earth. In similar fashion, writes LeRoi Jones, the urban blues addressed the needs of migrants dealing with the rigors of industrial work and the emotional challenges of being away from home. Migrants found solace in such forums of the urban blues as tenement parties, taverns, and dance schools, and at home through the playing of records. Along with the other agencies of assimilation, the blues that Broonzy and other musicians played helped migrants cope with the contradictions of the urban experience. [41]

Broonzy relocated to Chicago at a propitious moment in the evolution of the blues and jazz industry. The South Side was home to an entertainment district of open-air venues, informal tenement parties, taverns, segregated nightclubs, and upscale cabarets and theaters. In addition, the fledgling recording industry discovered profits by producing blues and jazz records for black consumers. Broonzy arrived in Chicago on February 8, nearly a week before Mamie Smith recorded "That Thing Called Love" and "You Can't Keep a Good Man Down" on February 14, 1920. The record sold well enough to convince producers of the existence of a black consumer market willing to support its own artists. On August 10, 1920, Smith returned to the studio to record "Crazy Blues" and "It's Right Here for You," a record that became a runaway hit and spurred the race record industry. With evidence of a potential market, the record labels searched for blues and jazz recording artists on the southern plantations, in the vaudeville troupes, and in the taverns and nightclubs of the ghetto.[42]

The many venues in the entertainment district offered an array of jobs and prospects to earn money for blues and jazz musicians. In the 1920s, Chicago, despite all its flaws, symbolized a dream of progress for migrants and, indeed, the city delivered new opportunities for many people. Men and women took on new occupations in the city's stockyards, steel mills, garment factories, railway yards, hotels, and kitchens. The ghetto gave rise to 75,000 wage earners who supported a middle class stratum of civil servants, politicians, teachers, professionals, and business owners. The black urban folk also had the leisure time and disposable income to support their own musicians. These were the "Fat Years" of industrial expansion and ghetto optimism in Chicago.[43]

Broonzy was part of a wave of black musical talent attracted to the city. Historically, the black community native to Chicago was too small to provide enough local musicians to meet the growing demand. The black talent pool had begun to expand at the turn of the century with the arrival of jazz musicians from New Orleans. By 1910, musicians such as Glover Compton, Charles Elgar, Jelly Roll Morton, and Tony Jackson were playing rag piano and jazz in the bars along State Street and Thirty-fifth Street. In 1912, heavyweight boxing champion Jack Johnson opened Café de Champ, and the word began to spread that Chicago offered opportunity for black entertainers. Chicago was the end of the line for the stage troupes of the Theater Owners Booking Association traveling from New York or New Orleans. As a road show terminus, the city became the new home of female vaudeville singers of the blues. Broonzy joined the postwar mass migration that drew songsters and folk blues singers to the city.[44]

Broonzy was incorporated into a community of blues and jazz musicians who shared the employment experience of the black urban folk. While the life of the musician seemed glamorous to outsiders, what went unseen was that the musicians faced the same obligations of marriage and family, and had the same needs for medical care and old-age pensions as everyone else. With few exceptions, black musicians could not earn a living through music alone, and, as a result, most worked in low-wage service jobs on either a regular or temporary basis to make ends meet. In the 1920s, most South Side musicians found their bread-and-butter jobs in the steel mills, rail yards, and meatpacking plants. Broonzy worked in a foundry and rail yard, as a redcap bag handler, store clerk, and in other jobs. Some of the best jazz and blues pianists worked in service occupations; Jimmy Yancey, for example, was a groundskeeper at Comiskey Park. Meade Lux Lewis washed cars in a Chicago garage. "Crippled" Clarence Lofton polished cars. Albert Ammons drove for the Silver Taxicab Company.[45]

Whatever their day jobs, these musicians saw themselves as part of a distinct class of entertainers. Broonzy was brought in contact with a network of musicians who embraced and nurtured him, and who understood his desire to express himself in music. Like these other blues and jazz artists, Broonzy considered himself first and foremost a musician. Chicago cornetist William Samuels, for example, was hired as an elevator operator and doorman, which were considered decent jobs for blacks. Nevertheless, he felt that jazz provided him with "more out of life than going up and down an elevator."[46] Broonzy was mentored by his musician friends both in the blues and in city life. This was a largely male-dominated society whose members had learned the secrets of musicianship in their families, fraternal orders, churches, and community groups, and sometimes in formal classes. Cornetist Joe Oliver guided a young Louis Armstrong in his development when Armstrong was a boy in New Orleans and as a young hornman in Chicago. Armstrong recalled Oliver's advice on ways to make his solos stand out: "put some lead on that horn, let the people know what you're playing."[47] The men shared ideas that shaped the occupational culture of musicianship based on such attributes as instrumental skill, instruments suitable for urban venues, storytelling, ability to swing, to read music, and to know popular songs. They also discussed gender norms such as women traditionally limited to the role of singer and piano player.

As a fiddler, Broonzy brought the Arkansas teachings of his uncle Jerry Belcher and See See Rider to the community of musicians in the South Side. He became acquainted with local players when working as a yardman at the Pullman Railroad Company. About 1924, he befriended banjoist Papa Charlie Jackson, who invited him to jam at the rent parties on the West Side and introduced him to other musicians like John Thomas. The men encouraged Broonzy to switch to guitar and tutored him on proper technique: "Charlie first got me started on guitar at that time and showed me how to make chords, and I played around a little with John Thomas."[48] In fact, Broonzy was late in switching to the guitar. Since the turn of the twentieth century, inexpensive guitars had become widely available either by mail order or in music shops. The guitar was more adaptable to the voices of blues singers and gradually replaced the fiddle and banjo in popularity. Broonzy remembered buying his first guitar: "I was jus' learnin' the guitar, I was playin' a fiddle all the time. I never started playin' the guitar until 1925, it was. I bought me a guitar, paid a dollar an' a half fer it, on Maxwell Street in Chicago." He also credited Brasswell with teaching him about the fundamentals of guitar playing at that time, saying that they practiced together for a year with his new guitar.[49]

Broonzy continued the practice of mentoring younger musicians throughout his career. His willingness to help musicians new to the South Side with a thoughtful word of advice or a favor was widely appreciated. Homesick James said, "That guy was just like a brother." J. B. Lenoir noted, "Big Bill he take me as his son."[50]

Broonzy's sense of identity as a musician and a working man was enhanced through his association with Local 208 of the Chicago Federation of Musicians (CFM). The local was the segregated chapter of the CFM (Local 10 represented white musicians). While black musicians had to deal with problems of racial segregation in the union, Local 208 helped migrants adjust to city life and to work in the rough-and-tumble entertainment venues. The union encouraged the occupational culture of musicians through education about and negotiation on such class-based practices as the closed shop, contracts, wage scales, hours, and work conditions.

Many blues singers new to Chicago performed for tips in the open-air market of Maxwell Street. They were comfortable with performing in the streets, which was a common way for itinerant bluesmen to get money in southern towns. The shopping district, designated as an open-air market in 1912, radiated out from Halsted Street in the West Side neighborhood of Jew Town. Maxwell Street drew crowds of working-class immigrant and black shoppers from nearby factories and tenements. They flocked to discount shops that sold everything from used furniture to car tires and records. Musicians seeking to earn money and make a reputation performed at sites along the thoroughfare. They played in weather good and foul, sometimes teaming up for jam sessions. In the streets, they could play with abandon the songs and styles of the rural South. Popular acts could garner more in tip money than a typical day's wages. If they were lucky, street performers gained notice from more established musicians, bar owners, and producers. It is unclear whether Broonzy played on Maxwell Street. However, he visited the district to buy records and to scout new blues talent.[51]

More established blues and jazz musicians worked the informal circuit of apartment rent parties. The parties were a ghetto variation of a southern custom of home entertainment. In the South Side, the parties were known by such terms as a "parlor social," "boogie," "percolator," "struggle," and "skiffle." Invitation cards were distributed to selected guests and friends. For example, guests were charged a twenty-five-cent admission fee in exchange for enjoying a party with music and food—and illegal booze for the cost of one dollar a jar. On a good weekend, South Side apartment dwellers were estimated to host ten thousand such parties in their units. The music typically featured guitarists, fiddlers, and harmonica players, or, in a more affluent home, a pianist. Blind Blake, for example, played at parties in tenements on South Parkway. Pine Top Smith entertained guests with boogie piano on Prairie Avenue.[52]

Broonzy was introduced to the rent-party circuit by friends he met when working at the Pullman Railroad Company. He soon earned a reputation as a reliable "down-home" fiddler: "In 1920, I came to Chicago and the people there asked me to come to their house. Some of them had known me at home and they knew I could play and sing the blues. So I went to their houses and they had fried chicken and pig feet and chittlins for seventy-five cents a plate, and if you could play and sing you got all the eats and drinks free."[53]

He found sustenance in an environment that reconciled the different interests of urban and rural cultures. The parties drew people from the same towns and counties of Arkansas, but also attracted migrants from other parts of the South (and northern blacks as well). The migrants enjoyed the company of fellow southerners, and the sharing of down-home cooking and moonshine with new friends.[54] The parties were settings where blacks exerted control over the space and creative process away from the interference of white club owners, producers, and spectators. They were forums where blues and jazz music helped people to cope with the challenges of adjusting to urban life. In this way, the parties nurtured an urban blues sensibility that expressed the new outlook of black modernity.

Some record producers understood the appeal of the rent party to black audiences and cut sides that re-created the mood of the skiffle, such as "House Rent Stomp," recorded by Broonzy in 1927. The ragtime blues conveyed to listeners the feel of a South Side party. Broonzy displayed his mastery of the guitar after switching over from the fiddle. He demonstrated trademark syncopated guitar picking and flashy embellishments to the accompanying bass lines of guitarist John Thomas. Broonzy sounds more like a square-dance caller than a bluesman as he evokes the joyous atmosphere of a successful rent party:

> Play it till the sergeant comes.
> Bring on that law.
> House rent's all paid.[55]

In the 1930 recording "Pig Meat Strut," Broonzy teamed up with guitarist Frank Brasswell and pianist Georgia Tom Dorsey. They recorded as the studio group known as the "Famous Hokum Boys," re-creating the clamor of a wild party that threatened to spill out onto the street:

> Aw, play it, boys, it's got good to Miss Betty now.
> Well, let's go down on Wabash.
> Saturday night.[56]

Broonzy developed his reputation in the rent-party circuit and was invited to perform in the segregated taverns and lounges of Chicago. The forums provided blues musicians with established venues in which to make money and nurture the urban blues. The bars were primarily located on the South Side along State Street and other major avenues, but a few were also located on the West Side along Lake and Madison streets. At the same time, jazz musicians found work in the segregated theaters and dance halls. Some jazz musicians entertained affluent audiences in the exclusive nightclubs and cabarets in the South Side.

In the 1920s, the South Side hosted hundreds of illegal speakeasies that played nightly to packed houses under the protection of the corrupt administration of Republican mayor Big Bill Thompson. Some of the jazz clubs were known as "black and tans" because they featured black artists performing for largely white audiences. During Prohibition, the clubs engaged in illegal activities such as selling bootleg liquor and prostitution. They were run by gangsters who received protection from the law in return for payoffs to police and politicians. The number of jazz and blues venues ranged from 12,000 in the early decade to 42,000 by mid-decade. The establishments ran the gamut from nondescript basement joints to elegant cabarets and offered jazz and blues to suit every taste. Many were owned or controlled by racketeers black and white. The district offered more regular employment to black entertainers than did any other city except New York.[57]

The center of the South Side entertainment district was Thirty-first Street to Thirty-fifth Street along State Street, Indiana Street, and South Parkway. Before the war, the area was a rundown industrial zone with lively saloons and brothels. In the interwar years, new theaters, dance halls, and nightclubs pushed out the old saloons as the district developed into a black entertainment alternative to the downtown establishments. Meanwhile, the downtown venues were segregated by custom and contract. For example, Local 10 of the Chicago Federation of Musicians restricted the hiring pool to white musicians for white customers and perhaps a token number of exceptional black musicians for private parties.

Bronzeville residents described the excitement of bustling streets and music radiating from doorways and storefronts. Among the well-known South Side theaters, dance halls, and nightclubs that featured jazz music was the Sunset. It was a major black-and-tan nightclub with a capacity to service six hundred guests. For an admission fee of from $1.20 to $2.50, the Sunset featured top jazz and blues entertainers such as Ethel Waters and the Louis Armstrong seventeen-piece orchestra. Other jazz establishments were the Pekin Theatre, Monogram Theatre, Vendome Theatre, Big Grand Theatre, Fiume Café, Royal Gardens, Edelweiss Gardens, the Plantation, the Apex, and the Dreamland Cabaret. In these establishments, people could watch the vaudeville acts or dance the black bottom, turkey trot, snake hips, and Charleston.[58] The working-class blues joints of the 1920s have been forgotten, but chronicled were some of the 1930s bars and lounges on Chicago's South and West Sides. Ruby Lee Gatewood's Tavern booked Broonzy, Memphis Minnie, and other major figures, 35th and State Club featured Tampa Red; George Wood's Tempo Tap had Sonny Boy Williamson; and the Boulevard Lounge hired Lonnie Johnson.[59]

Broonzy was fortunate to arrive in Chicago at the same time that the race record industry took off. OKeh Records had released "Crazy Blues" and "It's Right Here for You" by Harlem club singer Mamie Smith. The records were snatched up in black communities across America and demonstrated that the public would support black artists. In the years between the wars, the major labels began to make records for the black audience. The urban migration created a large pool of buyers of records, and later a clientele for jukebox songs. Mass advertisement by OKeh in the *Chicago Defender* spurred people to pay one dollar for a record, a price equivalent to almost a weekly wage for tenant farmers, but affordable for people who had migrated to the better-paying jobs of the industrial centers. The race record industry generated profits for both Smith and OKeh, and created a new line of work for blues singers capable of dealing with a studio setting.

Between 1920 and 1942, the race labels released an estimated 5,500 blues and jazz and 1,250 gospel sides recorded by 1,200 musicians and singers. Many of the sides were put out by the major labels of Brunswick/Vocalion, OKeh, Paramount, Victor, Victor's Bluebird, Decca, and Columbia. In addition, sides were produced by many independent labels, including black-owned start-ups such as Black Swan, Black Patti, Merritt Records, Sunshine, C&S Records, and Echo Records. The major labels created separate race lines to accommodate the marketing challenges of segregation laws and practices. In addition to the separate racial categories for record lists, the companies also maintained separate recording sessions for black and white bands.[60]

John Szwed credits the phonograph record with being the critical factor in shaping the direction of the urban blues. The race record industry was unique in satisfying the demands of black consumers. The comprehensive nature of the industry output—reflecting the diversity of rural and urban folk music—expanded the range of music available to record buyers. The labels disseminated the songs of artists both well known and without reputations; they spread the styles of isolated rural districts and accelerated a standardization of popular music generated in the studios. The technical limits of production encouraged singers to tighten compositions to fall within the three-minute track of the recorded side.[61]

The race record industry created new opportunities for black musicians, producers, technicians, advertisers, and owners. Broonzy aspired to make a record in 1927 after Papa Charlie Jackson introduced him to producer J. Mayo Williams. At that time, Jackson was a folk blues recording star under the management of Williams, the artist and repertoire (A&R) agent for Paramount Records. As the A&R representative, Williams was responsible for discovering and developing talent, and serving as the label's liaison to the blues community. Williams was a truly ambitious product of the black middle class. Raised in Monmouth, Illinois, he was a Brown University graduate who made his living recording working-class musicians. Besides being an Ivy League college graduate, he was briefly a professional football player, a sports reporter for the *Chicago Whip*, and a bathtub gin bootlegger at the Grand Terrace nightclub in Chicago. He entered the record business in 1922 as a collection agent for the black-owned Black Swan label, where a college fraternity buddy was executive treasurer. In 1923, Black Swan encountered financial problems that put it out of business. Paramount was one of Black Swan's creditors, manufacturing the records for Black Swan owner Harry Pace. When the label went out of business, Pace owed money to Paramount. He satisfied the debt by giving Paramount the record masters and discs of Black Swan.[62]

Williams approached Paramount for a job as director of its race labels. Despite his credentials, the company hired him as an unsalaried recording director and head of a publishing subsidiary called Chicago Music Company. Paramount had been founded in 1917 by the Wisconsin Chair Company of Port Washington, Wisconsin. The owners knew little about the music business in general, and even less about race records, but the Black Swan printing orders made them aware of the potential Negro market. Under the creative direction of Williams, Paramount became one of the major race record labels. But Williams was left to earn his salary on the backs of the musicians.

For illiterate blues musicians, Williams's role as go-between with Paramount had financial consequences, such as forcing them to cover the costs of the session and more. Williams squeezed singers in various ways to earn his money. One way, for example, was to keep copyrights and royalties. Williams encouraged singers to sign over publishing and mechanical rights. He kept entertainers focused on blues and jazz material, even when they had other musical interests. He scored songs for publication and placed them under copyright with the Library of Congress. He collected "recording fees" before studio sessions, and he kept one cent of the two-cent royalty fees paid by Paramount as he carved out a role as artistic director of black music.[63]

Williams also appeared to economize on studio expenses by limiting musicians on the number of takes per song. He ran a tight studio session, demanding that the musicians conduct themselves professionally, rehearse before recording, limit drinking during the session, and leave friends and family at home. If a musician failed to make a decent recording in two or three takes, the session would end. The records of new singers had to sell ten thousand copies on either the first or second release if they wanted to stay in the game. More than half of the artists discovered by Williams sold more than ten thousand copies of their first release.[64]

To discover new blues artists, Williams scoured Maxwell Street and South Side bars, lounges, nightclubs, and theaters. In this way, he recruited jazz figures Jelly Roll Morton and King Oliver, and vaudeville blues singer Ma Rainey, who became the label's best-selling artist with the 1924 release of "See See Rider." Williams captured the songs of folk blues singers who appealed to both urban migrant and rural buyers. When he heard Papa Charlie Jackson singing and playing the banjo on a street corner, he invited him to the studio. Born in New Orleans in 1885, Jackson had learned to play the banjo and guitar at fairs, carnivals, and traveling shows in the songster tradition. He first recorded for Paramount Records in 1924 and made best-selling sides like "Papa's Lawdy, Lawdy Blues," "Airy Man Blues," and "Shake That Thing." Williams followed up Jackson's success by recording Blind Lemon Jefferson and Arthur "Blind" Blake in the mid-1920s.[65]

Papa Charlie Jackson first brought Broonzy to the attention of Mayo Williams. After years of playing at rent parties and nightclubs, Broonzy and his friend John Thomas had gained enough confidence to ask Williams for a recording date. Broonzy recalled the secretary asking him what name he wanted to use on the records. When he answered, "William Lee Conley Broonzy," she responded, "For Christ's sake, we can't get all that on the label." According to Broonzy, "She said she'd think of a name for me and later on when she wanted me for something she said, 'Come here, Big Boy.' That gave her the idea to call me Big Bill and that's the way I've been known ever since."[66]

They played their best stuff during the session: "House Rent Stomp," "Big Bill Blues," "Gonna Tear It Down (Bed Slats and All)," and "Tod Pail Blues" (later renamed "Tadpole Blues"). As Broonzy recalled, the session failed to impress: "He said we didn't play well enough. I guess it wasn't very good because I was just starting on guitar." Broonzy remembered that Williams "told me to go back home and rehearse some more, because I wasn't good enough."[67]

Despite the disappointing audition, the session brought Broonzy in contact with the superb ragtime guitarist Blind Blake, one of several Paramount artists who helped him to develop his guitar picking. Broonzy would model the syncopated riffs of Blake demonstrated in recordings such as "Dry Bone Shuffle," where Blake put together intricate runs—including lines from the Charleston. Blake was one of Paramount's stars between 1926 and 1932, when the company folded, but details of his life were fragmentary. He was believed to have come from either Tampa or Jacksonville, Florida, and to have played in northern Florida and southern Georgia. He was an integral part of the coterie of Paramount country blues recording stars led by Papa Charlie Jackson and Blind Lemon Jefferson, and he cut all of his eighty titles for the label. Although his singing was considered ordinary, his guitar "gives him his place in the development of the twenties blues style." Most prominently, he played the cheerful ragtime tunes that evoked the mood of country dances.[68]

Broonzy recalled meeting Blake during an awkward encounter in the office of Mayo Williams. When a blind man asked Broonzy for his name, Broonzy answered abruptly and then asked the man to identify himself. Other players laughed at his haughtiness. When Broonzy learned it was Blind Blake, he felt humbled: "I like to fell out. Blake was the best guitar picker on records." Blake, taking pity on the novice, decided to give Broonzy a lesson in guitar virtuosity. "He took my guitar—my little dollar and a half guitar that I had at the time—and he set down and began to show me what a guitar could do. He made it sound like every instrument in the band—saxophone, trombone, clarinets, bass fiddles, pianos—everything."[69]

Charlie Jackson also continued to work with Broonzy. He not only motivated Broonzy to pick up the guitar, but apparently held sway in his development as a storyteller. According to Broonzy, "Charlie taught me how to make my music correspond to my singing."[70] Jackson may have shown Broonzy how to tell a story with humor, how to pace the narrative, and how to balance voice with guitar. His 1925 recording of "Salty Dog Blues" was a gem of ragtime narrative in which a man expresses appreciation for a beautiful woman and celebrates sexuality. Jackson provided a rendition of the popular dance song in which he offers more than five different verses accompanied by quick-paced, rhythmic guitar. This song was advertised in the *Chicago Defender* as "By Papa Charlie Jackson—the only Blues singing man who accompanies himself on a

Blues Guitar."[71] His song "Shave 'Em Dry," meanwhile, was an early example of a minstrel-influenced blues with an erotic punch line that would become a popular recording. The "dry shave" alludes to sexual intercourse without foreplay:

> Now here's one thing I can't understand,
> Why a bow-legged woman likes a knock-kneed man
> Mama can I holler, Daddy let me shave 'em dry![72]

Years later, Jackson and Broonzy worked together in the recording studio. On June 14, 1934, they cut "At the Break of Day" and "I Want to Go Home," on the Bluebird label with Broonzy on guitar, probably Black Bob on piano, and Jackson on banjo.[73] This was followed up with nine releases in October of that year. And in March 1935, Broonzy backed up Jackson in a session, but the three songs they recorded were not issued.

Although the early acoustic recording methods predated Broonzy, he described the process as though he had experienced it. Many musicians recalled the acoustic studio sessions of the early 1920s as hectic, makeshift affairs. The early sessions involved recording equipment that required musicians to play or sing into a horn, and it took a while for engineers to achieve good balance. Kid Ory, recording with the Hot Five jazz band of Louis Armstrong in Chicago, said the band members worked at different clubs and met in the studio after hours. Armstrong made the music selections and arrangements with advice from the others. They rehearsed a song several times before recording it. The tracks were laid down quickly, and a second take was rare unless the musicians disliked the results. In Harlem, Clarence Williams was known for conducting studio sessions on a "routine, mass production basis" with a "stable of musicians on a weekly payroll" of eighty-five dollars. He also recorded with his own band operating under different names like the Blue Four, Blue Five, Lazy Levee Loungers, Washboard Foot Warmers, and Jazz Kings.[74]

After the early 1927 failed studio session, Broonzy and Thomas continued to practice in the hope of earning another try out with Williams. Thomas also helped Broonzy to hone his guitar skills: "He showed me some more chords and we rehearsed and rehearsed around there about a year." They returned to Paramount for a second recording session in November 1927. Williams accepted the song "House Rent Stomp" for Paramount and scheduled another session for February 1928, when he accepted "Big Bill Blues." This led to a third recording session in October 1928, when they cut "Down in the Basement Blues" and "Starvation Blues." Paramount featured the duo as Big Bill and Thomps—the recording name of Thomas—with Broonzy on guitar and vocals, and Thomas on backup guitar.

Broonzy recalled an episode of "gramophone fright" during the session when singing into the horn of an acoustic recording machine. He probably misremembered the technology, though, since electric recording machines were in use by that time. Nonetheless, the studio environment was daunting to a novice musician with its stopwatch or light to indicate the end of a three-minute track. In this setting, producers expected singers to cut up to ten different sides in a two-hour session. Williams usually scheduled one recording session in a day with the intent of coming away with three or four songs. He preferred to release a strong song on the A-side and a weak song on the B-side to avoid packaging too much good material at once.[75] Broonzy believed the two records sold well, although he had no way of tracking sales; in fact, it appears that sales were disappointing. But Broonzy's method of calculating sales—whether accurate or not—was good enough for him: "There were two places on Maxwell Street in Chicago. I would go to one and Thomas to the other, and we did that every day. That's how I know that they sold good, because we two alone bought fifty of them."[76]

It was common for artists to buy large numbers of their discs both as keepsakes and as a way of boosting sales figures. This was an exciting time for Broonzy, but it also gave him a lesson in the fickle financial practices in the music industry. At that time, Paramount paid most of its new singers fifty to sixty dollars per usable side and an additional five to ten dollars for the publishing rights. It paid an accompanist ten dollars per side and backup studio musicians five dollars.[77] It appears that Williams had promised to pay the men a total of $150 for the four sides. When Broonzy asked for his money, however, Williams told him there had been a problem: "We was supposed to get a hundred and fifty dollars, but Williams told me that John Thomas got the money in front by telling some kind of tale that he had to go off and bury his father or something. Then they told me I broke the microphone patting my foot and singing and they had to take out of our money for that."[78]

But Broonzy told a slightly different story at another point, explaining that Williams had paid Thomas one hundred dollars after hearing the sob story but only gave Broonzy fifty dollars because he had damaged the recording machine. Even more, he said that Williams had gotten them drunk during the session supposedly to help them relax. But he also persuaded an intoxicated Broonzy to sign away the publishing rights. While the Paramount releases brought Broonzy and Thomas a sense of satisfaction, neither Williams nor other producers were clamoring for a new session. This probably meant that the records failed to make the ten thousand sales quota to merit a second session. It was eighteen months before Broonzy made another record—this time under various pseudonyms: Sammy Sampson for the American Record Company; Big Bill Johnson for Gennett Records; and Big Bill Broomsley for Paramount ("Broomsley" may have been a misspelling of "Broonzy").[79]

In the meantime, he returned to his job at Pullman and continued to play at rent parties and nightclubs. But Broonzy now had experience in the recording industry and no doubt walked the streets of the South Side with a new sense of pride. His community viewed blues musician with their own records as folk heroes. The records enabled audiences to bring the voices of favored singers into their homes and to share the music with friends and neighbors. The recorded blues singers had social impact even beyond that of the black press because they could reach audiences literate and illiterate. In this way, the artist whom the public identified as "Big Bill" began to record stories that expressed the feelings of average people.

4

"STUFF THEY CALL MONEY"

BIG BILL BROONZY WAS A LEADING FIGURE IN THE COMMUNITY OF South Side musicians whose recorded songs articulated the sentiments of urban folk audiences during the Great Depression. His records added his voice to the chorus of urban blues artists addressing such topics as work, unemployment, poverty, prostitution, disease, and death, and, in so doing, helped to create an oral/aural culture of solidarity. The blues recordings allowed listeners to share feelings of anxiety and despondence, and to better deal with the psychological effects of the economic crisis.

The recordings of Broonzy and others constituted a "speaking out" on issues of social and economic concern in the turbulent 1930s. The recordings engaged struggling audiences by allowing an exchange of viewpoints akin to the practice of "ritual condemnation," the informal use of everyday conversation to express discontent in black communities like the South Side. Affirming listeners through what James Cone terms "secular spirituals," the blues recordings provided emotional validation for an urban folk people grappling with social and economic disruption.[1] The blues songs offered supportive messages that filled a void created by the diminished role of folk culture and the church during the migration.

The Great Depression had profound social and psychological effects on the average person. Families accustomed to a middle class standard of living saw their income and savings disappear and their futures cloud with doubt. Individuals dealing with long-term unemployment and poverty suffered from physical and emotional illness ranging from anxiety and stress to malnutrition, alcoholism, and mental illness. Many men saw their social status as family providers undermined. Some experienced loss of self-esteem, humiliation, and shame. The values of individualism so espoused during the boom years of the 1920s were badly shaken as desperation led many people to seek charity. Writer Sherwood Anderson chronicled his visit to a basement soup kitchen in a southern city in 1930. As he stood outside, he watched seven hundred people enter for a meal, including one man who approached the kitchen three times before going in. "I am not here for the soup," he told Anderson. "I came here to meet a friend."[2]

During this period, the Chicago blues singers were in a prime position to relate to the needs of their audiences. They shared the problems of cultural dislocation and economic challenge with their listeners. They witnessed the broader despair across the city, and they were able to reach people through the medium of records. The musicians benefited from consolidation in the industry. The recording industry, centralized in Chicago, lowered production costs by using a small number of local performers to produce material. Although white corporations owned the black record labels, the studios were distant enough that blues artists had relative autonomy in the selection of songs and arrangements.

Musicians related to the struggle of ordinary people to find work because many of them, in fact, found it harder to find employment in bread-and-butter day jobs. In Chicago, for instance, blues pianists vied for work as poorly paid janitors at taverns. The jobs afforded them with access to a piano so they could maintain their skills, and in the evening, the chance to play for tips and drinks. For example, Sammy Williams worked on the staff of Gibby's Tavern for nearly twenty-five years and became a virtual ward of the owners.[3] Broonzy, like other musicians, had trouble finding steady work. His empathy for the struggles of ordinary people, and his sense that these issues would be popular, moved him to record topical songs on the Depression. He created a persona that articulated the frustrations of many people in recordings like the 1938 release "Unemployment Stomp":

> I haven't been in jail and I haven't never paid no fine (2×)
> I wants a job to make my livin', 'cause stealin' ain't on my mind.[4]

While the recording's upbeat rhythm inspired listeners to dance the blues away, the lyrics also allude to the notion of "acceptable theft" in light of the dire circumstances of the unemployed. The character describes the impact of unemployment on his family:

I broke up my home 'cause I didn't have no work to do (2×)
My wife had to leave me 'cause she was starving too.[5]

The realistic events depicted in the blues stories inspired audiences to use the songs to reinforce the sense of group identity. Moreover, urban residents used the new medium of jukeboxes, which replaced live bands in bars and taverns, to create needed centers for leisure activities. The taverns and lounges were the social centers where people came to talk, drink, and play the jukebox for a nickel. That so many taverns were called "lounges" was instructive: they were places where people could unwind after work, escape cramped kitchenettes, cool off after arguing with spouses, or recover from an afternoon of searching for a job. One reason why people fed hard-earned nickels into the jukeboxes was that the blues records added an affirmative soundtrack to daily life.

William Jones, in his study of black workers in sawmill camps, explores the role of barrelhouse blues joints in promoting the transition of migrant workers from rural to industrial culture. In the urban ghettos, the jukebox bars and lounges were migrant leisure environments that promoted a similar purpose. In these often white-owned venues, the urban folk were able to gather as communities of mutual support in the anonymous city. The music reflected their broader experience by addressing common events, figures, moods, and feelings.[6]

Broonzy saw the effects of the Depression on both the South Side and the plantations of Arkansas, and his recordings acknowledged the reality of hunger and malnutrition that poor people suffered during these years. His cover of the 1931 Charley Jordan recording "Starvation Blues" associated hunger with individual bad luck and the poverty of the community. It laments the downward spiral of hard times: the inability to pay rent, the prospect of homeless and family breakup, and the possibility of death represented in the image of the hearse:

Starvation in my kitchen, rent sign on my door (2×)
If my luck don't change, baby, can't stay at my home no more.[7]

Black musicians, in addition to losing day jobs, grappled with the closing of entertainment venues in the South Side. The district of taverns, nightclubs, theaters, dance halls, and record companies was dependent on the discretionary income of black industrial workers. As people cut back on spending, the establishments shut down, switched to jukeboxes, and laid off musicians. The

Depression ended the so-called "Golden Age" of the 1920s recalled by musicians as a time of an expanding employment in the jazz and blues industry.[8]

Moreover, musicians with engagements often played for lower wages and tips, even in the elegant nightclubs and theaters. Danny Barker came to Harlem from New Orleans in 1930 and found the entertainment districts in a terrible state, saying, "the depression for musicians in New York—man, it was a bitch." While he found work in clubs such as Harry White's Nest Club, Lenox Club, and Small's Paradise, the hours and payment were uneven. "Some days we'd make seventy-five cents, other mornings we'd get twenty-five," he said. "Everybody cooperated because there was nowhere else to go and, in fact, nobody had nothing." In addition, musicians put up with clubs cheating them out of wages. Coleman Hawkins, for instance, said that some Harlem clubs withheld payment to performers during the Depression even when they were union members. The musicians had little recourse for complaint.[9]

Meanwhile, some talented youths had to enter the business prematurely out of economic necessity. As child laborers, they worked under the radar of the laws and in the shady company of drunks and gangsters. Billie Holiday described suffering through the Depression at the age of nine. She lived with her unemployed mother in a tenement on 145th Street near Seventh Avenue in Harlem. Her mother was unable to find work as a domestic laborer, and they lived hungry and cold in the midst of winter. Holiday said she walked Seventh Avenue in search of work from 145th Street to 133rd Street until she came upon the Log Cabin Club. She entered and begged the manager for work as a dance girl; perhaps to stifle her anxiety, she asked for a shot of gin before the audition. The manager, after watching her dance awkwardly, turned her away. Holiday begged to be auditioned as a singer instead. The manager told the pianist to accompany her as she sang "Travelin'" and "Body and Soul" in haunting melancholy style. When the approving customers showered the girl with about eighteen dollars in tips, the manager hired her. Holiday ran home to tell her mother with the news, stopping long enough to eat a sandwich and buy a chicken for dinner.[10] If this story is true, Holiday was singing in a barroom when she should have been in third grade. In any case, the story illustrates her empathy with the hard luck of ordinary people.

The Depression also had a catastrophic impact on blacks in the rural South, with effects felt across U.S. agricultural production, but in particular on the cotton plantation farming where many black field hands and small renters worked. During the Depression, 2.8 million of the 6.8 million farmers in the United States worked as tenants. The South had the highest concentration of tenancy, with nearly half of the farmers working as such. The vast majority of black tenants were sharecroppers, the lowest class of tenancy characterized by debt peonage and landlord patronage. About 2 million black tenants lived in primitive conditions without electricity, appliances, education, or medical care, and enmeshed in debt and declining income. A 1934 federal government study found sharecroppers averaging a net income of $312 a year, or $71 per person. The lowest earnings were in Mississippi, where annual income was $38 per person (or ten cents per day) if wages were earned at all. Only 70 percent of sharecropping families earned cash after settling their account, and the average payout was thirty-three dollars.[11]

Broonzy, who had regularly returned to visit family in Arkansas after he left in 1920, understood the plight of the sharecropper and articulated the problems of hunger in songs such as the 1934 recording "Hungry Man Blues." The recording illustrates his continued awareness of the effect of poverty on the black family, and the shame felt by men unable to provide for their families. The song offers a father's lament over his inability to feed his family:

My wife is hungry, lord, and my baby too (2×)
I've got the blues so bad, baby, mama, I don't know what to do.[12]

In the 1940 recording "Plow Hand Blues," Broonzy drew upon memories of tenancy to compose a song of lament, taking a defiant stand against an economic system that led to the "death" (whether factual or symbolic is unknown) of his grandfather and contributed to the deterioration of so many people.

I ain't gonna raise no more cotton, I declare I ain't gonna try to raise
  no more corn (2×)
Lord, if a mule start to run away with the world, ooh, lord, I'm gonna
  let him go ahead on.[13]

Regardless of the sharecroppers' struggle, the transformation in U.S. agriculture was irreversible. During the 1930s, huge numbers of sharecroppers either left or were kicked off the plantations. The waves of migrants in search of food, shelter, and jobs strained the resources of individuals and families in ways not seen since the years of the Reconstruction era. Broonzy expresses the mood of many people in the 1937 recording, "Mean Old World":

This is a mean old world to live in, I'm just travelin' through (2×)
Yeah, sometime I get so blue till I don't know what to do.[14]

The experience of black workers in the industrial states was just as devastating. Urban League director T. Arnold Hill examined the growing economic plight of blacks in the depths of the Depression. In April 1931, Hill concluded that "at no time in the history of the Negro since slavery has his economic and social outlook seemed so discouraging." While black workers constituted 8 percent of the labor force, they comprised 22 percent of the national unemployed. The high level of joblessness among urban blacks was due to their concentration in occupations quickly undercut by the Depression, continued migration to the cities, and employer racism that targeted them, rather than white workers, for layoffs.[15]

In 1932, Chicago had an estimated 700,000 unemployed workers, or about 40 percent of the total number of gainfully employed persons. Evidence of the hard times was dramatized by images of idle men and bread lines. A desperate Mayor Anton Cermak allowed the public to dig up wooden street planks to use as firewood in the throes of a bitter winter. In the South Side, 43 percent of black men and 58 percent of women were jobless. In other areas, a 1934 survey of Massachusetts employment rates found that 19 percent of white workers were jobless compared to 32 percent of black workers, while about half of black males in the industrial centers of Philadelphia, New York, and Detroit were without jobs in the early years of the crisis. By 1937, the U.S. Census determined that skilled black workers generally suffered twice the rate of unemployment as white workers.[16]

As the job market contracted, blacks faced intense competition for the menial jobs once considered undesirable by whites. They were displaced from traditional "Negro jobs" such as domestic servants, garbage collectors, elevator operators, bellhops, waiters, and street cleaners—the range of low-paying service jobs that they had occupied in the boom years of the 1920s. In southern cities, black workers encountered racist campaigns to replace them with white workers. By 1932, partly as a result of such campaigns, nearly half of black workers in southern cities were unemployed. In Atlanta, for example, desperate white men pushed out black street cleaners and garbage collectors, organizing around the slogan "No Jobs for Niggers until Every White Man Has a Job!" In Marianna, Florida, a lynch mob attacked a store that hired black helpers. A white clerk, speaking after the incident, said, "A nigger hasn't got no right to have a job when there are white men who can do the work and are out of work." A white Georgia woman raised the issue with the highest political authority when she wrote to President Franklin Roosevelt in 1935: "Negroes being worked ever where instead of white men it don't look like that is rite [*sic*]."[17]

Companies in the northern industrial centers practiced racial discrimination in hiring as well. Employers replaced blacks with jobless whites, and required hiring agencies to select white applicants. Unions also shut out blacks from apprenticeships, training, and worksites. Many black job seekers went hopefully to employment offices knowing it was likely that they would be turned away. Broonzy illustrated the problem in a story about an experience in a Chicago employment agency. He went to the office to apply for a job listed in the newspaper by the agency. He and a woman were the only blacks among fifty people in the office. They took numbers and waited to be called, but by the end of the day, after all the other people had been interviewed, they remained uncalled. Finally, an agency manager told them that they did not hire Negroes. As they left, the woman expressed surprise at the rebuff, saying that she expected it in the South, but not in Chicago. Broonzy retorted bitterly that blacks should not be surprised to find racism practiced across the country.[18] He comments on the incident in the recording "Black, Brown and White:"

> I went to an employment office, got a number and I got in line
> They called everybody's number, but they never did call out mine![19]

In another incident, Broonzy recalled being set up for replacement in a steel foundry. He worked as a molder, a hot and dangerous job that had become a significant source of work for white immigrants and blacks until the lean days of the Depression. He had been employed for seven years, during which time he trained other men. One day, his boss asked him to train a new employee, an immigrant from Poland. Broonzy taught him the job, and the two worked together for a year. One night Broonzy invited the man to his house for dinner and drinks. The coworker, drunk on whiskey, teased Broonzy that he was blind to his own exploitation. When Broonzy asked what he meant, the man showed Broonzy his pay stub—he was earning one hundred dollars a week while Broonzy only earned fifty dollars, a wage considered sufficient for a Negro employee. The Polish immigrant had started at fifty-five dollars a week and in a year earned one hundred dollars. But the biggest irony was yet to come—the immigrant became his boss and fired Broonzy. Whether this incident actually happened cannot be confirmed; however, Broonzy raises an issue of injustice well known to black workers:

> Me and a man was working side by side, this is what it meant
> They was paying him a dollar an hour, and they paying me fifty
>   cents![20]

The middle class faced the challenge of maintaining its tenuous status as many families lost jobs and homes over the decade. The black Chicago business community was shaken by the loss of customers and the devaluation of assets. The 1930 collapse of the bank of Jesse Binga, a symbol of Bronzeville financial power, wiped out the uninsured deposits of the community. Among those touched by the bank failure were frugal musicians who had managed to accumulate savings. Bandleader and cornetist Joe Oliver, for example, claimed to have lost his life savings in the bank catastrophe. He died sick and poor in the midst of the Depression.[21]

People who kept their jobs still faced the threat of wage reductions, along with constant anxiety over employment security. One 1932 study of two thousand skilled workers in Harlem, for example, discovered that median income had fallen from $1,955 in 1929 to $1,003.[22] In 1937, Broonzy addressed some of the effects of poverty on ordinary life, such as the difficulty of paying for a ride on the streetcar, in the lighthearted recording "Stuff They Call Money." The song expressed the embarrassment of a passenger whose poverty was revealed publicly when confronted by a conductor. It perpetuated the image of the streetcar conductor as an authority figure with which the timid urban folk had to contend.

> I got on a streetcar one day, the conductor hanged out his hand.
> You can't get no free ride here, man, don't you understand.
> You must have stuff they call money.[23]

And in "Made a Date with an Angel," the protagonist laments having scheduled a date with a woman when he was broke:

> I've got a date with an angel, baby, and poor me, and I can't fly (2×)
> Gal, I can't do nothin', ooh, gal, but hang my head and cry.[24]

The Depression upset the traditional roles of family members. Unable to provide for their family, men lost status and respect in the eyes of their wives and children. For black men, the reactions may have been heightened be-cause of the severity of the conditions. The recordings of Broonzy and other singers contributed to the release of anxiety by talking out the problems faced by everyday people. Broonzy and other poorly educated blues singers often associated the real consequences of racism and poverty with the idea of "bad luck." Such superstitious beliefs were ways of explaining cruel situations and contradictory circumstances for which there were no easy explanations.[25] For example, in the 1940 release "I Wonder What's Wrong with Me," the narrator questions why he has problems when he has had avoided the actions thought to trigger bad consequences:

> I don't walk under no ladder, I don't play with no black cat (2×)
> I haven't been swept with no broom and I'm careful where I hang my
>   hat.[26]

While the church remained a key institution in urban black life, it no longer played the central role that it did in southern towns. Its agency was diminished as the needs of migrants were addressed by social service agen-cies like the Urban League and the YMCA. In addition, blues singers shared aspects of the traditional role of the preacher by validating the perceptions of a transplanted people. In this context, the blues ministered to the emotional needs of the folk, becoming what James Cone termed the "secular spirituals" of the Depression and helping people to transcend their suffering and feel better about themselves and the possibility of better days to come.[27] This role enabled Broonzy to reconcile his earlier desire to be a preacher with his ca-reer as a bluesman. Broonzy, for example, recorded songs that convey an im-age of death much like that found in the spirituals, such as the 1934 recording "Dying Day Blues":

> Did you ever get to sittin' down thinkin' of your dyin' day? (2×)
> Lord, it's no need to worry, you did not come here to stay.[28]

The talent of the blues singer to render stories of social realism came into full bloom when describing the effects of the Depression. Huddled to-gether in the congested slums, many blacks (and poor white as well) sought to forget their plight in the intoxication of the bottle and the joint; others succumbed to mental illness and suicide. Families incapable of providing for children smothered or abandoned newborn babies, while frustrated young people turned to crime for quick gains or turned on each other in rage, and

older people looked for answers in the church or in religious cults. Such reactions were chronicled in the songs of the urban blues artist, which raised
the existential dilemma of finding meaning in circumstances marked by
contradiction.[29]

The commentary on drinking in the songs of Broonzy and other blues artists
testifies to the easy availability of liquor in the ghettos and in the bars and
lounges where the blues were played. The availability spurred habitual con-
sumption of both brand-name and low-grade liquor with the result of high
levels of addiction. Cheap booze with names like "Sneaky Pete" wine, "White
Lightning" bathtub whiskey, and "Canned Heat" extracted from alcohol-based
solidified cooking fuel was distributed across the ghettos and rural areas during the Prohibition era, and continued to be imbibed with the repeal of Prohibition in the 1930s. The blues songs tagged alcoholics with such names
as "whiskey-headed man or woman," "liquorhead," and "wine-o." The blues
singer witnessed drinking in the taverns that served as forums for live music
and jukebox entertainment and for social contacts. But even more, the singers understood that alcohol helped people to cope with the disappointments
and frustrations of life as a racial minority.[30] Broonzy comments on alcohol
addiction and its destructive consequences in the 1935 recording "Good Liquor Gonna Carry Me Down":

> Now I wake up in the morning, holding the bottle tight,
> When I lay down at night, mama, just a gallon out of sight.
> Yeah, I just keep on drinking, 'till good liquor carry me down.[31]

The issue of poverty during the Depression cannot be fully understood
without exploring its particular effect on women. One of the tragic consequences of unemployment, poverty, and desperation was the spread of the
sex trade in the South Side. The reasons why women sold their bodies to men
were many, such as unstable family circumstances, feelings of inadequacy,
and drug addiction, but dire economic circumstances constituted a critical
factor. Black women were restricted to low-paying, labor-intensive jobs, and
as undesirable as these jobs were under normal circumstances, they faced
new competition for them from unemployed white women. During the early
1930s, the South Side experienced what one police official estimated as a 20
percent increase in prostitution. He based the claim on a rise in arrests during the midnight-to-8:00 a.m. shift, when an average of one hundred women
were arrested daily for practicing the trade.[32]

Prostitution had become a lucrative business of organized crime as mobsters gained control of South Side brothels. White patrons came to the area in the belief that it was safer and that black women were exotic, although middle-class blacks frequented the houses as well. The brothels were at the higher tier of the sex industry and actually experienced a decline in business as customers ran short of cash. The type of prostitution that grew during the Depression was the unorganized practice of streetwalking. The streetwalkers were likely to take customers into shared kitchenette apartments or the hallways and doorways of tenement buildings. Over time, the South Side contended with a disproportionate number of streetwalking prostitutes.[33]

The blues singers commented on this phenomenon in many recordings. Female singers, however, brought a different perspective to the issue. Perhaps because they had a better understanding of the circumstances that led women into prostitution, blueswomen composed songs that directly challenged conventional notions of the practice. In the 1930 recording "Tricks Ain't Walkin' No More," Lucille Bogan told a tale of the poverty and desperation from the vantage point of a streetwalker. As the character searches the streets and doorways for customers, she articulates the powerlessness of poor black women in the urban industrial economy. In the lighthearted "You Can't Sell 'Em in Here," Broonzy portrays a woman soliciting business in a tavern. In the 1939 release, the song's narrator—the tavern owner—debates whether to go with the woman or to send her elsewhere:

> Won't buy no whiskey, won't buy no wine,
> Get outa here before I change my mind.
> You can't sell 'em in here, you can't sell 'em in here.[34]

As the level of destitution rose, some of the unemployed justified theft committed to provide for their families. It was defended as morally different from stealing under normal circumstances. Some people even argued that the affluent were exploiters of the poor and deserved to be victimized in turn. The case for committing crime was furthered by the discriminatory practices of white relief in the urban ghettos. One letter writer in Memphis reported to FDR, "The most of us did not get no Wood or Coal this Winter + no cloths eather + hard words if we ask for enny."[35] As urban conditions worsened, so too did the potential for the ghettos to erupt. In 1935, Harlem exploded over a range of grievances but especially police misconduct and discrimination in hiring by local merchants. While the riot was an expression of rage without a coherent ideology or strategy, an investigative commission established by

Mayor Fiorella LaGuardia cited the systematic exclusion of blacks from the major companies, utilities, and unions as contributors to mass joblessness. The commission also underscored the deep distrust between the police and the community as an immediate source of the uprising.[36]

In "Police Station Blues," recorded by Broonzy in 1930, the protagonist comments on a police action of alleged racial profiling. He was arrested for an unstated reason, but insists he has done nothing wrong. Broonzy, though living in Chicago, was aware of the state of relations between police and blacks in both the South Side and Harlem communities, since the song was recorded in New York City:

> I was standin' on the corner, I was just sort of lookin' round.
> Lord, and the police come up and arrest me, Lord, and he carried me
>   down.[37]

The song is an adaptation of Nolan Welsh's 1926 recording "The Birdwell Blues," made with Louis Armstrong and pianist Richard Jones in Chicago. In Welsh's song, the protagonist is arrested in front of his home for no reason; after a brief trial, he is sentenced to hard labor in a rock quarry. Recorded in better economic times, but during the height of the urban migration, the song may have been interpreted differently by audiences:

> I was standing on the corner, did not mean no harm (2×)
> And the police came, dragged me from the house.[38]

In "They Can't Do That," recorded in New York City in 1930, Broonzy created a character that spoke about the abusive treatment of blacks in the hands of police and prison guards. The character describes the violent acts of police against black suspects even though people say that the police "can't do that." In fact, some guards were vicious "poor whites" ready to use their fists and feet, and fourteen-pound leather strap called a "bat" to bludgeon a man into submission.

> They take me to the jail before they put me in the cell.
> Kick me so hard until both of us fell.[39]

For urban migrants, the consequences of poverty were heightened by the additional challenge of living in overcrowded and blighted ghettos. In South Side Chicago, practices of residential segregation led to black residents living in levels of density that far exceeded those in white areas. During the

1930s, the South Side population density was estimated at 90,000 people per square mile compared to 20,000 people per square mile in white areas. The Chicago Plan Commission in 1942 concluded that the South Side had an estimated population of 250,000—about 87,000 more than it could accommodate without jeopardizing public health. Nonetheless, the formation of the ghetto was locked in place as more than 40,000 new migrants were herded into rundown tenement buildings. The overcrowding accelerated wear and tear on buildings, and inadequate city services such as garbage pickup and street cleaning left the place filthy.[40]

The range of housing available to black urban folk included flophouses for the most destitute and transient, one-room kitchenettes for lower-class families, and three- to six-room flats for established middle-class families. The most typical form of lodging by far was the kitchenette. The rooms were created from former six-room apartments that had rented for fifty dollars a month. Now the individual rooms, furnished with an icebox, bed, and gas hot plate were each rented for eight dollars a week—bringing in $192 a month. Yet the combination of overcrowded rooms and shared bath led to rapid deterioration of the buildings. Federal government photographers documented the deplorable state of housing conditions in the ghettos. One series of photographs, for example, portrayed the dilapidated kitchenette home of a South Side Chicago family: the bathroom had suffered water damage, causing plaster to peel away and leaving chunks of plaster, wood, and debris strewn around the clogged toilet bowl, and a cracked toilet seat lay against the wall. Another photograph showed three boys sleeping on a dirty mattress without linen or pillows, just a ragged blanket to stave off the cold. There were clothes and schoolbooks piled in a basket like trash, and shoes lay in the middle of the floor. In a third photograph, a man and wife and eight children crowd around a dinner table covered by tattered cloth. Behind the family, the wall is bare and cracking, and in one section a cardboard patch is placed over an area of exposed wood.[41]

Without needed medical care or the ability to maintain their appearance, many of the long-term unemployed deteriorated physically. One deadly consequence of the combined circumstances of declining health and congested slum housing was the higher rates of infectious disease. Outbreaks of influenza, pneumonia, and tuberculosis were common in the tenement buildings. In South Side Chicago, for example, the level of tuberculosis was five times higher than in white areas, and the rate of venereal disease (syphilis and gonorrhea) was twenty-five times higher, or about seventy-five cases per one thousand blacks versus three cases per one thousand whites.[42] In the 1936 recording "Pneumonia Blues," Broonzy created a persona that gives witness to the public fear of the scourge of that disease:

> My friends told my wife they had did all they could,
> They said, "Put him in the hospital before he ruins the neighborhood."
> I keep on achin', yes, I ache both night and day.
> Yeah, doctor, doctor, please drive this old pneumonia away.[43]

In the 1938 recording of "Sad Letter Blues," Broonzy explores the theme of the death of a parent. The story begins at the moment the man learns the tragic news. The recording was not released, perhaps because of the quality of the performance, or perhaps because of the sensitive nature of the subject:

> I got a letter, it come from where I was born.
> It was just to let me know that my mother was dead and gone.[44]

Considering the difficulties faced by migrants adjusting to a mean urban environment in the Depression, it was understandable that Broonzy found incentive to record a song in 1941 called "Going Back to My Plow."[45] The title illustrates sympathy for those people who may have contemplated giving up on the city.

The Great Depression sparked militant reactions by the dispossessed of the nation. In black Chicago, a leadership class of community activists, journalists, and politicians organized the discontented to fight back against a variety of ills, but especially against employment and housing discrimination. For instance, the community supported a campaign of economic boycott against white-owned retails stores called "Spend Your Money Where You Can Work." The movement, which began by targeting chain grocery stores, Woolworth department store, and other substantial retail outlets in 1929, resulted in an estimated two thousand new jobs for black workers. Over the decade, the community had some success with other economic justice campaigns such as the fight against the building trades unions to open up skilled construction jobs, and the confrontation with transit companies over hiring black bus and train drivers.[46]

The social consequences of the Depression illustrated the pitfalls of the market economy absent a social safety net. As a consequence, a public that had idolized Wall Street financiers and captains of industry a decade earlier became receptive to government intervention in economic affairs. Five days after being sworn in, President Roosevelt submitted emergency legislation to a special session of Congress. The New Deal policies took steps to restore public confidence in the banking system by providing government assistance to ailing banks, ensuring the deposits of the public, and regulating the practices of commercial and investment banks. It sought to foster confidence in the equities market by passing a Truth-in-Securities Act that mandated transparency in stock issuances. For the downtrodden, the government created the Federal Emergency Relief Administration to quickly distribute cash to the unemployed.[47]

Broonzy, along with other black Americans, found hope in the possibilities of the New Deal as FDR initiated programs on behalf of the "Forgotten Man." Still, black voters initially viewed FDR with trepidation. They had supported the Republican Party from the time of Reconstruction. Northern black voters continued this tradition in the 1930s, even supporting Hoover over Roosevelt. But the black community had little to show for its support of Republicans over the decades. The party took the black vote for granted, and the Democrats now began to seek it. The Democratic Party, dominated by southern segregationist politicians who held key committee posts in Congress, did not seat a black delegate to a national convention until the New Deal. The New Deal economic policies neglected the special needs of the black unemployed because of opposition from southern Democrats. However, FDR's appointment of sympathetic figures in the administration, effort to reach out to civil rights leadership for advice, and promotion of redistributive policies with the potential of benefitting black workers brought a sense of hope to the community.[48]

The Depression led the federal government to assume the role of employer of last resort in recognition of the economic insecurity created by the lack of jobs. Under New Deal policy, the U.S. government initiated a broad range of employment programs known by the public through acronyms such as the WPA (Works Progress Administration), CWA (Civil Works Administration), PWA (Public Works Administration), CCC (Civilian Conservation Corps), and NYA (National Youth Administration). The New Deal also underwrote massive hydroelectric projects to bring power to the Tennessee Valley Authority, and it established the social insurance programs of unemployment relief and old-age pensions.[49]

For the average black person, the New Deal programs offered a combination of benefit and detriment, possibility and disappointment, as the government contended with the complex problems of mass unemployment, diminished consumer purchasing power, cutbacks in corporate spending, and overproduction of goods and services. In addition, President Roosevelt's reliance on congressional committees dominated by southern Democrats to steer New Deal bills to law meant that the particular concerns of blacks were usually ignored.

The Agricultural Adjustment Act, initiated in 1933 and revised over the years, was an example of a program in which poor black tenant farmers fared badly. The AAA was designed to help commercial farmers but had little to offer the great bulk of the 5 million distressed tenants, sharecroppers, and farm laborers. Under the AAA program, farmworkers were entitled to an equitable share of government payments made to the landlords. However, the program had poor tools to require or measure the fair allocation of payments. As a result, black sharecroppers were denied their cut of the benefit as the landlords kept the money to themselves. Moreover, many landlords found the tenant redundant to their operations and kicked them off the land.[50]

The New Deal created publicly funded jobs that typically paid modest wages and offered limited hours but provided hope to millions of men and women desperate for employment. The Civil Works Administration (CWA) was the first jobs program, initiated in November 1933 with the intention of rapidly creating employment and putting wages in the hands of the jobless. The CWA reached peak employment of 4.2 million in January 1934. Intended to be a short-term emergency initiative while the federal government developed more extensive jobs policies, the CWA spent over $951 million on 180,000 projects related to the betterment of public property such as school buildings, roads and streets, parks and airport landing fields before it came to an end in July 1934.[51] The program is celebrated in the 1934 recording "C.W.A. Blues" by Walter Roland, in which the protagonist comments on taking care of his woman with good CWA wages, and in a different version, also titled "CWA Blues," released by Joe Pullum:[52]

> I was hungry and broke, because I wasn't drawing any pay,
> But in stepped President Roosevelt, Lord, with his mighty CWA.[53]

A year after the CWA shut down, the federal government unveiled its major employment program, the Works Progress Administration (WPA). The

WPA went into operation in August 1935 with funding of $4.7 billion to be used to create jobs on public projects with the intent of preserving the skills and self-esteem of workers, and of adding to structures of public value. Congress continued to fund the WPA until 1944. Over the years, the agency undertook more than 250,000 projects, from highway construction to the publication of books in Braille. It oversaw the building of an estimated 35,000 public projects including 2,500 hospitals, 5,900 schools, 1,000 airport landing fields, and 13,000 playgrounds either newly constructed or renovated. From 1937 to 1941, the agency spent $11.3 billion primarily on various construction and conservation projects, but also on community service programs such as education, the arts and humanities, school lunches, and public health.[54]

Broonzy worked on WPA projects in Chicago and recalled the experience with mixed, although mostly positive, emotions: "In that time just about all the men and women was on the WPA. That was the only work you could get at that time and it last a long time, too."[55] He also admired the WPA for giving consideration to World War I veterans: "WPA, PWA, CWA, all of these was work projects for men and women. Me and my manager both was on the WPA together. There was no recording at that time. It was easy for us to get a job on the WPA because we had been in the army in 1918 and they called us old veterans. All old veterans had no trouble getting on the WPA."[56]

Broonzy wrote about working on a street construction job laying concrete on Forty-seventh Street in Chicago. His story gave the impression of a supervisor having to stay on top of some workers to prevent them from taking unscheduled breaks. At the same time, he wrote about several friends falling ill from laboring under the hot sun but noted that he was used to such work conditions from sharecropping and foundry jobs. As a result, he claimed in a fanciful story, the boss selected him to dig a ditch some six feet deep. He proudly accepted the job, but upon completion he made the startling discovery of snakes at the bottom of the ditch! The snakes had been placed in the hole by coworkers as a joke.[57]

Broonzy recorded one song in recognition of the WPA, the 1938 "W.P.A. Rag." The song celebrates the joy of receiving a paycheck in the year of the highest employment of the agency and was one of the most popular jukebox selections of the decade. It was a dance tune that encouraged listeners to go out and spend some of the money on a good time: "I want all you women and I mean all you stags / Just to spend your money while you play this W.P.A. Rag."[58] Both the WPA and the program for major public works projects, the

Public Works Administration (PWA), established a good record for fair employment. In 1935, FDR issued executive order 7046, banning racial discrimination in the hiring for government projects. As a result, blacks comprised an
estimated 15 to 20 percent of the WPA employees. In 1936, blacks made up
an estimated 31 percent of the PWA workers under a system of hiring targets
used to ensure the meaningful employment of black workers.[59]

By 1940, an estimated 19 percent of black men and 12 percent of women
were employed on government projects compared to 3 percent of white men
and 2 percent of women. The substantial presence of blacks on the government payroll helped to offset their lack of representation in private industry:
an estimated 52 percent of black men and 23 percent of women worked in
private industry compared to 70 percent white males and 33 percent of females. However, while blacks made strides in gaining public employment,
they gradually recognized the shortcomings of the development. They remained dependent on the government rather than making inroads in the
larger sector of private industry. In addition, the private-industry occupations
opened to black workers were largely in doing servants' work, manual labor,
and unskilled factory work.[60]

Meanwhile, the WPA hiring practices raised some concerns over whether
the jobs in fact were better than receiving direct relief. Unlike the relief agencies, for example, the WPA wages did not take into regard the size of the
family. Workers found that they were hired in positions that paid less than
their skills should have commanded, their wages were reduced due to illness
and weather stoppages, and they were limited in the number of work hours
and laid off to share the jobs with other unemployed.[61] This reality led Peetie
Wheatstraw to comment on the trend of people receiving the "304" dismissal
form on a WPA job. The protagonists complain of being fired in the 1937 release "New Working on the Project," and the 1938 recording "304 Blues":

> When I was working on the project, I had everything I need ($2\times$)
> But since I got my 304, ooh, well, I can't even get any feed.[62]

The Civilian Conservation Corps (CCC) was created in March 1933 to
address the problem of jobless young men between the ages of seventeen
and twenty-five. The 1937 census reported unemployment rates at 18.5 percent for teenaged workers between fifteen and nineteen years, and 19.2 percent for workers between twenty and twenty-four years. An estimated 4.1
million young adults were looking for work in the summer of 1940, with an
additional 1.7 million new young workers coming on the job market annu-

ally. The proportion of unemployment was even worse for young women and members of minority groups. The CCC was one of two programs to tackle the problem of youth unemployment, the other being the National Youth Administration, which provided benefits to all groups. The CCC created labor-intensive jobs for durations of six to twenty-four months. During its existence, the agency grew to manage 1,500 camps, to which it assigned about two hundred city youths per campsite. The work involved improvements to bridges, trails, landing fields, and fire towers as well as activities to control erosion, floods, and fires. The agency employed more than 500,000 youths in 1935 and a total of 2.2 million over seven years. The jobs paid thirty dollars per month, of which twenty-two dollars was sent to their families. The CCC also offered basic literacy and vocational education courses.[63]

Broonzy was a member of Local 208 of the Chicago Federation of Musicians (CFM), founded by black musicians in 1902 after they were shut out of the white chapter, Local 10, a year earlier. Like many urban migrants in the 1930s, Broonzy witnessed both the advantages of organized labor and the limits placed on black participation in the trade unions. During that decade, Local 208 reduced the membership fee from fifty to twenty-five dollars. The annual dues were twelve dollars per year. The union attempted to promote the welfare of musicians in a number of ways. Perhaps foremost, it sought to protect musicians from unfair competition by fighting for a union shop at major venues. It supported a closed shop throughout the ghetto but had a limited ability to monitor employment practices at smaller bars and lounges.[64]

Under President Harry Gray, Local 208 created a pay scale in accordance with the finances of the venue. For example, the salary for an engagement at a top "Class A" theater or nightclub was ten dollars per night; at a "Class B" venue, eight dollars; at a tavern, five dollars; and at a road house, three dollars. Many blues singers worked as scab performers for tips, thereby avoiding union dues. Bar owners had a mutual interest in allowing musicians to entertain customers with performances that ranged from a few songs, to an intermission, to a full-night repertoire. Some female blues figures like Ma Rainey and Bessie Smith shunned the union, but others like Lil' Armstrong joined Local 208. In addition to setting wage rates, the CFM provided hospital insurance, death benefits, and assistance for destitute members such as baskets of food.[65]

During the 1920s, the membership of Local 208 was estimated to be in the hundreds. As the Depression deepened, however, its membership became harder to calculate but was clearly on the decline. The CFM grappled with severe job losses across the city as a result of the business failure and techno-logical displacement. In the theaters, as an example, the number of employed musicians plummeted from 2,000 to 125 during the decade. The union tried numerous tactics to encourage the employment of musicians. It endorsed a government proposal to have musicians voluntarily limit engagements to four weeks to create openings for other musicians. It cosponsored "Living Music Day," where merchants hosted live concerts to publicize the bands, and it promoted free concerts in the city parks and charitable institutions.

Finally, the CFM and the national American Federation of Musicians supported the New Deal program to hire musicians under the WPA, which hired musicians for positions where they could use their skills rather than as general laborers. The intent was to help musicians preserve their talents and to provide the public with concerts. At its peak of relief employment, the WPA hired about 12,500 union members and 2,500 nonunion musicians and music teachers. They performed for an estimated 2.8 million people in orchestras, bands, choral groups, and community concerts.[66] However, most black jazz and blues musicians who sought WPA work had a better chance of being employed as laborers than as artists. This was the case with the unem-ployed Broonzy, who was happy to be hired for a South Side street construc-tion project.

Like blacks across organized labor, members of Local 208 had second-class status in the Chicago Federation of Musicians and the American Federa-tion of Musicians. The president of CFM Local 10, James Petrillo, was known as a thug who used intimidation and fear to enforce segregationist policies. As a result, black musicians had few opportunities to compete for higher-paying jobs outside of the South Side and West Side.[67] Such experiences en-abled blues singers to relate to the everyday problems of their working-class audiences.

The outbreak of war in Europe led to industrial revival in the United States as factories geared up to provide armaments for allied nations and national defense. The large pool of surplus labor was absorbed into the factories, war-related industries, and eventually the military itself. Some of the black unem-ployed gained from the initial period of economic expansion. Peetie Wheat-straw celebrates the benefits of factory employment in the 1940 recording "Chicago Mill Blues":

I use to have a woman that lived up on the hill, (2×)
She was crazy 'bout me, ooh well, well, 'cause I worked at the
Chicago mill.[68]

For most blacks, however, employment in the defense plants continued to be elusive as the custom of last-hired, first-fired played out. It took organized lobbying and protests to open up jobs in the factories in Chicago and other cities. In 1940, trade union leader A. Philip Randolph organized discontented blacks for a threatened mass march on Washington, D.C., calling for jobs and justice. The threat persuaded President Roosevelt to issue an executive order in 1941 that banned racial discrimination in defense hiring, and to establish the Fair Employment Practices Commission to oversee complaints of discrimination. The movement succeeded in opening defense jobs for blacks during the war years.

In the chaotic transformation of U.S. society during the Depression years, the blues singer stepped to the forefront as the representative voice of the black working class. Against this backdrop, Broonzy played an important part in creating songs that expressed the discontent of the ordinary people. His recordings provided emotional support at a time when the church and traditional culture were in a state of transition. In bars and taverns across the urban ghettos, people used the music, characters, scenarios, and sentiments to help themselves deal with the insecurities of racism and unemployment. In this way, Broonzy supplemented the role of the preacher by nurturing a culture of solidarity.

5

"DONE GOT WISE"

BILL BROONZY WAS A LEADING NIGHTCLUB PERFORMER AND RECORDING
star during a decade when the blues reflected the transformation of black
culture from rural to urban industrial conditions. During the 1930s, the folk
blues of migrants evolved into the blues of an emerging working class. The
music was an indication of the changing outlook of the public—and the record industry's interpretation of those changes. Broonzy was part of a class of
South Side musicians articulating the new preferences of the blues community. He shifted from the traditional form of solo blues and fiddle music to a
modern form that expressed his coming-of-age as an urban black man.

The urban blues signaled the transformation taking place in the ghettos
that the cultural historian Raymond Williams describes in *The Sociology of
Culture,* his exploration of the relationship between social change and popular
arts: "The real dynamics of the socio-cultural process are most evident in the
transformations of 'popular,' which moved not only along a trajectory from
late forms of 'folk' culture to new and partly self-organizing forms of urban
popular culture, but also along a trajectory of extended—and finally mas-
sively extended—production of 'popular' culture by the bourgeois market."[1]

Broonzy was part of both the urban migration and the industry of blues
production. The urban blues arose during a period of upheaval in the recording industry. The Depression forced many companies out of business and
led to consolidation. The race labels abandoned expensive field recordings,
concentrated production in the Chicago and New York studios, and relied on
the talent pool of artists in the local ghettos. The surviving labels promoted
discount records to cash-strapped fans. The jukebox was an additional source
of revenue in taverns across black communities. As the labels caught on to
the changing tastes in blues music, they sought to reproduce it by working
with singers like Broonzy.

In the 1930s, Broonzy was a central figure in the production of urban blues. His skills had evolved in the informal training ground of the tenement rent parties, taverns, and nightclubs in the South Side and West Side. He proved to be comfortable with studio technology, a prolific session musician, and a confident and reliable lead singer. As a result, he was in prime position to be a representative of the new blues genre.

Within the urban black music scene, the fleeting but intense popularity of hokum music provided a kind of interlude from the late 1920s into the deepening of the Great Depression in the early 1930s. This good-humored music served as an antidote to the somber unfolding of the economic decline. Exactly how the music began was a mystery. "Hokum" was a term used by musicians to describe nonsense lyrics. The origin of the word may have been derived from the French phrase "hocus-pocus," a mock-Latin phrase used by jugglers to divert attention from a trick. In U.S. culture, the word "hokum" had its roots in the comedy of minstrelsy.

In the 1920s, hokum music, with its lighthearted, naughty stories, was encouraged by producer J. Mayo Williams. At the center of the performances was the unlikely pianist Thomas Dorsey. The son of an upwardly mobile minister, Dorsey spent years moving back and forth from the secular to the sacred genres of music. He began playing blues piano in Atlanta and would continue to seek music jobs in the nightclubs of Gary, Indiana, and Chicago. He also had the advantage of studying music at the Chicago College of Composition.

Like Broonzy, he arrived in the Windy City at the time when its popular culture was being impacted by the arrival of both migrants and jazz musicians chased out of the brothels and clubs of New Orleans by the U.S. Navy. Dorsey wrestled with the conflict of wanting both to pay homage to God and to seek fame and fortune. His best work eventually would appear in the form of gospel hymns he wrote like "Precious Lord, Take My Hand," published in the National Baptist Convention hymnal *Baptist Pearls*.[2]

Dorsey credited the origin of hokum music to Papa Charlie Jackson and his 1925 recording of "Shake That Thing." The actual craze, however, began with the 1928 Vocalion release of a risqué song composed by Hudson "Tampa Red" Woodbridge and Dorsey called "It's Tight Like That." Dorsey recalled Whitaker coming to his home one night with the double entendre lyrics written on paper, but needing music. At this time, Dorsey had dedicated himself to sacred music and did not want to return to secular songs, but he was broke, and Woodbridge promised, "there is big money in it if it clicks."

Dorsey looked around at the meager furnishings in his home and his wife's shabby clothing and agreed to write the music. They took the song to Williams, now a producer at Vocalion, and it was released in November 1928 to popular reception.[3] From there, Woodbridge and Dorsey cut a series of sexually suggestive hokum records with titles such as "Pat That Bread," "You Got That Stuff," "It's All Worn Out," and "Somebody's Been Using That Thing." In an interview with the BBC, Dorsey remembered: "Blues, Hokum; now they had such a thing they called Hokum. It had live beats to it. We didn't want to call ourselves blues singers, and we didn't want to call ourselves popular singers. I don't know what the word Hokum means. . . . But it was a good word to carry, for nobody knew what it meant and they say 'Hokum, Hokum Boys, we going to see something.'"[4]

At about this time, Broonzy fell in with Dorsey and producer Lester Melrose, a white sponsor whom he met when working in a grocery store. Melrose was born in 1891 on a farm in southeast Illinois near the town of Olney. He moved to Sumner, Illinois, as a teenager and worked in his father's livery stable and grocery store. He talked his way into a job as a fireman on the Baltimore and Ohio Railroad, but was let go when the company discovered that he was underage. In 1912, he moved to Chicago to be with his brother Walter; the two opened a grocery store where Melrose worked until he was drafted into the army and, like Broonzy, served in France.

When Melrose returned from the war, he and his brother Walter opened Melrose Brothers Music Company on Cottage Grove Avenue, which sold sheet music, piano rolls, musical instruments, and records. The business took off when the Tivoli Theater opened nearby. The brothers moved to a larger space and began to get "inquiries from various composers, including colored, about publishing music or getting it recorded on phonograph records. It was impossible for us to publish pop tunes at that time, so we decided to take a whirl at the blues."[5]

They served as publishers and as agents for small labels like Gennett at first, eventually working for the major labels Columbia and Victor. It should be noted that their younger brother, Frank Melrose, was a respected jazz pianist who recorded with Wingy Manone, Johnny Dodds, E. C. Cobb, and Bud Jacobson. Lester and Walter Melrose would publish the music of King Oliver, Jelly Roll Morton, Bix Beiderbecke, and other jazzmen, and arrange their recording sessions. In the interim, the music store became a hangout for musicians seeking to hear the latest records and to make connections.

In 1926, Lester Melrose sold out his interest to Walter and dedicated himself to producing for the race record labels. He first hit pay dirt by copying the swing-influenced productions of J. Mayo Williams, from whom he bought the rights for "It's Tight Like That," which he rerecorded with Tampa Red and Thomas Dorsey. In 1930, Melrose received a request from the American Record Company (ARC) in New York City to record some of the Chicago blues artists: "I got together a dozen musicians and vocal artists and went to New York City and recorded about thirty selections for them."[6] Among the artists Melrose recorded were Broonzy and his buddy Frank Brasswell.

ARC was created in 1929 by the merger of three small companies that issued numerous labels. The Plaza Music Company carried the Jewel, Domino, Oriole, Banner, and Regal labels; the Pathé Phonograph and Radio Corp. issued Pathe, Actuelle, and Perfect; and the Cameo Record Corp. had Cameo, Romeo, and Variety. ARC supplied the ghettos with inexpensive records by instituting an aggressive distribution strategy to offer twenty-five-cent discs in department stores such as S. H. Kress and McCrory's. It developed a marketing strategy to maximize sales from each release by distributing the same recordings on different labels in different stores, thus creating the phenomenon of the "dime-store" labels.[7]

More than fifteen years later, Broonzy spoke about the road trips to the ARC studio in New York: "One day in 1930, we all piled into a Ford and drove to New York. There was Georgia Tom and I, a girl named Mozelle, Lester Melrose—he was the manager of the record company—and two members of the Hokum Boys, Arthur Pettis and Frank Brasswell. They sang but they didn't play and we made records like 'Come On In,' where Mozelle, Tom and I sang and Tom played piano and I played guitar."[8] In fact, Broonzy confused the personnel during two different road trips to the ARC studios in 1930. Between April 9 and 11, Broonzy, Dorsey, and Brasswell cut fifteen songs as the Famous Hokum Boys. Broonzy also played on nine songs released under the name of Georgia Tom. In addition, he recorded three songs under the name Sammy Sampson with Brasswell: "I Can't Be Satisfied," "Grandma's Farm," and "Skoodle Do Do." Finally, he recorded two songs as Sammy Sampson with Tom Dorsey, "Tadpole Blues" and "Bow Leg Baby." In the releases can be heard the evolution of the maturing Big Bill as a singer and guitarist. He unveiled a mixture of blues shouting and vibrato phrasing akin to the sermon style of a country preacher; meanwhile, he experimented with fast-fingered runs and one-string blues licks.

From September 15 to 17, Broonzy returned to the ARC studio with Dorsey, Pettis (recording as Bill Williams), and Mozelle Alderson (recording as Hannah May or Jane Lucas). They recorded eighteen sides released under various names: the Famous Hokum Boys, Hannah May, or Georgia Tom and Hannah May. This was a period when Broonzy recorded either with the hokum band or under the recording name of Sammy Sampson. For example, he recorded two songs as Sammy Sampson with Pettis: "Police Station Blues" and "They Can't Do That," and three songs as Sammy Sampson with Dorsey: "State Street Woman," "Meanest Kind of Blues," and "I Got the Blues for My Baby."

The ARC sessions began Broonzy's creative association with the better-educated pianist and composer "Georgia Tom" Dorsey. Over the next year, Dorsey taught Broonzy to integrate elements of jazz and blues, and probably to read music well enough to be competent in the studio. They formed the core of the revolving studio band that put out a lighthearted hokum music, combining risqué lyrics with jazz, ragtime, and blues. The popular music often was played at other labels using some of the same studio musicians. The bands featured such names as the Hokum Jug Band and the Hokum Trio. In 1930, Broonzy and Brasswell recorded "Saturday Night Rub" and "Pig Meat Strut" with a different hokum band called the Famous Hokum Boys. The studio recorded the band in numerous arrangements, such as the members playing under different names and as accompanists. During his hokum years, Broonzy perfected the ragtime guitar style that listeners would come to identify as his trademark. The rhythmic guitar choruses in "Black Cat Rag" and "Pig Meat Strut," or in backing the vocals of Dorsey and Hannah May in "Eagle Riding Papa" and "Papa's Getting Hot," displayed the sound of syncopated guitar accented by bends and slides.

The hokum fad played itself out in the early 1930s, but the style spread and may have encouraged future experimentation with blues combos. The music marked the departure from the slower folk blues and indicated a gradual shift in the tastes of the urban folk.

As the stock market crash of October 1929 broadened into a full-fledged economic crisis, nowhere was the impact greater than in urban black communities. Phonograph recordings were a barometer of the hard times. As the record industry experienced declining sales, from $104 million in 1927 to $6 million in 1932, the race record series faced possible extinction. The sale of race records declined from an estimated 5 percent of total industry sales in 1927 to about 1 percent in 1931. The price of race records eroded to the point where major labels were unable to turn a profit.

The companies that managed to stave off bankruptcy often stopped producing race records or focused on very limited output. Columbia, for instance, was forced to reduce the number of copies it made of new blues and gospel records from about 11,000 in 1927 to 1,000 in 1931. In better times, it had bought the OKeh label only to witness a steep decline in the fortunes of both companies. In a similar vein, Paramount was forced to suspend operations in 1932. The Starr Piano Company scrapped the seventy-five-cent Gennett label in 1930 and closed down the Superior label in 1932, and the Champion label in 1934.[9]

Despite the seeming collapse of the market for race records, the sales figures in fact illustrated that a segment of the black community continued to buy existing and new records despite economic hardship and the availability of radio. Rural families often did not own radios because their homes lacked electricity, but even migrants in the cities eschewed radio because the programming was geared to the white audiences. However, many rural black families did own phonographs—from 20 to 30 percent of black families in certain counties of Georgia, Mississippi, and the Carolinas—and continued to buy records because the songs addressed subjects they cared about.[10] The record player popular with blacks was an inexpensive Columbia graphophone that required no electricity. It was operated by a mechanical spring device that spun the turntable—the owner simply had to crank it up.

Through its bare-bones survival, the race recording industry preserved a venue for Broonzy's continued evolution as a musician. He continued to experiment with his music throughout the 1930s, increasingly merging elements of ragtime, jazz, and blues in his recordings. While the eclectic nature of his recordings may put off some blues "purists" today, Broonzy's varied musical output illustrates the range of music considered to be "blues" at that time— and demonstrates the evolution of a modern voice. By 1932, Broonzy was able to dispense with his various pseudonyms and stick with the moniker Big Bill.

In March, Broonzy participated in several sessions for the inexpensive ARC-produced labels of Banner, Melotone, Perfect, Romeo, and Oriole, using an early 1900s Gibson Style O guitar. In one session, he released the sides "Too Too Train," "Worryin' You off My Mind," "Shelby County Blues," "Mistreatin' Mama Blues," "Bull Cow Blues," and the impressive "How You Want It Done," where he showed awesome guitar virtuosity. In a second session, he led the studio band called the Jug Busters. The band integrated folk instruments like jugs with jazz instruments, and it brought together for the first time Broonzy and the swinging pianist known as Black Bob. These were the last recordings Broonzy would make as the industry sagged under the weight of the Depression.

During this time, Broonzy made his nightclub debut as a band leader. In 1932, he began playing in a broad range of Chicago venues from small taverns to theaters like the Regal and Savoy. The names of the well-known blues establishments included Ruby Lee Gatewood's Tavern ("The Gate") at W. Lake and N. Artesian Avenue; 1410 Club at 1410 Roosevelt Road; Triangle Inn at Fourteenth and Racine; Club Claremont at Thirty-ninth and Indiana; Club Georgia at Forty-fifth and State; George Wood's Tempo Tap at Thirty-first and Indiana; and the Du Drop Lounge at 3609 Wentworth. There were also the lesser-known spots whose names suggested weekend fun: Romeo's Place, the Squeeze Club, Brown's Village, the 708 Club, the Chicken Shack, and the Ebony Lounge.[11] In the segregated social life of Chicago, these clubs were forums for the development of urban blues culture that, in later years, became informal social laboratories where blacks and whites could party together at ease. "My first personal appearance in Chicago was in 1932," Broonzy recalled. "I mean in a public place and playing music for a living. None of us would ever make enough money just playing music. I had to have my day job and play music at night. Friends who were interested in us would pick us out for jobs for parties and maybe in small taverns, like Ruby Gatewood's and Johnson's Tavern. The biggest was in theaters. I played off and on at the Regal, Savoy and Indiana Theaters and once for four nights at the Morrison Hotel."[12]

Since his first failed effort, Broonzy had developed as a recording artist, and he now was in a position to draw crowds for his live performances. He stood poised to become an industry star. He had mastered combining his singing and playing, as well as performing solo and with various band formats; and he had laid the groundwork for the emergence of a modern blues that appealed to a mass audience. Now he waited for the industry to come back from the depths of the Depression.

The race recording industry revived around 1934, in the early years of Franklin Roosevelt's New Deal, but with an altered structure. Even big corporations like ARC became takeover targets for movie companies, which sought to gain both the profits from record sales and the audio technology to use in motion picture sound. In the early 1930s, the Consolidated Film Industries bought out both ARC and the Brunswick Record Corporation with its Brunswick and Vocalion, Columbia, OKeh, and Melotone labels. In response, music companies carried out their own mergers. Decca had its own label and purchased Gennett records and its subsidiary label, Champion. The Radio Corporation of America soon had the Victor and Bluebird labels.[13] By 1934, the industry was dominated by a small number of manufacturers distributing large numbers of cheap records.

The mass production of records led to aggressive campaigns to sell the discs through a distribution network of record stores, department stores, and jukebox owners. Long gone were the early days of selling discs by mail order, traveling phonograph salesmen, railroad porters, and furniture stores. While records sold for as much as one dollar before the Depression, the dime-store labels now sold them for as little as six for fifty-five cents.

Moreover, the new record market created by jukebox owners should not be neglected. In 1927, the Automatic Music Instrument Company distributed the first multiselection electric phonograph. During the Depression, the availability of jukeboxes enabled owners of taverns and lounges unable to afford live bands to offer music to patrons for five cents per song. Over the decade, the jukebox came to dominate in black bars and taverns. It was both a market in its own right and an outlet for advertising songs to customers. The combination of discount records and jukeboxes gave the urban blues artists, and the race record industry, a unique level of market penetration. The music of Broonzy and other urban blues musicians reached deep into the black community.

The popular reception of the blues reflected the increasingly secular outlook of urban migrants. The experience of city life caused many to turn away from traditional folk religion. Without the emotional support and social structure the rural churches had once provided them, poor industrial migrants began to adopt a more rational, material conception of life, and increasingly sought answers in worldly practices such as the policy game, the bottle, the trade union, and the urban blues.

Consolidation of ownership brought with it a consolidation of production in Chicago and New York. More and more, the industry relied on the pool of talented musicians based in those cities. Broonzy emerged from a two-year hiatus to find the Chicago studios looking for established stars. The Melrose-dominated labels initiated an assembly-line method of production in which members of studio bands rotated lead and sidemen positions. The new division of labor made stars of top-flight talent like Tampa Red, Roosevelt Sykes, and Big Bill, who could reliably create good sides every few weeks.[14]

Under this system, the studios increased the pace of output in race music production. In the 1920s, for example, the labels offered a wide variety of music from the studio and field recordings of vaudeville blueswomen, songsters, preachers, and bluesman like Blind Lemon Jefferson and Charley Patton. In the 1930s, however, the companies built a stable of musicians capable of producing an increasingly standardized blues style that would appeal to an urban working-class audience. In the 1920s, Jefferson released an unprecedented 100 titles, compared to other top singers like Patton with 30 to 40, or Son House with six. In contrast, the recording stars of the 1930s cut many more releases: between 1927 and 1942, for example, Broonzy accounted for 228 sides, Tampa Red for 251, Lonnie Johnson for 191, Bumble Bee Slim for 174, and Peetie Wheatstraw for 161.[15]

By necessity, the studios encouraged artists who could thrive in a mass-production studio band environment. They sought to build up the names of in-house singers to ensure reliable sales in a market where the jukebox had expanded the potential for sales. As a result, the blues singers of the Depression were semi-professional artists—even if they still had to work day jobs because of low advances and few royalties.

Concentrated corporate ownership invested managers with awesome power over the publishing rights and recording contracts of artists—and the ability to exploit them with impunity. The new business structure empowered white producers and labels at the expense of black artists and independent labels. White producers like Fred Hager and Ralph Peer at OKeh, Frank Walker and Dan Hornsby at Columbia, and H. C. Speir at various labels were gatekeepers for the selection and production of black music.[16] In this environment, Melrose became the leading white producer of race records in Chicago and captured the evolving sound of the urban blues. During the 1930s and 1940s, he managed the blues artists for the Columbia and RCA Victor labels. "In February of 1934," Melrose wrote, "taverns were opening up and nearly all of them had juke-boxes for entertainment. I sent a letter, which was just a feeler, to both RCA Victor and Columbia Records, explaining that I had certain blues talent ready to record and that I could locate any amount of rhythm-and-blues talent to meet their demands. They responded at once with telegrams and long-distance phone calls. From March, 1934, to February, 1951, I recorded at least 90 percent of all rhythm-and-blues talent for RCA Victor and Columbia Records.[17]

The urban blues integrated elements of swing, ragtime, boogie-woogie, and folk blues in a new musical form. It signaled an urban sensibility through the song topics, language choice, beat, instrumentation, and arrangements. Rural musicians were influenced by associations with jazz musicians from

New Orleans and other cities, and by the records of popular swing bands from Kansas City. The urban blues arrangements were akin to the popular small jazz combos of the era. In similar fashion, the urban blues combos featured swinging rhythm and powerful horn sections. Some of the names selected by the artists illustrated their transition to and affinity for urban life: Kansas City Bill, St. Louis Jimmy, and Memphis Slim.

Because the record labels no longer had the finances to underwrite field recording trips, Chicago-based musicians came to dominate the studio sessions. Meanwhile, the ongoing migration made it easier for scouts to discover new talent in the streets, parties, and bars of the South Side and West Side. Prolific studio musicians like Broonzy were used by Melrose as informal musical directors and scouts for new talent. Besides Broonzy, the stable of recruiters and recruits included Tampa Red, Washboard Sam, Merline Johnson, Lil Green, St. Louis Jimmy, Walter Davis, Memphis Slim, Big Maceo, Jazz Gillum, Red Nelson, Punch Miller, Ransom Knowling, Blind John Davis, Josh Altheimer, Sonny Boy Williamson, and many others. The arrangements integrated modern and folk instruments, including at various times guitars (acoustic and electric), piano, washboard, bass, harmonica, drums, clarinet, kazoo, trumpet, and saxophone.

While entertainers usually negotiated control of their performances, white producers exercised their power in the studio. They could limit the range of music selected for recording and narrow the definition of the blues. Melrose, unlike some white supporters who pushed their musical vision on musicians, seemed willing to allow the artists to shape the urban sound. His concern was with generating profits, and as long as the records found a receptive buying market he stayed out of their way. As one writer noted, "Melrose, it must be remembered, was a music publisher and his primary interest in promoting blues recording sessions seems to have been to enlarge the Wabash and Duchess Music catalogs he operated.[18]

Interpreting a photograph of Broonzy with Melrose and the popular urban blues recording artists Jazz Gillum, Roosevelt Sykes, St. Louis Jimmy, and Washboard Sam, Shaw notes Broonzy's central role as a contractor in the Melrose studio operation. Broonzy dominates the photo by holding his guitar, thereby communicating his status as the house guitarist and leader of the studio band.[19]

The guitar-piano duo became a standard of the urban blues. Broonzy collaborated with pianist "Black" Bob Hudson to form one of the best guitar-piano duos of the era. Black Bob was a talented and prolific musician whose boogie-woogie figures backed many of the top recording artists of the decade such as Tampa Red and His Chicago Five, Lil Johnson, and the Hokum Boys. The pairing of Broonzy with Black Bob may have been a Melrose-backed studio gambit to take advantage of the popularity of the piano-guitar duos of Tampa Red/Georgia Tom and Leroy Carr/Scrapper Blackwell. The Carr-Blackwell band reportedly sold more than 1 million copies of different versions of "How Long, How Long Blues" between 1928 and 1935. Broonzy admired Carr and called him "the greatest blues singer I heard in my life."[20]

While not as popular as the Carr-Blackwell duo, Broonzy and Black Bob were a respected guitar-piano recording team. In 1935, they started an association that raised the level of sophistication from the rustic folk blues of individual performers to the hard-driving pulse of the urban blues. They experimented with the gritty sound of piano-guitar blues in dozens of songs and later expanded to a small band combo. The arrangement incorporated the string bass beat of Bill Settles. With Settles's driving bass and Bob's rolling piano choruses, Broonzy developed a style of confident, hard-edged blues that expressed the tough migrant experience in Chicago's factories, rail yards, and meatpacking houses. The band hit its stride with "Bricks in My Pillow," "Big Bill Blues," "Married Life's a Pain," "Match Box Blues," and "Pneumonia Blues," each recording a powerful combination of storytelling and thumping rhythm.

From 1935 to 1937, Broonzy recorded with musicians who evolved a style of swinging blues that articulated the outlook of black urban modernity: He led bands that brought together New Orleans jazz musicians such as Ransom Knowling on string bass and Ernest "Kid Punch" Miller on trumpet with folk instrumentalists such as Charlie McCoy on mandolin, Washboard Sam on washboard, and a percussionist identified only as "Heebie Jeebies" (a slang description for delirium tremens) on woodblocks. One of the early studio bands was the State Street Boys with Broonzy; Black Bob; probably Bill Settles; Jazz Gillum harmonica and vocals; Carl Martin, guitar; and Zeb Wright on violin.

The group released eight sides on Vocalion and OKeh records in 1935. In January 1937, Broonzy was part of a studio band called the Chicago Black Swans. It teamed Broonzy, Black Bob, Tampa Red, clarinetist Arnett Nelson, and trumpeters Alfred Bell or Herb Morand (who played with the Harlem Hamfats, a band with similar arrangements managed by J. Mayo Williams). The Chicago Black Swans featured trumpet introductions, Big Bill's rhythmic narratives, and the chorus exchanges of trumpet and clarinet. Its swinging sound can be heard on "Don't Tear My Clothes" and "You Drink Too Much." The recordings "Barrel House When It Rains," with Broonzy, Black Bob, Bill Settles, Punch Miller, and Fred Williams on drums, was another example of the excellent pairings.

During this time, Broonzy continued to put out the tough blues of small band combos. He turned to the studio pianist Blind John Davis, one of the few native-born Chicagoans among the house musicians, with a background more steeped in jazz than in the blues. While northern-born, Davis was caught up in the camaraderie of the migrant studio musicians. Blinded early in life, he got involved with the migrants in the rent-party culture of the city and would go on to become a reliable player for the Melrose labels—all the while deny-ing interest in the blues. Big Bill, Blind John Davis, and Fred Williams con-tinued to put out a stream of urban blues releases such as "I Want My Hands on It" and "Made a Date with an Angel."[21]

The blues writer Elijah Wald questions the importance of this period of blues innovation. As a blues traditionalist, however, he displays the bias of the folkie purist—a tendency to undervalue the modern urban blues pref-erences of urban migrants in favor of the interests in country blues of later white fans.[22] Such attitudes hint at an exotic conception of black cultural development. One noted blues writer had this to say about the traditional-ist approach to this era of modern blues: "Instead of analyzing the music of this period, their tendency has been to speak of a 'Bluebird Sound,' of pat recording formulas, and to express a certain dissatisfaction with the music of the period—since it does not measure up to their standards of excellence for country blues or the later electronic blues. The truth, I feel, lies in the fact that the blues of this middle period not only gave birth to the subsequent modern style but had a definite, distinctive style of its own."[23]

Nonetheless, a case can be made that by 1940 the urban blues had become somewhat stylized because of studios copying the arrangements of the best recordings. Yet musicians like Broonzy, Sonny Boy Williamson, Jazz Gillum, Tampa Red, and Big Maceo continued to put out songs of distinction. Their legacy paved the way for the postwar R&B sound of Louis Jordan, Fats Dom-ino, and Eddie "Cleanhead" Vinson.

With his reputation firmly established, Broonzy became a father figure to a generation of migrant musicians in Chicago, and contributed to many of the Melrose-created studio bands. He played with the top musicians of the urban blues such as Bumble Bee Slim, Washboard Sam, Jazz Gillum, Red Nelson, Casey Bill Weldon, Sonny Boy Williamson, Lil Green, and Merline John-son. Collectively, the recordings of such artists expanded the lyrical depiction of the black urban community. Consider the partnership with Bumble Bee Slim in 1934 and 1935, when Broonzy supported him on recordings such as "Burned Down Mill," "Policy Dream Blues," and "When the Sun Goes Down." The 1935 song "Policy Dream Blues" tells the humorous story of a poor man looking to the illegal numbers racket to make a score. But his love of gambling becomes an addiction that deepens his poverty:

> Policy's a racket and it's awful hard to beat
> I've played my last dime and couldn't even eat.[24]

In 1938, Broonzy backed Jazz Gillum and His Jazz Boys on "Reefer Head Woman," "Sweet Sweet Woman," and "I'm That Man Down in the Mine." The recording "Reefer Head Woman" featured personnel from the Broonzy-led studio band the Memphis Five. It included Broonzy, Gillum on vocals and harmonica, George Barnes on electric guitar, Washboard Sam on washboard, and an unidentified bassist. The protagonist lamented his troubled relationship with a marijuana smoker:

> I can't see why my baby sleep so sound (2×)
> She must have half smoked her reefer and it's bound to carry her
> down.[25]

It should be noted that songs like "Reefer Head Woman" were part of a legacy of blues and jazz tunes celebrating, condemning, or simply commenting on marijuana and cocaine. In 1938, even Ella Fitzgerald stepped away from her image as an innocent to record "Wacky Dust," a song about cocaine. The popularity of the topic alluded to the blues community's frequent use of reefer, which was rendered taboo by new laws making it illegal.

Broonzy accompanied Red Nelson on such numbers as "Eva Mae Blues," "Working Man Blues," and "Jailhouse Blues" in 1937, and "Prowling Ground-hog" and "Don't Tear My Clothes" in 1938. Recording as Red and His Wash-board Band, the session brought together Broonzy, Nelson on vocal and gui-tar, Black Bob, Washboard Sam, Fred Williams, and Arnett Nelson on clarinet.

Broonzy respected Washboard Sam as a good blues singer and worked with him as both an accompanist and songwriter. Washboard Sam led the hard-swinging studio band that commented on such topics as the Civilian Conservation Corps ("CCC Blues") and gambling ("Policy Writer's Blues") during the Depression. Broonzy told a story that alluded to the possibility of him and Sam being half brothers. He wrote that his father had an affair with a woman in Arkansas who may have been Washboard Sam's mother. The affair ended after his mother and the young Broonzy confronted his father while he visited her in the shack on another plantation. Of course, the accuracy of the story could not be verified.[26]

Despite his involvement in so many recording sessions, Big Bill was never able to gain substantial financial benefit. He achieved a semi-professional status—meaning that he earned part of his livelihood from music—but he continued to work regular day jobs. He appeared to earn more from playing in clubs than from cutting records, but even the money earned from club dates was minimal. He recalled his disappointing club earnings in an interview, saying, "Little I made out of um, I couldn't have bought a car, let alone a house for my mama. . . . [Y]ou ain't gonna make enough out of playing in no club to buy stuff like that; you eat and live it all up."[27]

Broonzy became a recording star during a period when the musicians' union had little influence in the record industry. Local 208 had problems getting information from the studios on the hiring and payment of musicians for studio sessions. According to bandleader and Local 208 executive William Samuels, blues musicians like Broonzy, Ma Rainey, Blind Lemon Jefferson, and others received little payment and no royalties for their work. "They would get ten dollars to cut a record," he said. "They worked for peanuts." He noted the experience of Joe Oliver as an example of the studio treatment of a major jazz artist. Oliver's band worked five- to six-hour recording sessions, with the entire band receiving a payment of sixty-five to seventy-five dollars. They never received royalties from the sale of their records. "The industry made all the money. The white manager made money," said Samuels.[28]

In the 1930s, Broonzy began to work for producer Lester Melrose. Melrose stands as a controversial figure in modern blues recording history. The historian Benjamin Filene, in *Romancing the Folk*, identifies Melrose as the driving force of modern blues, bestowing upon him a status superior to that of the musicians. William Kenney similarly downplays the achievements of black musicians in granting Melrose the credit for shaping the urban blues sound and placing him on a pedestal as the "white blues entrepreneur [who] thereby guided the emergence of the "Bluebird Beat."[29] Both scholars minimize the impact of earlier white producers, and of black producers like Clarence Williams and J. Mayo Williams, who went from being a creative force with Paramount in the 1920s to chief black A&R representative for Decca Records in the 1930s.

The jazz writer and impresario Bob Koester suggests that Melrose was "remembered with unusual fondness by the artists he recorded." But if the musicians' own accounts of their experiences are to be believed, a different portrait of Melrose takes shape. The musicians describe a producer with a history of questionable business practices. For example, Broonzy and other musicians accused Melrose of appropriating their songs and royalty checks. The musicians accepted such treatment because they lacked the education and institutional support to stand up to him. Melrose could operate in a manipulative fashion because of the segregationist culture of the industry, which empowered white producers by shielding them from competition with black producers. In this powerful position, Melrose assigned composer credits and performance rights to himself and paid artists whatever he chose—treating them in a manner similar to that of a plantation boss.

During their long relationship, Broonzy complained of Melrose refusing to tell him how much he earned in royalties from his recordings with the various labels. He argued that when Melrose did pay him something, he used tricky methods to shortchange him. For example, Broonzy said that on one occasion Melrose wrote Broonzy a check for twenty-five dollars and asked him to cash it, buy liquor and beer for a party, and bring back the change. Several months later, Melrose repeated the action and after the party told Broonzy that it was time to settle his account. He calculated that he owed Broonzy one hundred dollars in royalties, but deducted fifty dollars to repay himself for the two checks he had written, saying it had been an advancement of wages. He paid Broonzy fifty dollars. Thus, if Broonzy's story is to be believed, he was cheated out of half of the royalty earnings and tricked into paying for the parties as well.

Broonzy complained to Columbia Records about the underpayment and asked to be paid directly, but he was told that he had to work through Melrose. He asked Melrose to see the royalty statements from Columbia but was told that the label only sent him a grand tally for all the artists under contract. Melrose argued that only he could determine how much each artist had coming to them.

Finally, Broonzy said that Melrose gave his songs "Black Mare" and "Rocking Chair Blues" to Big Boy Crudup with the new titles "Black Pony" and "Rock Me Mama." Melrose refused to pay Broonzy for the songs, saying that they were different than the originals; however, he also refused to pay Crudup for the recordings, arguing that the songs and money belonged to Big Bill. (Crudup also claimed that Melrose cheated him of royalties when he allowed Elvis Presley to record "That's Alright, Mama" and "My Baby Left Me.")[30] The end result of such practices was the large-scale theft of the wealth of black musicians: "They all say we blues singers live too fast and drink and run around with other women and get clipped of our money," said Big Bill. "Well our manager did it too but we got the blame for it, and they is living in a mansion now and still receiving royalties from the blues we blues singers wrote and made records of and a lot of the blues songs have been released in different parts of the world. *Who gets the money?*[31]

The year 1938 marked the transition point for Broonzy from which there was no turning back. His success as an urban blues star was mirrored by the popularity of other modern bluesman, such as the boogie-woogie piano trio of Albert Ammons, Pete Johnson, and Meade Lux Lewis, and swinging small band jazz combos. For Broonzy, this peak recording year marked his break from the guitar-piano recording format and expansion into creative small band arrangements.

In 1938, Broonzy confidently recorded with ever more innovative bands. One quartet featured Bill on vocals and guitar, Davis on piano, Bill Owsley on tenor sax, and George Barnes on electric guitar. In embracing the teenaged Barnes, a white musician who went on to play with jazz great Bucky Pizzarelli, the band made one of the earliest recordings of electric guitar blues. The band demonstrated an impressive level of interplay in the 1938 recording of "Sweetheart Land." A second band involved Broonzy, Punch Miller, Joshua Altheimer on piano, and Fred Williams on drums. Altheimer had migrated to Chicago from Pine Bluff, Arkansas, and found in Big Bill an older mentor and Arkansan soul mate. Taking over from Blind John Davis in 1937, Altheimer brought a nimble, boogie-woogie piano style to the urban blues trio. They executed marvelous trumpet solos and straight-ahead singing on "Got to Get Ready Tonight," "Trucking Little Woman," and "Unemployment Stomp."[32]

Formed in 1938, the band Big Bill and the Memphis Five announced the arrival of the sophisticated urban black man. The band featured the powerful front-line horn section of Walter "Mr. Sheiks" Williams on trumpet and Buster Bennett on alto saxophone, Blind John Davis on piano, Ransom Knowling on bass, and Big Bill on guitar and vocals. In "W.P.A. Rag," Broonzy introduces the song with a field holler that testifies to his plantation origins. But he quickly follows up with an irreverent vocal "wink" that signifies the transition to industrial working-class life, switching to a fast-paced dance tune in celebration of New Deal optimism. The music featured Broonzy's single-string guitar licks interweaved with thumping bass lines and horn exchange. Until 1939, the band released recordings such as "Going Back to Arkansas," "Fightin' Little Rooster," and "You Can't Sell 'Em in Here."

The innovative nature of the urban blues arrangements provided alternative ways to express the modern black aesthetic. The artists displayed a technical mastery and social maturity that knowledgeable listeners recognized as articulating a different meaning than the earlier folk blues. Of course, neither Broonzy nor the other musicians had a theoretical approach to changing the style of the blues—they did not seek to abandon blues traditions, but they did attempt to create a music that addressed the new realities of the urban industrial experience. While the traditional blues was the skillful statement of a talented field hand, the modern blues was a collaborative endeavor requiring the expertise of technically sophisticated artists.

Some of the change occurred in response to the transformation of the record industry, which continued the trend toward concentrated ownership. In 1938, the conglomeration of recording and film corporations became acquisition targets of powerful radio corporations. In February 1939, the Columbia Broadcasting System bought the Brunswick Records Corporation—American Records Corporation labels from Consolidated Film Industries. CBS now controlled the Brunswick, Vocalion, Columbia, and OKeh labels of BRC and the ARC dime-store labels Perfect, Oriole, Romeo, Banner, and Melotone.[33] It closed down the ARC dime-store labels in 1940, ending an important source of distribution for Big Bill and other blues artists in the ghettos, and brought to a close the most prolific recording period of Broonzy's career.

From mid-1939 to 1940, Broonzy played notable urban blues with Joshua Altheimer on piano, and either Ransom Knowling on string bass or Fred Williams on drums. It is unclear why Melrose disbanded the Memphis Five, but perhaps the cost of maintaining a studio band of that size without the revenues from the ARC labels played a role. While Melrose still supported a few larger studio band arrangements—such as bringing in clarinetist Odell Rand on "Keep on A-Smilin'"—the bulk of Broonzy's recording sessions were with the trio. With fellow Arkansan Altheimer at his side, Broonzy brought new energy to his singing. Some of his most powerful blues shouting, backed by Altheimer's impressive piano choruses, can be heard on 1939 titles such as

"Cotton Choppin' Blues," "I'm Still Your Sweetheart, Baby," and "Messed up in Love." Broonzy hit his stride as a blues shouter in 1940 with the accompaniment of Altheimer and percussionist Washboard Sam. The trio was capable of evoking a sense of taut drama on recordings such as "Medicine Man Blues" and "Looking up at Down." "But my favorite piano player," Broonzy asserted, "and the one who worked on all my records from 1936 until he died on Feb. 18, 1940, was Joshua Altheimer. He played a boogie-woogie style and he seemed just right for me. I think he was the best blues piano player I ever heard. He wasn't very big and he couldn't have been very strong because he died when he was only 30."[34]

Altheimer passed away just as the group hit its peak. In the years to follow, Broonzy returned to reliable sidemen from previous sessions such as Horace Malcolm (a New Orleans–trained pianist who had recorded with the Harlem Hamfats) and Blind John Davis, whom he considered to be "the best all-around piano player I ever recorded with."[35] He would use a variety of pianists in club performances during these years such as Georgia White, who played with him about 1949–50 but never recorded with him. He recorded with upcoming pianist Peter "Memphis Slim" Chatman in the early 1940s. As Broonzy recalled it, they met in Chicago about 1939 and became friends. Broonzy offered career advice to the younger musician, such as encouraging Slim to develop his own sound and avoid sounding too much like Roosevelt Sykes. (Slim initially took offense at the comment but later saw its value.) Broonzy turned to Slim after the death of Altheimer, and they played together in studio sessions and nightclub dates. He said that as Slim improved his skills, he advised him to start his own band.[36]

Broonzy recalled meeting Big Maceo in Chicago about 1941, when he played piano with Tampa Red at the Flame Club. They became friends, and Broonzy soon asked Big Maceo to stand in at club dates. They successfully performed at Ruby Gatewood's Tavern and decided to continue performing in clubs and theaters and in recording sessions in 1945. Paul Oliver considered Big Maceo one of the great boogie-woogie pianists of his generation and cited his recording of "Chicago Breakdown" as an urban blues classic. Broonzy commended Big Maceo for helping him to expand his awareness of chord structures. Broonzy remembered when Big Maceo threw a birthday party for himself. He wrote about partygoers ganging up on Big Maceo so they could deliver birthday whacks with a belt in imitation of the good-natured birthday celebrations of their boyhoods on the plantations.[37]

Broonzy's bands appeared to lose some of the dynamic interplay after Altheimer's death. The results of some recording sessions were uneven—to be sure, the bands still reached heights of swing on numbers like "Rocking Chair Blues," "When I Been Drinking," and "I'm Having So Much Trouble," but the sessions sometimes sounded formulaic. Perhaps searching for inspiration, Broonzy returned to a ragtime style with the accompaniment of harp player Jazz Gillum in "Key to the Highway," and tried his hand at jazz singing in "Why Should I Spend My Money?" In 1942, he resurrected the urban blues arrangement of the Memphis Five with a new studio band, Big Bill and the Chicago Five. It featured Broonzy, Punch Miller on trumpet, Buster Bennett on alto saxophone, Memphis Slim on piano, and Judge Riley on drums. The output was modest, perhaps the best number being the Casey Bill Weldon/Andy Razal song "I'm Gonna Move to the Outskirts of Town," a tune recorded earlier by Weldon and covered later by Louis Jordan and the Tympany Five band. By now, as Oliver writes, Broonzy was established as one of the most talented and prolific recording artists of the urban blues: "Big Bill emerged in the Thirties as one of the major artists of his day, and remaining in Chicago, he was a prime mover in the blues music of the city."[38]

Big Bill Broonzy's image among his white fans was an outgrowth of his late career transition to "authentic" folksinger. This image was slowly crafted beginning in 1938, when he introduced a combination of country and urban blues to white fans in New York. Over the next two decades, he cultivated a second career as a folk bluesman among white fans in the United States and Europe, evoking the sharecropper's life and American roots culture. The blues writers, nearly all of whom admire Broonzy, have seemed reluctant to disturb white audiences' folkie image of Broonzy by discussing his role among black audiences as a modern bluesman.

As Broonzy moved further outside of the context of black Chicago, he played the role of the trickster, typified by such characters in black folklore as B'rer Rabbit or John the Slave who use the gullibility of stronger adversaries to outwit them.[39] In this way, Broonzy followed the path of earlier crossover folk blues singers like Huddie Ledbetter (Leadbelly).

Broonzy, of course, was no stranger to entertaining white audiences. As a boy performer in Arkansas, he played fiddle at "two-way" picnics—picnics for white families that hosted separate bandstands for black and white musicians. He no doubt entertained white customers who ventured into black nightclubs in Chicago as well. When he first performed for whites in the

1930s, the Depression had created a climate of distrust in commercial practices and a public mood receptive to alternative economic arrangements. In the cities, hard times created common interests between black and white workers, rivals over jobs and housing in years prior.

As workers suffered mass unemployment, wage cuts, and home evictions, radical labor and political organizations encouraged them to work together. For example, blacks and whites cooperated in the organization of unemployed councils and industrial unions, the march on Washington of World War I veterans, and the campaign for legal justice for the Scottsboro Boys. Even in the rural South, blacks and whites found common ground in the organization of the Southern Tenant Farmers Union. The mass movements brought about a greater effort on the part of the American Left to work with—and often appropriate—black social and cultural activities.

The financial turmoil spurred intellectuals to question the corrosive effect of capitalism upon the American character. In this climate of activism, the American Left looked to folk culture as a means of rediscovering the soul of the nation, the innocent democratic spirit of pre-industrial America. They looked to the music of the rural and small-town folk, the people who had gotten by outside of modern industrial society. The songs of blacks—of a people with a history of oppression—captured their attention as a native source of folk music.

Broonzy debuted before white New York society at the "From Spirituals to Swing" concert at Carnegie Hall in December 1938. The unique musical event was produced by John Hammond, a young New York aristocrat who came up with the idea of staging a festival of "Negro music from its raw beginnings to the latest jazz," with the intent of introducing white elites to the value of music that they would have deemed as lowbrow. Despite Hammond's misgivings, the communist-oriented magazine *New Masses* sponsored the event.[40] In Harlem, meanwhile, black cultural nationalists viewed the event with suspicion, seeing in it a larger effort of the white Left to appropriate black culture and to control its interpretation for their own interests.[41]

Hammond was related to the wealthy family of the nineteenth-century industrial capitalist Cornelius Vanderbilt, and had developed an interest in black culture as a young man. He attended Harlem rent parties and, like other white managers of black musicians at the time, believed he had a special understanding of black people. What he actually had were connections in the music industry that the artists needed, and a desire to build up his career by serving as a gateway for black talent. As a scout for Columbia Records, Hammond sought out jazz players and produced records and concerts, including Bessie Smith's last session. He brought the voice of Billie Holiday to the attention of white jazz fans, publicized the Count Basie and Benny Goodman bands, and connected Josh White with the Café Society. His idea for the Carnegie Hall concert was born out of such relationships: "For many years it has been an ambition of mine to present a concert that would feature talented Negro artists from all over the country who had been denied entry into the white world of popular music."[42]

This was an era when the omnibus category "Negro folk music" included ballads, work songs, spirituals, ragtime, blues, and jazz, and "From Spirituals to Swing" promised to be "the first major concert to be produced in New York for an integrated audience." At one point in the concert, Broonzy was featured as a singing sharecropper in a minstrelsy performance Hammond had concocted, a portrayal that undercut the reality of Broonzy's adjustment to urban life. Hammond initially sought to bring in the younger Robert Johnson, believing him to be "the best there was," but after discovering that Johnson was dead, he turned to Broonzy. He asked Big Bill to participate after listening to his records, describing Broonzy as "another primitive blues singer whose records I loved."[43] Hammond's depiction of Broonzy as a "primitive" bluesman showed his appreciation of Broonzy's folk blues materials but also his reluctance to fully understand Broonzy's role in the expression of urban blues modernity. While Hammond no doubt admired the talent of the black artists, his stereotyping of Broonzy as a sharecropper catered to the romantic visions of the audience.

Hammond was not alone in this regard, of course. This was a time when blues culture was stifled from crossing racial boundaries on its own terms. The folk music revivals of midcentury sometimes appeared to border on creating a "new minstrelsy." In the nineteenth century, the minstrel shows enabled northern working-class audiences to grapple with issues of slavery, abolition, and racial superiority, while at the same time establishing the basis of a national music. In the folk revivals between the 1940s and 1960s, the presentation of blues and jazz artists encouraged audiences to negotiate perceptions of race while seeking to rediscover a "distinctive American culture" lost in the dynamics of industrial capitalism.[44]

The Hammond event provided an uncertain white audience with a secure vantage point from which to enjoy and interpret black music. While some people ventured up to Harlem nightclubs in the years of Prohibition, few gave serious consideration to the music as worthy of a forum as esteemed as Carnegie Hall. Yet the building was packed that night by patrons of black culture such as writer Carl Van Vechten, who came to witness the panorama of black music: a recording of West African drumming accompanied by a lecture from Howard University professor Sterling Brown; New Orleans jazz and boogie-woogie piano by Albert Ammons, Meade Lux Lewis, and Pete Johnson; gospel songs by Sister Rosetta Tharpe, Mitchell's Christian Singers, and the Golden Gate Quartet, and blues by Sonny Terry, Helen Humes, and Big Bill.[45]

Because Hammond had arranged for Broonzy to be portrayed as a Delta sharecropper recently arrived to entertain New York society, Broonzy—often depicted in stylish suits in the promotion photos disseminated to ghettos stores and clubs—appeared at Carnegie Hall wearing the overalls of a field hand. Hammond allegedly had spread a rumor that Broonzy had bought his first pair of shoes for the event. Broonzy accommodated the fantasy of his white supporters to make a foray into the lucrative folk music circles. In dramatic fashion, he pretended to be shy, approaching the stage with trepidation. Helen Humes coaxed him out, saying, "Bill, are you ashamed or scared to go on stage? "Both," he said. "Forget that you were ugly as hell when you came to New York. It's too late to change that mug you're wearing, so forget how you look and how you're dressed, go out there and sing and play just like you did in Mississippi to them mules and cows."[46]

Broonzy, with good-natured humor, played his role to the hilt for the audience. He evoked the enduring power of the minstrel image. Yet as he wore the costume of the cotton picker and the grin of "Zip Coon," he must have wrestled with conflicted feelings over the presentation. After all, he had spent the last decade creating an urban blues for rural migrants. He had come to New York to share the blues with a new audience on an honored musical stage but found himself trapped in the predicament of racial imaging.

Among the selections performed were "Louise, Louise Blues" and "Just a Dream"—where he referred to visiting President Roosevelt in the White House, only to realize that he was dreaming. It was a story about a working-class man who believed his presence was respectfully acknowledged by the leader of the New Deal but came to realize the fantasy of it all:

> I dreamed I was in the White House, sitting in the President's chair
> I dreamed he shaked my hand, said Bill I'm glad you're here
> But that was a dream, just a dream I had on my mind.[47]

Years later, when reflecting on that evening, what Hammond most re-membered was the shock value of the minstrel skit: "Bill, who farmed in Ar-kansas with a pair of mules, shuffled out and sang about a dream he'd had in which he sat in President Roosevelt's chair in the White House. The audience screamed. It had never heard anything like this."[48]

Years later, Broonzy described the minstrel incident as an opportunity to introduce himself to New York society: "I do believe that I never would have been heard in a big hall like that and nobody would have ever heard of Big Bill and a lot more if it hadn't been for that man, John Hammond." He also expressed gratitude for Hammond's role in helping to arrange performances in Town Hall, Café Society, and the Village Vanguard in New York, and in the Million Dollar Club in California.[49]

Hammond later enabled white audiences to see Broonzy perform in nor-mal fashion at the second "From Spirituals to Swing" concert in 1939. Broonzy, playing guitar and accompanied by pianist Albert Ammons, played the urban blues. This time he wore a suit as he demonstrated the guitar-piano combos popular with black audiences.[50] At end, the "From Spirituals to Swing" con-certs helped to raise the status of black music in white cultural circles, while at the same time illustrating the conflicts posed for black artists by the expec-tations of white audiences.

During 1938, the American Federation of Musicians tried to boycott stu-dio recording sessions to protest the use of records in jukeboxes. The action was unsuccessful, but it did raise awareness of the issue among musicians. In 1942, the American Federation of Musicians called a second boycott of studio recording over the issue of jukeboxes. The "Petrillo Ban," named after union leader James Petrillo, opposed the widespread use of jukeboxes in small estab-lishments, contending that they displaced live musicians by the hundreds.[51]

During this period, the recording industry faced production cutbacks due to the scarcity of shellac from government rationing for the war. Shellac was an essential ingredient in the manufacturing of records. The result was a steep reduction in the making of records, and in particular, the production of black music. At the same time, the U.S. War Production Board took control of jukebox manufacturers to provide music to military bases around the nation and world. Young people compensated for the decline in record production by forming jukebox clubs and turning to live bands.

For Broonzy, the combined effect of the boycott and the scarcity of shellac resulted in a three-year hiatus from any significant recording activity. However, he still had a strong following in the taverns and nightclubs. Expanding employment during World War II meant that blacks had stable incomes from work in defense plants. During these years, the audiences for urban blues music continued to grow as southern migrants moved in accelerated numbers to the ghettos of Chicago, New York, Detroit, and Los Angeles. In some areas, radio stations began to introduce the music to larger audiences by remote broadcast.

Meanwhile, white clubs and dance halls once closed to blacks began to serve them in light of their disposable income and the heightened sensitivity to racism. Musicians also found work in bars and clubs in and around military bases. Some of the more popular bands toured with military goodwill shows and broadcast on the Armed Forces Radio Network. During the war years, musicians had more places to play and larger audiences to entertain, even though the production of race records was at a standstill.

Looking back, Broonzy remembered with fondness the lucrative performances in the saloons, nightclubs, dance hall, and theaters in those years, saying, "I made more playing in taverns and nightclubs than I ever did out of records."[52] A sense of his earnings in midcareer can be gleaned from club payments in 1942 and 1944: The Indiana Theater paid Broonzy and Memphis Slim $7.75 each for midnight performances. The two men split thirty dollars for weekend performances (Friday, Saturday, Sunday) for four months at Ruby Gatewood's Tavern. Meanwhile, union contracts showed that he was paid about ten dollars on weekend nights and six dollars on weeknights.[53] These documents provide a sense of what a popular urban blues singer could earn during the war years. For most musicians, however, the pay was irregular and the working conditions difficult.

Also during this time, Broonzy used the positive reception from the Carnegie Hall concert to build a following in the white jazz and folk music circles of New York. He made trips from Chicago to perform at Café Society in New York City, established by Barney Josephson as a club for integrated audiences. In New York and Chicago, Broonzy gained the attention of the American Left, which was engaged in a folk revival that linked progressive politics with the music of working people. Progressive fans admired the ballads, spirituals, blues, and protest songs sung by such figures as Paul Robeson, Leadbelly, Josh White, Billie Holiday, and Big Bill.

6

BLACKS, WHITES, AND BLUES

THE POSTWAR YEARS WERE A TIME OF CAREER TRANSITION FOR BROONZY. While he continued to record urban blues music for the black market, he experienced declining support as young black audiences moved on to bands performing the new electrified rhythm and blues. At the same time, he extended his career by building a following with new white audiences. Broonzy's ability to cross over to white fans, first discovered in the "From Spirituals to Swing" concert in 1938, garnered him an international base of support.

Broonzy's decision to cater to the interests of white folk blues fans, which sometimes required him to don the mask of the sharecropper bluesman, was not without complications. But by returning to the traditional ballads, blues, and spirituals that he had learned as a boy in Mississippi and Arkansas, Broonzy came full circle in his career. He mixed the folk music with stories about life as a field hand.

White audiences rarely recognized Broonzy as an innovator of the urban blues. While some people no doubt were aware of his earlier recording career, most were uninterested in that aspect of his repertoire. Nevertheless, at the end of his career Broonzy was able to maintain the black folkloric tradition of using song and story to express truth to power. He used the opportunity to promote ideals of racial justice and human dignity in the hope of raising the consciousness of his new fans.

At the end of World War II, Broonzy returned to the recording studio as a respected but aging urban blues recording star. Between 1945 and 1953, he recorded forty-seven sides with the Hub, Columbia, OKeh, Mercury, and Chess labels. While the sides lacked the vitality of the 1930s sessions, they illustrated his continued interest in expressing a modern blues sound. As such, his body of studio recordings contributed to the development of swinging rhythm and blues in the postwar era.

The rhythm and blues (R&B) sound evolved from the musical amalgams created in the interactions of musicians on street corners, house rent parties, nightclubs, dance halls, and recording studios. It took advantage of the dramatic sound of electrified guitars and commanding horns, and the amplification of voices and harmonicas. The R&B craze was defined by the infectious boogie-woogie beat of the jump blues, ignited by the popular Kansas City bands, but embodied by Louis Jordan and his Tympany Five Band, Big Joe Turner and Pete Johnson, and the small band combos of Wynonie Harris and Eddie "Cleanhead" Vinson.

At end, however, the term "rhythm and blues" described a wide variety of black popular music, ranging from cabaret jazz to street corner doo-wops, and featuring singers from the aging Big Bill to the salty Dinah Washington and the shouting Muddy Waters. The recording industry advertised the music as rhythm and blues to get away from the offensive semantics of the old "race record" category.[1] The advent of radio stations with black music programming, radios installed in cars, and the spread of music through jukeboxes enabled rhythm and blues to leap the walls of the ghettos and reach white audiences.

In 1945, Broonzy teamed with Don Byas, alto saxophonist; Kenny Watts, piano; John Levy, bass; and Slick Jones, drums, in a moonlight session in New York City for Hub Records. (The label identified Broonzy as "Little Sam," perhaps to avoid contract complications with Columbia.) The liveliest number was the remake of a 1940 Washboard Sam release, "Why Did You Do That to Me?" They also remade the 1930s release of "Just a Dream"—in which Broonzy relates a dream he had of visiting FDR—at a time when the president had recently passed away.[2]

From 1945 to 1947, Broonzy was involved in studio sessions producing rhythm and blues. He worked with a studio combo called Big Bill and His Rhythm Band, which featured John Morton, trumpet; Sax Mallard, alto sax; Bill Casimir, tenor sax; Charles Belcher, piano; Ransom Knowling, bass, and Judge Riley, drums. The band displayed a strong front-line horn lead-in and chorus on "I Can Fix It"; in 1947, it recorded without Morton and with pianist Bob Call replacing Belcher, and released foot-tapping numbers such as "Big Bill's Boogie," "Just Rocking," and "Shoo Blues." After that, Broonzy worked with the fledgling Mercury Records, the first independent label based in Chicago in 1945.

Mercury was founded during an explosion of independent record labels seeking to satisfy the pent-up demand for records after years of wartime scarcity, especially in black music. Mercury was joined by other labels such as Atlantic, King, Specialty, Imperial, Hit, Philo/Aladdin, Exclusive, Savoy, National, Chess, and Vee-Jay. Mercury used both established artists and emerging bands, introducing musicians who would later come to be identified with a golden age of rhythm and blues. Some of the early bands included Albert Ammons and His Rhythm Kings, Eddie "Cleanhead" Vinson and His Orchestra, Gene Ammons Sextet, the Four Jumps of Jive (Willie Dixon on bass), T-Bone Walker, and Dinah Washington.[3]

In 1949, Broonzy recorded with the Fat Four, a band featuring Antonio Casey, alto sax; Carl Sharp, piano; Ransom Knowling, bass; and Alfred "Big Man" Wallace, drums. (About this period, he was engaged at Silvio's Tavern on West Lake Street in Chicago with the Fat Three band, personnel unknown.) In 1951, he recorded with the Big Little Orchestra, comprised of the former band members of Big Bill and His Rhythm Band. The session results included impressive bass and saxophone introductions and flights of improvisation on "You've Been Mistreating Me" and "Tomorrow."

Broonzy also cut folk blues sides that stood in stark contrast to the R&B tracks. Perhaps Mercury sought to market these tracks to a crossover audience in recognition of the growing popularity of folk music. Of particular interest was the recording of the protest song "Get Back (Black, Brown and White)." It was a remake of a side he had recorded in Paris a few weeks earlier, but while the song was quickly released in Europe, Mercury held it back for a later release on an LP.[4] Broonzy was moved to compose the song during a time of growing civil rights activism such as the lunch counter sit-ins organized by the Congress on Racial Equality (CORE) at Chicago restaurants that discriminated against blacks.

Broonzy's final recording session for black audiences was with Chess Records, which was formed several years after Mercury Records. Leonard and Phil Chess had emigrated from Poland in 1928 to escape Russian anti-Semitism. In the early 1940s, they owned liquor stores and the Macamba nightclub on the South Side. In 1946, they bought into the independent label Aristocrat Records started by Evelyn Aron and her husband. The label featured jazz and rhythm and blues, and in 1947, expanded into the blues. In 1950, the Chess brothers bought out their partners and changed the named to Chess Records. Chess offered records from both emerging and established musicians. While it produced a broad range of R&B talent—including Gene

Ammons, Memphis Slim, Willie Dixon, Washboard Sam, and Big Bill—the label was best known for the amplified urban folk blues of Muddy Waters. In the 1953 recordings, Broonzy returned to the small band format, bringing together Lee Cooper, guitar; Ernest "Big" Crawford, bass; and Washboard Sam. Perhaps the most noteworthy side was "Jacqueline."

In the 1950s, Broonzy's stature in the black community was on the wane. He regularly played at Moore's, a small bar near Thirty-fifth Street and Cottage Grove Avenue. Broonzy apparently was romantically involved with the owner, whom he once described as "one of my wives." It should be noted that Broonzy's marital status over the decades was in flux. There was no information available on his relationship with his first wife in Arkansas, Gertrude Embrie. In addition, there was scant information about his second wife, Rose, whom he may have met in Chicago in the 1920s, and whom he married later on. At Moore's, Broonzy played urban blues with a pianist and drummer whose skills were beneath him. During this period, he had switched to electric guitar, but his playing was more subdued than the loud postwar style of Muddy Waters. Broonzy described his conversion to electric guitar as a concession to the tastes of the bar's clientele, new migrants from the rural South: "Most of the people in this place are just up from Mississippi. They don't want to hear no acoustic blues—they're happy to be in the city and acoustic blues just reminds them of a miserable place they're glad they got out of."[5]

During this time, Broonzy was hired to perform at the gatherings of the United Packinghouse Workers of America (UPWA), which was formed in 1943 after decades of frustrated attempts to organize the meatpacking plants. Since 1900, packinghouses like Armor and Swift had exploited ethnic and racial differences to thwart workers' efforts to form a union, but in 1937, organizers began a series of successful campaigns that laid the foundation for the creation of the UPWA. The organizers used folk culture to help bridge racial and ethnic differences among workers. During the 1950s, the union, which had substantial black membership, was known for its militant activism and participation in the struggle for racial equality in Chicago. Broonzy's records continued to receive occasional attention in the South Side when played on jukeboxes or broadcast by disc jockeys like Holmes "Daddy-O" Daylie, one of Chicago's premier black DJs in the 1950s, along with Al Benson, Sam Evans, and Jack Cooper. In 1956, Daylie became the first black DJ to regularly host a show on a network station, WMAQ, an NBC affiliate, and he continued to play Broonzy's records even after the singer had fallen out of favor.[6]

After more than twenty-five years, Broonzy's career as a recording artist

for black urban audiences came to close. While some of his recordings remained in distribution, he produced no new records for black audiences. This
was a time of transition in the blues industry as independent labels sought out
new stars for a younger audience. The Chicago labels recognized the changing tastes of young audiences and turned to R&B figures like Muddy Waters,
Jimmy Reed, Howlin' Wolf, Johnny Shines, Bo Diddley, and J. B. Lenoir to
lead the way. Their confident, defiant, boisterous, electrified sound reflected
the energy and optimism of young urban migrants. At the same time, audiences tuned in to jazz-influenced R&B talents like Ruth Brown, Etta James,
and Fats Domino.

As Muddy Waters grew in stature, he wanted to show his appreciation to
Broonzy for his role as a mentor. Aware that Broonzy no longer commanded
the youth audience in the South Side, Waters invited him to perform during
intermissions.[7] By the mid-1950s, Broonzy, now in his sixties, had given all
he had to the blues. For more than two decades, he helped to forge the music
that had articulated the sensibility of black modernity. Nevertheless, he found
an eager new audience outside of the ghetto.

While black fans knew Broonzy as a singer of urban blues, he continued to
build a following as a folk blues singer with white audiences. After John Hammond brought Broonzy to the attention of New York society, Alan Lomax
went on to promote him to a national and international audience of cultural
elites. Lomax wanted to build on the work of his folklorist father, who had
argued that black rural music was among the most authentic representations
of American folk culture.

John Lomax, who had begun documenting American folk music in 1910,
came to conclude that black music and song had significantly influenced national music. In 1932, Lomax received a contract from Macmillan to create a
new book of American folk songs. With his son, Alan, John Lomax traveled
the country in search of material, recording the songs on-site to capture the
full power of the artists.

The project was underwritten by the Archive of American Folk Song of
the Library of Congress and by the American Council of Learned Societies.
The archive had been founded in 1928 under Carl Engel, head of the Music
Division of the Library of Congress. Engel had raised money for a national
folk song repository with the encouragement of folklorist Robert Winslow
Gordon and poet and journalist Carl Sandburg, who published a collection of
folk songs, *The American Songbag*, in 1927.[8]

The story of John Lomax's meeting singer Huddie Ledbetter (Leadbelly) in the state prison in Angola, Louisiana, and the exploitative relationship that later developed between them has been well told and is not relevant to this work. However, Lomax's romantic portrayal of Leadbelly as the embodiment of the primitive folk hero would greatly influence the perceptions of white folk supporters for decades. Many adherents looked to black folk music as a means of revitalizing commercial American culture generally, and as a vehicle for fostering common community when mobilizing political campaigns specifically.

In 1940, Alan Lomax was one of the most knowledgeable folklorists in the country and a driving force behind the folk revival, and he skillfully promoted folk music in concert halls and through the mass media. That year, for example, he and Nicholas Ray (director of the 1950s classic *Rebel without a Cause*) produced the CBS network radio show *Back Where I Came From*, which featured fifteen-minute episodes on traditional songs.

Lomax marked 1940 as the beginning of the folk revival from a political standpoint. One noteworthy event was the March 1940 "Grapes of Wrath Evening." Hosted by the actor Will Geer to raise money for migrant workers in California, the fund-raiser attracted a number of folksingers involved in left-wing causes such as Leadbelly, the Golden Gate Quartet, Woody Guthrie, and Josh White. Also in attendance was a young Pete Seeger. While Lomax sometimes performed, he preferred mentoring young musicians like Seeger, encouraging them to seek "authenticity" by copying the experiences of indigenous folksingers. Lomax also directed the Archive of American Folk Songs from 1942 to 1945, and oversaw the folk music division of Decca Records in the late 1940s.[9]

As director of the Archive of American Folk Song, Lomax approached Broonzy in 1942 for help with his research on race, blues, and American life. He apparently wanted to portray Broonzy as the embodiment of black folk culture much as his father had done with Leadbelly in the 1930s. Lomax believed he could use blues music and performers to provide an insider's account of race relations in the South. Lomax questioned white America's racial assumptions in a wartime climate of fascist beliefs where Nazi Germany proclaimed Aryan racial superiority, and where FDR countered by touting America as the arsenal of democracy. In this context, Lomax viewed the caste system in the South in the same light as the fascist regimes sweeping Europe. He questioned the common perceptions of whites that blacks were happy living under the laws and customs of segregation and tried to use oral documentary

to let whites know what blacks thought of racial oppression. He was influenced in this approach by oral history projects conducted in Soviet Russia.[10]

While Lomax's political mission was well intended, he clearly displayed a
naïve hope that black southerners would open up to a white stranger. In fact,
it was unlikely that people taught to protect themselves from white violence
through silence and accommodation would speak to him at all. To overcome
this reluctance, Lomax tried some clumsy stunts to "fit in" with black subjects
over the years; for example, when recording people with Zora Neale Hurston
in Florida, he put on blackface makeup; and when interviewing a blind beg-
gar in Mississippi, he pretended to be a black preacher.[11]

In taking on the oral history project, Lomax appears to have bypassed this
barrier by relying on Broonzy as an informant. Broonzy, no doubt, found it
advantageous to curry favor with a man so well connected in Washington,
D.C., and New York folk circles. Lomax met Broonzy while he was research-
ing blues clubs in Chicago, and the singer invited him home: "I visited Big
Bill in his rented single room, lit by single lightbulb hanging at the end of a
flyspeckled wire, and watched as he wrote lyrics for his next blues session
with a stub pencil on a school tablet. Bill struck me as wise as he was big, and
warm and talented."[12]

Broonzy later introduced Lomax to band members Memphis Slim and
harmonica player Sonny Boy Williamson. The meeting came shortly after
Lomax's 1941 folk music concert at the Library of Congress, where he staged
a performance for the Roosevelt White House. The idea behind the concert
was to encourage the use of music in the armed forces as a way of bringing together people from different racial and ethnic backgrounds. It also provided a
vehicle for Lomax to impress FDR and gain support for the folk song archive.[13]

In 1946, Lomax, perhaps seeing the opportunity to build on the theme
of improving race relations through folk music appreciation, arranged for
Broonzy, Sonny Boy Williamson, and Memphis Slim to play at a series of concerts at Town Hall in New York City called "Midnight Special." For Broonzy,
who was once again depicted as a rural blues singer, the experience must have
been reminiscent of the "From Spirituals to Swing" concert: "That night, the
trio tore the house down at Town Hall, discovering that their Delta music was
appreciated by an audience that they had never known about."[14]

Once again, Broonzy was cast in a narrow role that served the interests
of white promoters. Lomax's characterization underplayed the reality that
Broonzy had been a top recording artist of the urban blues for nearly two

decades. His band members also were longtime residents of Chicago and performers of the urban blues. Furthermore, the Hammond concert had made Big Bill well aware of the New York society audience. It appears, therefore, that Lomax was more interested in promoting his investigation of black rural culture than in depicting the reality of the black blues musicians. Such appearances, nonetheless, sparked interest in Broonzy in the New York jazz community, and led to requests for him to tell his story. In 1946, he had a chance to summarize his career as an urban bluesman in an article for *Jazz Record*.

After the concert, Broonzy, Williamson, and Memphis Slim stayed with Lomax at his apartment in Greenwich Village. As Lomax told it, the good feelings after the concert led to an impromptu tape-recorded conversation on race relations in the South. Broonzy wound up interviewing his band members for Lomax, more than likely relaxing with generous shots of whisky, and telling his own stories to draw them out. Lomax threw in questions from off-mike. In this way, Lomax relied on Broonzy much as his father had relied on Leadbelly to encourage prisoners to sing their songs.

Most of the topics Lomax dealt with had less to do with the musicians' current lives than with their pasts or their knowledge of race issues: experiences with chain gangs, prison camps, work camps, and racial murders and rapes. The discussion also probed their beliefs on the social origins of the blues. Lomax interspersed field recordings from the national archive with the stories of the men. For decades, he kept the identities of the three informants anonymous, citing concerns for the safety of their families. Just as likely, however, was that he withheld their identities to dramatize the program and perhaps to forestall challenges to the veracity of their account.[15]

The limits Lomax placed on the topics of discussion raised questions about the integrity of his research method. Broonzy, for example, had lived away from Arkansas for more than twenty years. Although he returned to visit family, he was hardly the best person to interview on contemporary race relations in the rural South. Broonzy would have been a far more effective witness in a discussion of conditions in South Side Chicago—or in the recording industry. Lomax, however, appeared to have had little interest in exploring these topics. While the interview was somewhat contrived, it nonetheless provided valuable historical insights on the blues musicians' recollections of growing up in the South.

In the early 1950s, Broonzy's association with Lomax led to a job at Iowa State College. Lomax apparently had a connection with an English professor at the college, located in Ames, which resulted in a concert appearance. The concert was part of a folk song revival occurring among a new generation of fans on college campuses. The professor then helped Broonzy get a job as a janitor at the men's dormitory, Friley Hall. Some people thought the position was an insult to a musician as accomplished as Broonzy, and painfully symbolic of the place that educational institutions deemed proper for the blues. But this may have been an overreaction in light of Broonzy's lack of education and need for a regular paycheck.[16]

It cannot be overstated that Broonzy earned little from his music, and that he made much of his living as a laborer. Even during his prolific recording years, he continued to work as a dishwasher, a helper in a funeral home, and a clerk in a furniture store. At the age of fifty-seven, he wanted financial stability and no doubt welcomed the opportunity for a steady paycheck—and the chance to "go to college." When Broonzy revealed to the English professor that he could barely read and write, the professor was so concerned about the situation that he made a deal with Broonzy: he would teach Broonzy to read in exchange for Broonzy teaching him to read music. Broonzy soon improved his reading and writing skills, but he would never become proficient.[17]

Broonzy became a popular figure on the Iowa State campus, playing guitar at student gatherings and other occasions. At one point, a controversy arose over a picture taken of him clowning with his work tools. The photo was published in the school newspaper with the title "Mopper's Blues," after one of his recordings. The photo showed him carrying a mop, broom, and toilet swisher, with one foot propped up on a pail filled with cleaning utensils. To critics, the photo portrayed Broonzy as a minstrel figure once again, but he asked supporters to avoid making a fuss over it. Yet he probably harbored some conflicted feelings about the janitorial position. Interestingly, he once told a British magazine that he held the title of head caretaker with a staff of five janitors under his supervision.[18] Probably more fancy than fact, this claim alludes to the larger issue of his sense of pride, and perhaps a desire to make the job appear more important than it was.

Pete Seeger became acquainted with Broonzy from his work in the Library of Congress during the postwar years. Seeger was reared in the milieu of progressive folk culture and seemed destined to become a leading figure in the folk revival. He was a protégé of Lomax and recalled him as the "single most important person in the folk song revival" movement of the Popular Front in 1940. The Popular Front was a broad coalition of political groups in the United States and Europe, often with leftist and centrist views, that united to oppose fascism and Nazism during World War II. Born in 1919, Seeger was the product of a privileged upbringing. His father was Charles Seeger, an academically trained classical composer and musicologist who integrated folk music with the campaigns of progressive causes. Charles Seeger's efforts in this regard would span three decades, from the Depression to the Cold War. His mother, Constance de Clyver Edson, was a classical violinist and teacher. His parents divorced when Seeger was seven years old. His father later married Ruth Crawford Seeger, a major female composer of the twentieth century.

In 1931, the elder Seeger was a member of the Composers' Collective of the Workers Music League. Along with other artists, such as Elie Siegmeister and Aaron Copeland, Seeger composed propaganda songs intended to arouse the radical sentiments of workers. The activity failed, however, apparently because the writers had problems connecting with the working-class audiences. Accepting that his effort had gained little traction, in 1936 Seeger turned his attention to working with the New Deal Farm Security Administration (FSA). During his travels for the FSA, the elder Seeger took his son to the Mountain Dance and Folk Festival in Asheville, North Carolina, founded by folklorist Banscom Lamar Lunsford to promote Appalachian culture. Lunsford, known as the "Minstrel of the Appalachia," also worked for New Deal congressman Zebulon Weaver of western North Carolina. When Pete Seeger heard a musician play a five-string banjo, he was encouraged to pursue a career as a folk singer.

The family lived in Washington D.C., where Ruth Seeger was hired to transcribe the field recordings of John and Alan Lomax. She brought the folk music to the attention of her son, Pete, who listened to the recordings and played along with his banjo. Three years later, Pete Seeger was employed as an intern for Alan Lomax, a friend of his father's, in the Archive of American Folk Song in the Library of Congress. His job was to transcribe and catalogue the field recordings of race and hillbilly music to select the songs that best represented traditional American culture. The project was underwritten by the music division of the Pan American Union, which his father headed, and which later became the Organization of American States. Seeger absorbed the folk music legacy and attempted to re-create the sounds in his performances; and in the tradition of Lomax, he sought to persuade white audiences to embrace the multicultural heritage of the nation's folk tradition. In this vein, Lomax encouraged him to learn a variety of folk music styles, to perform with other musicians, and to value the musicians with authentic folk origins.[19]

Seeger immersed himself in a wide array of blues, gospel, and prison songs in the archives of the library as well as in commercial recordings. He later learned from Leadbelly, and went on the road with Woody Guthrie, who became the leading voice of leftist folk culture. At one point, Seeger and several other singers rented a communal loft space in lower New York that became a crash pad and cultural laboratory for young, politically active folk artists. The singers, heeding the advice of John Hammond, copied the Harlem rent party practice to raise money and share musical ideas.[20]

In 1948, Seeger worked on behalf of the presidential campaign of Progressive Party candidate Henry Wallace. Supporters turned to folk songs to help advertise the peace platform of the campaign. Seeger was a cofounder of a leftist folk music organization and journal, *People's Songs*, designed to "create, promote, and distribute songs of labor and the American people." (Guthrie was a member of the organization, and Lomax served on the board and created songs for the Wallace campaign.) This was the same year that Seeger met Broonzy. As he recalled it, Broonzy was performing at the Village Vanguard with Tampa Red and Lonnie Johnson. That night, he performed "Black, Brown and White." Seeger, impressed at the poignant commentary in the song, asked Broonzy if he would send a copy for publication in the journal *People's Songs*. Seeger said that several months later—after he had forgotten about the incident—he was surprised to find in the mail a record of the song sent by Broonzy.[21] The song drew from aspects of Broonzy's life and articulated the sentiment of an emerging postwar civil rights activism:

> I helped win sweet victory,
> With my little plow and hoe.
> Now I want you to tell me, brother,
> What you gonna do about the old Jim Crow.[22]

Broonzy had spent his own money to record the song and submit it for publication in *People's Songs*. He saw it as a chance to raise the awareness of white folksingers on issues of racial inequity without the censor of promoters, and he seized the opportunity to protest racism to a group of artists who might carry the message to other audiences.[23] Seeger remembered that Broonzy was admired by young singers, who viewed his music as "authentic" working-class folk art because it was derived from life experience. Broonzy's music held great appeal to white middle-class fans disenchanted with banal commercial music.

Many white fans learned of the blues through jazz societies, record collectors, and folk music concerts. The recordings also became increasingly available with the distribution of vinyl LP records and portable radios, allowing some to pick up the music from the programs of powerful radio stations. Music preferences soon emerged, with white fans tending to prefer the folk blues standards and black fans gravitating toward the urban blues and emerging rhythm and blues.

From 1952 to 1997, Louis "Studs" Terkel communicated to well-educated, progressive audiences of Chicago through his show, *The Studs Terkel Program,* on radio station WFMT. Over the decades, he earned the respect of listeners as a thoughtful chronicler of city life and culture, putting writers, actors, classical musicians, and folk artists on the air. Terkel had moved to the Windy City from New York City in 1920 at the age of eight. His family owned the Wells-Grand Hotel from 1926 to 1936, a rooming house in Bughouse Square where Terkel met a broad range of people, nurturing his interest in colorful characters. He earned a law degree at the University of Chicago in 1934, but he never practiced. Instead, he performed with the Chicago Repertory Group for a short time. Then he took a job in the Federal Writers' Project of the Works Progress Administration, where he worked in a variety of writing and on-air capacities on radio. During the Depression, Terkel teamed up with the folklorist Win Stracke to promote the use of folk songs for expressing the sentiments of the working class and for building bridges between different ethnic groups.

Terkel, like Alan Lomax and other cultural scholars of the Left, viewed the blues as indigenous American folk music, and he valued the country blues style as the most authentic. Terkel met Broonzy in the late 1940s, and they became friends and collaborators in a music revue. Just as Lomax built a historical context around the presentation of folk blues, Terkel produced a traveling revue that featured different sources of American music. The show was called "I Come for to Sing," and it introduced college audiences to the roots of American folk culture. With Terkel as the narrator, the concert featured Broonzy singing the blues, Win Stracke performing songs of the frontier, and the English folklorist Laurence Lane singing Elizabethan songs. They performed at about twenty different midwestern colleges and universities. Terkel recalled the camaraderie established between the men as they traveled to concerts and some of the social challenges they faced in out-of-the-way places.[24]

Terkel recalled a nasty incident that occurred in Lafayette, Indiana, on the way to Purdue University. They had stopped at a noisy tavern for beer and sausage sandwiches, but when they entered the establishment the room grew quiet. As they approached, the bartender said he would serve the whites but not Broonzy. When Stracke began to argue with the man, Broonzy turned around and left. Outside, Broonzy told them that he wanted to avoid a scene, and he tried to laugh off the incident. Terkel remembered the laugh as one edged with pain and anger.[25] Broonzy later incorporated the incident in a story about racism in a bar in the North. In the story, Broonzy went to a bar with three white friends, and though the bartender served everyone, he broke Broonzy's glass after each drink. The more they drank, the higher the mound of smashed glass. Finally, the owner threw them out of the bar.[26] This revised version of the incident was meant to make light of the painful encounter, but it illustrates the lingering sting of the insult, as does its inclusion in a stanza of "Black, Brown and White":

> I was in a place one night,
> They was all having fun.
> They was all buying beer and wine.
> But they would not sell me none.[27]

In the early 1950s, Terkel introduced Broonzy to the listeners of his radio show on WFMT. Influenced by Lomax, Terkel focused on the country blues style that had captured the imagination of young white fans. While Terkel presented folk blues, it should be noted that powerful midwestern stations were spreading rhythm and blues outside the wall of the ghettos—not only in Chicago, but in West Helena, Arkansas, where KFFA featured Sonny Boy Williamson (Rice Miller), and in Memphis, Tennessee, where WDIA arose as the self-styled "Mother Station of the Negroes."

In 1956, Terkel produced the album *Big Bill Broonzy Sings Folk Songs* for Folkways Records that included an interview with Broonzy focusing on his years on the plantation and his training as a songster. Big Bill spoke of growing up in Mississippi and Arkansas while intermixing guitar playing and folk standards such as "Plough Hand Blues," "C. C. Rider," "Joe Turner Blues," and "Bill Bailey." He also performed a version of "This Train" with a civil rights theme: "This train you don't need no transportation / No Jim Crow and no discrimination." He recorded "Black, Brown and White" for a second time as well. In this way, Broonzy once again made use of an opportunity to stir the progressive sentiments of the audience.

Terkel truly admired Broonzy and was aware of the role he played in the development of urban blues. In fact, Terkel frequented record resale shops to buy 78 rpm records of the 1930s studio sessions with Broonzy, Washboard Sam, Jazz Gillum, Blind John Davis, and other innovators of the modern sound. However, Terkel met Broonzy at the start of the folk revival, and he knew that his radio audience wanted to hear the folksinging Broonzy, not the Broonzy of the Memphis Five era. LeRoi Jones notes that the walls of segregation created a cultural dissonance in which white fans tended to "discover" black music at times when black audiences had moved on.[28]

Terkel was shocked by the negative reaction to the country blues displayed by some black youths. He recalled an incident where a young man disrespected Broonzy in the middle of a performance. In a voice loud enough to be heard by the rest of the audience, the man derided the folk blues as slave songs and scraped his chair against the floor on his way out the door.[29] Broonzy, too, commented on evidence of disinterest in folk blues among young black fans. For example, regarding the poor reception he received at a Washington, D.C., nightclub, he said, "They never lifted their heads from their plates." And he apparently drew small audiences in New York City, which, perhaps defensively, he blamed on the interest in bebop. "New York's dead," he told a newspaper reporter. "It's those crazy guys with the bebop that are killing the business."[30]

Meanwhile, in Chicago, Broonzy was attracting the attention of young whites in the folk clubs and universities. Robert March, a member of the Folklore Society, a University of Chicago student organization, recalled Broonzy as an admired figure among young leftists. "We were biased towards acoustic blues so Bill was one of our heroes. It was a very tough time for any blues musician—only Muddy Waters could count on a fairly steady gig," he said. Broonzy, although not politically active in a traditional way, became a "darling of the labor left" because of his union performances and his protest song "Black, Brown and White."

In 1954, the Folklore Society sponsored a concert at the University of Chicago to raise money for the organization. Broonzy was the opening act, and the featured performer was Pete Seeger. At this time, Pete Seeger, along with 151 other musicians, actors, writers, and journalists, had been named as a threat to U.S. security in the pamphlet *Red Channels: The Report of Communist Influence in Radio and Television*. *Red Channels* was a blacklist published in 1950 by the right-wing journal *Counterattack* as part of the Red Scare created by the House Un-American Activities Committee investigation of the entertainment industry. In addition to Seeger, *Red Channels* named Lena Horne, Langston Hughes, Burl Ives, Leonard Bernstein, Aaron Copeland, and other artists and entertainers with progressive associations. Artists cited in the pamphlet suffered public scorn and cancelled engagements. By sharing the stage with Seeger, Broonzy made himself a target for political attack. Recalling the event, March said, "Though Pete and Bill didn't meet until an hour or so before the concert they managed to work out a few numbers to sing together."[31]

Meanwhile, Terkel remembered Broonzy playing to audiences at folk music clubs such as the Gate of Horn, the Blue Angel, and the Blue Note on Monday nights (known as "dark night" because the clubs were usually closed). In particular, he recalled being at one performance where Broonzy failed to show up. As the audience grew restless, Memphis Minnie hustled onstage in his place. "Big Bill sends his regrets for not being here tonight," she said. "He's on his way to Europe."

In the 1950s, European fans learned of the blues through jazz societies, record collectors, occasional radio programs, U.S. military radio shows, and goodwill cultural programs. They had contact with jazz musicians during the interwar years, but not with blues singers of the caliber of Big Bill. Eventually, the European jazz societies created opportunities for blues singers to perform, and they reached out to Broonzy, who, in 1951, crossed the Atlantic Ocean for the second time. He was the first blues singer with commercial success in both the black and white worlds to tour Europe. As such, he served as an ambassador of the blues to Europe, and his performances influenced the practices of European musicians. His trip was sponsored by a European jazz fraternity of nightclub owners, journalists, record collectors, musicians, and managers. Among the sponsors were Hugues Panassié, a French jazz impresario; Yannick Bruynoghe, a Belgian jazz writer; Herbert and Stanley Wilcox, talent agents; Max Jones, a writer for the jazz review *Melody Maker*, and Humphrey Lyttelton, a musician and founder of the London Jazz Club.

From the beginning, however, two of Broonzy's American sponsors—Alan Lomax and Win Stracke—worked behind the scenes to establish European connections for him. Lomax—cited as a suspicious figure in the blacklist handbook *Red Channels*—had left the United States to escape the rising anti-communist hysteria, moving in 1950 to the United Kingdom, where he would live for eight years. Lomax and Stracke had alerted Panassié to Broonzy's superb talent.

In 1951, Lomax helped to produce a radio series on the folk music of England, Scotland, and the United States. He interviewed Broonzy on the air and had him demonstrate various forms of black folk music. The show was a hit and raised British interest in the blues.[32] The involvement of Stracke and Lomax no doubt swayed the European perception of Big Bill as a folksinger, although the sponsors seemed only too eager to believe in the image. Panassié would say, "He came to Europe on a kind of vacation, and his work, for the time being, is to open his heart and soul to us over here."[33]

Broonzy was following in the footsteps of an earlier generation of African American jazz musicians who had won the admiration of Europeans. Coming out of the First World War, European musicians strove to learn about jazz culture by sponsoring black artists like Louis Armstrong, Sidney Bechet, and Coleman Hawkins, who had received enthusiastic receptions in the jazz dens and concert halls of Paris and London. Now it was time for Broonzy to introduce the music of the plantation and the ghetto to this new audience.

During his European tour, Broonzy performed for small but appreciative audiences emerging from the years of wartime austerity in England, France, Belgium, Germany, Italy, Denmark, and the Netherlands. The audiences, primarily comprised of jazz enthusiasts and record collectors, had learned about Broonzy through jazz societies and journals, concert and nightclub appearances, radio programs, and, in later years, television appearances. In addition, Broonzy recorded for various European labels, and completed a small number of sessions with European bands.

Broonzy arrived in Brussels on July 18, 1951, to begin a three-month tour. He was met at the airport by a "few fans," such as English trumpeter Johnny Evans, who asked if he intended to give public performances. Big Bill reinforced the image of the sharecropper singer, saying that he was "too old to be a musician now" and that his style of blues had died out in America. Nevertheless, he had brought along his guitar and blues compositions, crammed with other items in a steamer trunk. After a few hours with fans in Brussels, Big Bill caught a train to France.[34]

Hugues Panassié sponsored Broonzy's debut in Paris, a city with a reputation among black musicians as a place of social freedom and art appreciation, where jazz was admired as native American culture. Over the years, Paris had attracted a community of American musicians, writers, and painters, and the expatriates no doubt embraced Broonzy. Panassié had begun writing about jazz in the 1920s, promoting a version of the concept of "negritude" explored by pan-Africanist poet Leopold Senghor, a concept that argued for a common culture shared by people of the African Diaspora. He believed that American jazz derived from an experience of nation, race, and culture and therefore considered black jazz musicians superior to white.[35] Panassié was cofounder of the famed Hot Club de France and the journal *Jazz Hot*, and authored several books on jazz. He was worshipped by his French disciples, who referred to him as "the Pope of Montauban," the town he lived in during the war.

Broonzy, depicted by European writers as "the living embodiment of an untutored folk musician," once again donned the mask sought by his audience. He accepted the romantic delusions of fans, although not to the extent of wearing overalls as he had for the concert at Carnegie Hall. Since the European audiences were comprised of a large number of record collectors, Broonzy performed more numbers from his urban blues repertoire as a solo performer than traditional folk songs. A collector who attended one of the performances in France described the event in a letter, reporting that Broonzy sang a mixture of blues and ballads, including "How Long Baby, How Long?" "Trouble in Mind," and "Mama Don't Allow It," as well as guitar rags. The writer deemed the performance a success.[36] Broonzy left Paris for a session in Düsseldorf, Germany, where he recorded with Graeme Bell and His Australian Jazz Band on September 15, including such standards as "John Henry," "In the Evening, When the Sun Goes Down," and "When the Saints Go Marching In."

Back in Paris a week later, he attended a recording session arranged by Panassié and engineered by American jazz clarinetist Mezz Mezzrow. He recorded sixteen songs for Vogue Records in two sessions on September 20 and 21. Charles Delaunay, a business associate of Panassié who cofounded the Hot Club and the magazine *Jazz Hot* in 1934, started Vogue Records in 1949. The titles included a mix of blues and folk ballads, some of which went back to his first recording sessions, such as "House Rent Stomp." Among the releases were "Backwater Blues," "Hollerin' and Cryin'," "Feeling Low Down," "John Henry," "Big Bill Blues," "Blues in 1890," and "Black, Brown and White"—the first recordings of this political song.[37]

It should come as no surprise that Mezz Mezzrow was part of the session where "Black, Brown and White" was recorded. In a way, Mezzrow was able to overcome the French preference for black artists by portraying himself as a type of "white Negro," and thereby sharing in a measure of authenticity. Coming out of the Chicago and New York jazz scenes of the 1920s, Mezzrow formed an integrated band in the 1930s called the Disciples of Swing. Mezzrow was known as an antisegregationist who had rebelled against the racism of white society and embraced African American culture, sometimes to the extent of passing as a person of interracial background to perform with black bands in segregated venues. In the 1930s, he recorded with Bechet and Tommy Ladnier in a famous session arranged by Panassié. In the late 1940s, Mezzrow moved to Paris, where he played with visiting musicians and helped to foster an appreciation for jazz.

Broonzy said that he was well received in Europe but unprepared for the variety of reactions from fans, which ranged from admiring to hysterical. "I remember, I left Belgium, going to Germany on a train, and I got off in Hamburg," he said. "Some of the white girls who were there to welcome me when I got off the train looked strange. When I went to shake the hand of one of the girls, she fainted." He encountered another type of reaction when touring in Denmark, which led him to conclude that some Europeans had difficulty relating to a black man in circumstances other than performance: "In Copenhagen, a bunch of girls meeting the train ran when they saw me get off; but whenever I played, they liked me. They have to get used to black people."[38]

Broonzy arrived in England on September 22 under the sponsorship of the Wilcox agency and the London Jazz Club. There was a question over whether he could play because of visa restrictions. Apparently the musicians' union had supported bans on performances by foreign jazz musicians to protect the market for local artists. However, there was opportunity for intermission performances and for "variety artists" such as blues singers if venues were arranged.[39] Broonzy was scheduled to give performances on the afternoon and evening of Saturday, September 22, at Kingsway Hall in Holborn, London. The event was billed as a "Recital of Blues, Folk Songs, Ballads" and advertised in two articles in the leading jazz magazine *Melody Maker*, as well as in a separate program. The newspaper announcement depicted Big Bill as a solo Delta blues singer, and indeed, the sponsors asked Broonzy to play "the old field blues, the country blues":[40] "He is a plain blues singer, always sticking to the pure idiom of the early blues; by this I mean the blues as they were sung and played before jazz music really started, and as they are still sung and played today way down in the State of Mississippi and other States in the South of the USA."[41]

The newspaper articles included two photographs of Big Bill dressed in cabaret attire: one had him standing tall with shirt open at the neck, cigarette dangling from his mouth, and guitar held waist high with the neck pointed toward the viewer at an assertive angle. The second showed him in a fedora worn at a rakish tilt, a dark suit with shirt open at the collar, and two-toned shoes. He stood in front of a building with his guitar case resting upright against him. The images contrast strikingly with the articles: the photos depict Broonzy as a modern cabaret singer, while the articles promote the sharecropper persona. Despite the dissonant messages, the audience generally responded to the folksy portrayal.[42] The program carried the cigarette photograph with an introduction by Max Jones drawing information from Broonzy's 1946 article in the *Jazz Record*. Referring to Broonzy's folk recordings, Jones noted that his "expressive voice and shouting style, matched by vivid and varied guitar accompaniment, have made him a great favourite with collectors of folk-blues recordings." He cited an endorsement from Panassié that Broonzy was the "greatest remaining exponent of authentic Negro blues."[43]

Arriving at Kingsway Hall in the red sports car of Max Jones—a jazz writer who would later author a biography of Louis Armstrong—Broonzy wore an ill-fitting suit that may have been selected to evoke the image of the country bumpkin. The cozy forum served as a church, with a backdrop of pulpit and organ pipes. Broonzy sang into a microphone that afternoon to a "small crowd that clustered round him at the bottom of the steeply ramped seats." He picked from a selection of blues, spirituals, and folk songs listed in the printed program—some of which were performed with the accompaniment of British musicians Roy Sturgess, piano; George Hopkinson, drums; and Bryce Ford, bass.[44] One reviewer raved about the afternoon performance, singling out such high spots as Broonzy's guitar playing in "John Henry" and "House Rent Stomp," his emotive singing of "Careless Love," and the compelling ballad "Black, Brown and White": "During his performance of this I found myself deeply moved—yet Bill sang the song with a very slight smile on his face—there was no hatred there, just a great tolerance and love of the Human Race. Here one felt, was a man who had experienced all the horrors of racial discrimination, but had come through the ordeal with a smile, tinged with sadness, perhaps, but never with resentment."[45]

That evening, Broonzy performed some of the same ballad and blues standards he had played in the afternoon, including "In the Evening," "Keep Your
Hands off Her," "Key to the Highway," "Back Water Blues," and "Just a Dream."
This concert attracted about three hundred fans, including Alan Lomax, who
had arrived from Scotland and joined Broonzy onstage, a surprise appearance
that several reviewers criticized as an unnecessary distraction. Paul Oliver
remembered Broonzy for both his music and his infectious personality, in
particular, his warm manner of addressing the audience and telling stories to
win them over.[46]

While reviewers wrote that the evening concert was better attended and
even more successful than the afternoon show, one called Lomax's participation the "one let-down." Lomax's effort to provide an introduction, promote
his book, and offer commentary between the numbers was deemed a "dismal
failure." Reviewers felt that Lomax had wasted time that Broonzy might have
used to sing more songs, had encouraged an encore with British accompanists not up to the task, and perhaps worst of all, had invited the audience to
participate by singing along and stamping their feet, which degenerated into
noise pollution.[47] Another reviewer, however, offered a more supportive view
of watching the two men interact: "Both of them were still talking and arguing and asking for news about old friends when they were already on stage—
with the result that the audience felt as if they had wandered more or less by
accident into one of those fabulous jazz parties of which the books are full."[48]

At end, the concerts were highly regarded by reviewers: "Without doubt
the coming of Big Bill Broonzy to London for his two concerts was the most
important and exciting jazz event of the year—in fact, for the blues lover, this
great singer's arrival bordered on the fantastic." Another concluded that the
recital was "the best and most memorable" of the last few years, and a third
asserted that it was "generally acknowledged to be the finest ever heard here
in that field."[49]

During his stay in London, Broonzy met with musicians like Lew Stone,
Joe Crossman, Wally Fawkes, Micky Ashman, and Humphrey Lyttelton—the
core of a fledgling London jazz scene. Lyttelton, a thirty-year-old jazz trumpeter and bandleader at the time, recalled the joy English musicians experienced watching Big Bill perform that day, noting especially the way he sat on
a chair in the middle of the floor playing the blues and talking about the music. "He was one of the first to come over," he remembered, "billed as one of
the last of the Mississippi bluesmen."[50] Lyttelton, the son of an Eton College

headmaster, had organized his first band only two years before Broonzy's visit and was performing at the London Jazz Club, also known as the Humphrey Lyttelton Club, in the Soho district. Broonzy's contact with these musicians, along with his recordings and later appearances on radio and TV, influenced their understanding of the folk blues.[51]

Meanwhile, George Melly, then a twenty-five-year-old blues singer and art critic, remembered Big Bill lying about his background, telling people, for example, that he owned eight farms in Mississippi. "One got the impression he'd come straight from the delta into the studio then into fame," he said, only to discover later that "the real truth was he came out of Chicago where he'd sung rhythm and blues."[52]

During the London tour, Broonzy was able to squeeze in a recording session where he sang "Keep Your Hand off Her," "Stump Blues," "Five Foot Seven," and "Plough Hand Blues" among other selections. His impression of Britain was favorable except for an incident that could have occurred in most areas of the United States. He remembered, "I never was mistreated, except for once in Nottingham, England, when the hotel man said they don't rent rooms to Negroes." In late September, his fans saw him off at Waterloo Station on his way back to work in Ames, Iowa. Upon leaving, he composed an impromptu farewell song and played it before boarding the train.[53]

His first European tour a success, Broonzy returned to Britain, France, and the Netherlands for a second engagement in 1952. At the time, the jazz press was praising a newly released album of eight songs recorded during his 1951 Paris session on Vogue Records. During this trip, he performed with Mahalia Jackson in a concert hall outside London. However, Broonzy apparently encountered financial difficulties with his agent, Herbert Wilcox of Wilcox Ltd. in London. The agency brought in American musicians to perform with British bands and tried to find creative ways to bypass protective visa restrictions on jazz musicians by presenting artists like Sidney Bechet under the legally accepted category of variety or intermission act.[54]

Broonzy wrote that Wilcox had helped to make arrangements for performances in England, Holland, and Belgium between November and December. However, he claimed that Wilcox not only cheated him out of concert payments, but charged him for rent, meals, and heating costs when staying at Wilcox's house, cab fares in London, and plane and cab fares for both men when traveling to Holland and Belgium. In addition, Broonzy asserted that Wilcox used his passport to acquire a book of government ration stamps but never turned over the book. Finally, he said that Wilcox took a concert check, cashed it without his permission, and kept the money. Wilcox promised to deposit money in a bank account for Broonzy in London and to wire money to his account in Chicago, but Broonzy wrote that he never received the money. He described the incident in a letter to folklorist Win Stracke (in his phonetic writing style), saying that he was "never wose treeted by no boddy like mr wilcox treeted me in my life i dont think he hase a hart in him at all to say one thing to day an change so soon in too weeks time he must have dollar sind for eyes."[55]

Broonzy used Paris as his base of operations when traveling back and forth between the United States and Europe between 1953 and 1957. During this period, he returned to Britain and Belgium in 1955, the Netherlands, Denmark, Belgium, and Italy in 1956, and Britain for a final time in 1957. During this era, Broonzy was able to travel to Africa for the first time. The nature of the visit, whether for pleasure or business, is unclear. In 1953, he sent a postcard to Win Stracke from Algeria noting that he was in "africar" and would return to Paris from there. He asked Stracke to express his regards to friends and family and wrote that he hoped to come back to Chicago soon.[56]

Younger musicians remembered watching Broonzy perform on British television during this period. In November 1955, for example, he appeared on the Independent Television program *Downbeat*. The young Eric Clapton recalled: "he was big here because they showed him on TV. It was so spellbinding that I think anyone that was leaning in that direction got it from there." He also introduced British audiences to Blind John Davis, Brother John Sellers, and other bluesmen who accompanied him in concerts. An admiring young John Mayall said, "Think about all the people that came up through Big Bill Broonzy—he was like the Art Blakey of the blues world."[57]

Broonzy's warm reception overseas led him to encourage Muddy Waters to follow in his path. Heeding the advice, Waters went to the United Kingdom in 1958. Upon arriving, he met writer Tony Standish and guitarist Alexis Korner, with whom Broonzy had stayed during the 1955 and 1957 tours. Korner, respected as the "Father of British Blues," was a musician, historian, and broadcaster. In 1955, he formed the London Blues and Barrelhouse Club and was a major figure in the British blues community in the 1960s. That day in 1958, as Waters unpacked his guitar, he handed it to Korner and told him to play something. As Korner played a few ragtime licks, Waters nodded knowingly and said, "Aha, Bill learned you that."[58]

During his 1953 extended visit to Paris, Broonzy wrote to Lomax that he was living at 29 Rue du Paris with a woman named Jacqueline and that he planned to marry her. It should be noted that he was still married to Rose Broonzy at this time. The state of the marriage was unclear, but whatever the circumstances, he apparently planned to make a commitment to his new woman, Jacqueline. From the letter, it appeared that Lomax had visited the couple before returning to the United Kingdom. Broonzy asked Lomax to bring him wedding bands and a new shirt the next time he came to France.[59] He later recorded a song in her name for Chess Records:

Lord , she has got my heart, someday she have my name (2×)
Lord, we have pictures made together, and put them in the same
    frame.[60]

How their relationship evolved is unknown. During this period, the state of Broonzy's love life was cloudy indeed. He seemed to have been involved with women at home and abroad. In Amsterdam, however, he fell in love and had a special relationship with a Dutch woman in the mid-1950s, Pim van Isveldt. They had a son named Michael. Broonzy was pictured pushing the boy in a stroller down the streets of Amsterdam. He sent two photographs of the child to Studs Terkel: one showed him serenading the infant with his guitar, and the other showed the boy several years later standing next to a scooter on a street in Amsterdam.[61]

Broonzy proved to be as prolific a recording artist in Europe as he had been in Chicago. During the tours, he recorded songs for such labels as Vogue in France, Black and Blue in Holland and Belgium, Savoy in Denmark, Ricordi in Italy, and Spotlight in England, offering a repertoire of spirituals, ballads, work songs, jazz standards, and folk blues in the fashion of Leadbelly. Examples of the sides released were "Nobody Knows the Troubles I've Seen," "John Henry," "Down by the Riverside," and "Going to Chicago" from the 1952 sessions; "Glory of Love," "Swing Low Sweet Chariot," "I'm Gonna Sit down at the Feastin' Table," and "When Do I Get to Be Called a Man?" from the 1955 sessions, and "Take This Ole Hammer," "Blue Tail Fly," "Sixteen Tons," "Irene," and "The Crawdad Song" from the 1956 sessions. The sides illustrate his astonishing skills as a folksinger, offering richly expressive singing supported by rhythmic guitar runs and phrases.

Broonzy's recording history was unparalleled. He was one of the most consistent recording stars of his generation. He produced for black audiences a phenomenal 744 sides as both a lead singer (275) and accompanist (469) between 1927 and 1953. For white audiences, between 1951 and 1957, he issued 97 sides for the U.S. market and 156 sides on international labels. His performances and recordings can be credited with shaping the direction of the British blues. For example, his work influenced the guitarsmanship of Alexis Korner, the arrangements of Humphrey Lyttelton, and the repertoire of Lonnie Donegan, who called his interpretation of black folk blues "skiffle," apparently taking the name from the Chicago rent parties in the 1920s and 1930s. Moreover, Broonzy was an inspiration to up-and-coming English and Irish singers influenced by the blues such Eric Clapton and Van Morrison.

During this period, Broonzy continued his tradition of using song to speak truth to power. In the 1950s, the Cold War was transforming political relations both domestic and international. In the struggle for world influence, American leaders sought to persuade newly independent nations that its economic system was superior to the socialist model. At the same time, black civil rights leaders were engaged in campaigns to end segregation. The nation wrestled with the impact of the 1954 U.S. Supreme Court decision in *Brown v. the Board of Education* and the 1955 boycott of segregated buses in Montgomery, Alabama. These issues raised the political awareness of an international audience in the midst of the Cold War.

Such was the U.S. racial dynamic in 1955 and 1956 when Broonzy recorded in Europe and the United States, and published the song "When Do I Get to Be Called a Man?" The song—along with "Black, Brown and White"—stood out in a repertoire of folk standards. Clearly, the lyrics were meant to prick the conscience of white fans. Big Bill drew upon events both personal and social in portraying the quest for equal rights—things that should have resulted in respect from white society. Instead, the achievements meant little to nothing because of the laws and practices of white supremacy. In this ballad, the one-time field laborer turned working-class entertainer questions if he will ever be considered as an equal:

> They say I was undereducated, my clothes was dirty and torn.
> Now I got a little education, but I'm a boy right on.
> I wonder when will I be called a man.
> Or do I have to wait 'till I get ninety-three?[62]

When visiting Belgium, Broonzy made the acquaintance of the writer Yannick Bruynoghe, and they maintained a regular correspondence afterward.

During these exchanges, Broonzy expressed a desire to write an account of his life. He shared his thoughts on the blues at a time when no other musicians were doing so, and before scholars had begun to define the culture. Broonzy wrote his series of letters in phonetic English. Bruynoghe and his wife, Margo, who were fluent in English, read the letters aloud to correct spelling, and arranged them in rough chronological sequence. The collaboration began in 1953 with the preliminary title of "The Truth about the Blues" (presumably to correct the half-truths of journalists). The memoir was published in Britain under the title *Big Bill Blues* by Cassell & Co. Ltd. in the fall of 1955 and distributed in the United States by Grove Press the next year. Excerpts of the books were released as a five-part weekly series that ran from August to September 1955 in the jazz magazine *Melody Maker*. Both the book and series included illustrations created by the blues historian Paul Oliver.[63] It was ironic that Broonzy selected a European to help him tell this "truth," but perhaps he had achieved a level of trust with Bruynoghe that he did not share with his American supporters. It also was evident that Bruynoghe was eager to recognize Broonzy's role as an urban blues artist in addition to his contributions as a folksinger.

Broonzy's "truth about the blues," however, was sometimes as much fancy as fact. Bruynoghe, noting that Broonzy wrote the account based on memory and story, identified it as a "faction" work of autobiography. Some of the anecdotes were the tales of a master storyteller and revealed more about the psychology of the author than about actual events. Yet within the stories is evidence of the collective experience of a people and of the blues singer as a class: "So Big Bill may have sometimes adapted for his own use stories that happened to others, or that he had heard of, coloring them with his lively imagination. But it is nevertheless evident that he led a very hectic life, typical of most southern blues singers of this time."[64] Thus, the book was valuable both for the skeleton chronology of his life it offered and for the larger truths it revealed about his perceptions of the black experience in the age of blues. Moreover, the book gave a somewhat more balanced depiction of his career: for example, it highlighted the urban blues artists of the 1930s and 1940s, and downplayed the romantic folk blues image.

The Bruynoghes visited Broonzy and his American wife, Rose, in Chicago on December 19, 1957. They arrived at his apartment at 4716 South Parkway and remained in the city for several weeks. Broonzy gave them a tour of the South Side blues culture, a panorama of places and persons that few white supporters had seen. They met musicians such as Memphis Slim and Tampa Red, visited clubs like Silvio's, Smitty's Corner, and the 708 Club, and interviewed producer J. Mayo Williams, folklorist Win Stracke, and Studs Terkel.[65]

The previous year, Bruynoghe had assisted filmmaker Jean Delire with the production of an eighteen-minute film noir documentary called *Low Lights, Blue Smoke: Big Bill Blues*. The story was set in a smoke-filled cellar club in postwar Brussels. Broonzy emerged from the shadows of the night to walk down the narrow stairway and enter the tiny, low-ceilinged club. As he entered, a white jazz band left the cramped bandstand to make way for an authentic blues musician. On top of a piano was a burning candle set in an old wine bottle. He took off his coat and hat, laid a smoldering cigarette on the piano keys, strapped on the guitar and got comfortable. In an atmosphere of shifting lights and shadows, with customers drawing their drinks through straws, he played a set of standards such as "Why Did You Leave Heaven?" "Saturday Night Blues," "Just a Dream," and "Guitar Shuffle." The elder Broonzy exuded confident sexuality; he was dressed in casual shirt unbuttoned at the chest, smoked a cigarette, and played acoustic guitar as customers swayed and danced to the music. All the while he traded seductive glances with a female admirer. The set ended to great applause as he packed up his guitar, put on his coat and hat, and stepped out into the night. Delire entered the film in the 1957 Berlin International Film Festival, one of the "big three" European film festivals along with Cannes and Venice. The film won a Silver Bear Award, a special prize in the short documentary and cultural film category. Bruynoghe brought the film to Chicago during his visit and showed it at the debut of the Old Town School of Folk Music in January 1958.[66]

In his association with European jazzmen, Big Bill emphasized that the blues sensibility came from life experience, and that instruments should conform to the character of the singer, rather than the singer adapting to the standards of the instruments. This was a lesson difficult for some formally trained jazz musicians to accept. For example, a few overseas accompanists found it confusing to perform with Broonzy unless he played within a strict chord structure. One London pianist went so far as to take a snooty attitude with Broonzy, believing that his academic training gave him a leg up. During rehearsal Broonzy told him that his music did not correspond with the guitar. "Of course, if you just want the common chord . . ." the pianist sniffed, but he was stopped in midsentence by Broonzy's retort, "Well, I'm only a common blues singer."[67]

Broonzy established a bridge of cultural exchange between the black American and European blues communities in the 1950s. Lyttelton gave him credit for laying the groundwork for hundreds of other musicians to follow in his wake, such as Muddy Waters and Buddy Guy, and for helping foreign audiences learn about the urban blues. During these years, he set the standard through both live performances and prolific recordings. In fact, his legacy of 156 song releases for the European market exceeded the 97 folk songs released for the white American market, and cemented his place in the pantheon of American folksingers with the likes of Leadbelly, Josh White, Woody Guthrie, Paul Robeson, Sonny Terry, and Brownie McGhee. Through his consummate professionalism and irresistible charisma, Big Bill truly became an ambassador of the folk blues.

7
FINAL DAYS

BROONZY WAS A CIGARETTE SMOKER AND PROBABLY A HEAVY ONE AT that. In the documentary film *Low Lights, Blue Smoke: Big Bill Blues* and in some photographs, he was pictured either holding or smoking a cigarette. A cover photo of *Melody Maker* caught him in the midst of a song with eyes closed, guitar under arm, and cigarette dangling from his mouth. Decades earlier he was photographed with cigarette in hand on a Chicago street with Jack Dupree, Jazz Gillum, Little Bill Gaither, Tampa Red, and his dog, which "drank whiskey just like we did and helped us sing." It was probable that smoking contributed to the lung cancer that would end his life—he learned the devastating news of his diagnosis from a doctor friend in July 1957.[1]

The month of July was a grim one for Big Bill and his family, but not without days of triumph. One high point was performing at a folk music concert at Roosevelt College, Chicago, with Sonny Terry and Pete Seeger on July 6, 1957. The college was founded in honor of the deceased President Roosevelt in 1945 with a mission of educating qualified students without regard to class, race, ethnicity, age or gender. Another high point was a final epic recording session for the Verve label. Broonzy began work on a folk blues album characterized as his "last musical will and testament" by producer Bill Randle. "My prime motive for recording Bill Broonzy," Randle recalled, "was to preserve as much of the blues complex as he was able to give us. When I arrived in Chicago at the height of one of the worst storms in that city's history, Bill Broonzy greeted me in the studio with: 'Man, this is a helluva night. Is there gonna be any whiskey?'"[2]

The album stayed with the folksinger format, involved recording sessions at Universal Studios on July 12 and 13, and generated ten hours of material. Big Bill sang, told stories of the past, ruminated on the blues, his travels, his friends, family, and other homespun topics addressed in prior sessions. The album expanded on the autobiographical information covered by earlier interviewers and was released as *Big Bill Broonzy—Last Session* on Verve Records in 1957. It featured a compendium of his folk repertoire including "Key to the Highway," "Tell Me What Kind of Man Jesus Is," "Joe Turner Blues," "See See Rider," "Take This Hammer," "John Henry," and "Bill Bailey."

That summer, Broonzy left Chicago to work at Circle Pines, a folk school and camp located halfway between Kalamazoo and Grand Rapids near Delton, Michigan. The camp brought together families interested in supporting cooperative enterprises and in promoting peace and social justice education. Circle Pines was used by a grocery co-operative with a store in Hyde Park, Chicago, and another in Detroit. The camp was accessible as a year-round retreat by co-op employees and as a summer camp for city kids. Broonzy was hired to do kitchen duties and to perform at informal gatherings as early as December 1956, and had entertained guests at the camp on December 13. Robert March, a camp visitor that summer, remembered an incident involving Broonzy and an attractive college-age female counselor. She came on to him shamelessly, but Broonzy carefully fended her off. Broonzy and March, who accompanied Big Bill during the informal concert, left the event together. Broonzy, thinking about the woman, said to him: "I decided to leave Europe and the young women to the young men."[3]

Pete Seeger visited the camp that summer and filmed Broonzy performing while sitting on a cabin porch. On a sunny day, with birds chirping off camera, Broonzy sang in public for the final time. He wore a white shirt with pen in pocket, a wristwatch, and a pinky ring. Using a guitar pick and singing in a weak voice, he performed, with as much cheer as he could muster, "How You Want It Done," "John Henry," "Worried Man Blues," and the instrumental "Blues in E." The next day he underwent surgery to remove the cancerous lung.

The months after the operation were difficult for Broonzy physically and financially, although the support of admirers helped him keep up his spirits. On November 23, 1957, Broonzy made a final public appearance before an estimated crowd of 1,500 well-wishers. The benefit concert was held at the KAM Temple, the largest synagogue on the South Side. The event raised about $2,500 on his behalf to help pay his medical expenses. The concert was organized by Studs Terkel and promoted by radio station WFMT and local newspapers. For more than two and a half hours, Broonzy's colleagues performed an array of blues, gospel, jazz, and folk standards in celebration of his illustrious career. The performers included Sunnyland Slim, J. B. Lenoir, Little Brother Montgomery, Odetta, Pete Seeger, and Mahalia Jackson. Broonzy was brought onstage by Jackson, who walked him back and forth, and sang "Just a Closer Walk with Thee." Her inspired tribute left many fans in tears.[4]

On this day, Broonzy was able to reconcile the conflicting visions of his blues talent. For the first time, he looked out upon both his black and white admirers. He witnessed the coming together of the urban migrant audience that had confirmed him as a voice of blues modernity, and the white audience that had subsidized him as an authentic folksinger. One writer noted: "Despite the weakening effect of his serious operation, Big Bill wanted to share this evening with those honoring him. He stood onstage, tall and proud, as the performers and audience paid tribute to him."[5] An eyewitness reported that the recovering Broonzy could barely speak but played his guitar with tears streaming down his face. Then he stepped up the mike and whispered, "Thank you! I love you! God bless you!"

The surgeon had removed a cancerous lung and part of his vocal cords, in effect stripping away one of his great musical gifts. However, his guitar-playing skills remained strong, and on December 1, 1957, he helped folklorist Win Stracke inaugurate a school of folk music on the North Side. Stracke, who had promoted the idea of folk music as a vehicle for labor organizing in the 1930s, teamed up with guitarists Frank Hamilton and Dawn Greening to found the Old Town School of Folk Music. The school debut featured Broonzy demonstrating his best guitar licks to an enthusiastic audience: "That night Big Bill Broonzy gave us a demo of his powerful guitar playing. Big Bill, black and handsome, could stir a roomful of uptight humans into a bowl of instant throbbing rhythmic jelly."[6]

Later that month, as Broonzy convalesced at home, he composed a new song and took a few days to show Bruynoghe around the ghetto blues scene. Bruynoghe was struck by the diminished voice of the once powerful singer: "Fortunately, Bill is physically unchanged; just as wonderful and young-looking as ever, and in excellent spirits. A short while later, some other guests joined the party: Little Brother Montgomery, Memphis Slim, his wife and four kids, and Tampa Red. Bill played us a tape that he had made the day before. Every day he played and sang—he tried to sing; he had written a new blues called 'Problem Child' and it was extremely moving to hear this weak, broken, faded voice expressing just as much feeling as it always did, but with all its power lost."[7]

A few months later, Broonzy was interviewed by a reporter for *Down Beat* magazine. The writer noted that Broonzy lived with his wife, Rose, and pet cat, Ananias. Among their possessions were a television, a stereo console, and an ample collection of blues records. He spent the days walking around the neighborhood or sitting in his apartment strumming the guitar. He had been unable to sing since the operation. A British visitor concluded that Broonzy looked well, his face appearing healthy and his smile ever-present. But his voice had been silenced. "When he opens his mouth to talk, Big Bill Broonzy isn't there. There's only a whisper of the man."[8]

The combination of sickness and unemployment apparently took a heavy toll on his finances. In an effort to return to work, he scheduled a second operation to restore his voice by realigning his vocal chords. However, he could not afford the medical costs—even worse, the cancer had reappeared. The British jazz community came to his aid by establishing the Bill Broonzy Benefit Fund Committee with Pat Brand and Max Jones of *Melody Maker*, Alexis Korner, and other supporters. They sponsored a concert on Sunday, March 9, 1958, at the London Coliseum.

This was the first time a benefit concert had been organized in the United Kingdom for an American musician. It featured seven bands and six singers, and among the participants were trumpeter Humphrey Lyttelton and His Band, guitarist Johnny Duncan and the Blue Grass Boys, the Dill Jones Trio, and singer Cleo Laine. In addition, Alan Lomax and Sister Rosetta Tharpe dropped by in support of the effort. The concert raised five hundred pounds with a value of about $1,400 in 1958.[9] A second concert, held later that month by the National Jazz Federation of England, raised another five hundred pounds. This concert involved a midnight matinee at the Dominion Theater with the Lonnie Donegan Skiffle Group—the early folk blues band that would influence English rock—the Chris Barber Band with Ottilie Patterson, and the Ken Colyer Band. Patterson wrote new words to a blues song taught her by Big Bill, "When Things Go Wrong." This group constituted the British wing of musicians influenced by Broonzy across the trajectory of his career. The Chicago concerts, on the other hand, provided a window on the U.S. wing—but only a glimpse of his influence. His career had touched the lives of two generations of blues musicians from Ma Rainey and Papa Charlie Jackson in the 1920s, to Georgia Tom, Blind John Davis, and Joshua Altheimer in the 1930s, to Muddy Waters, Lil Green, and Don Byas in the 1940s, and to Pete Seeger, Humphrey Lyttelton, and Eric Clapton in the 1950s.

Broonzy sent a telegram thanking his British admirers for their generosity and informing them of his failing state of health: "Please don't think hard of me for not writing you all. I can't see. I am almost blind and my mind is not good. I am so nervous. I am writing to let you all know I haven't forgot you. I am yet thankful for what you all did for me."[10]

Broonzy took a turn for the worse on the morning of August 15, 1958. With the assistance of Win Stracke, he summoned an ambulance from the Capitol Ambulance & Oxygen Service. The ambulance picked up Broonzy at his home at 4716 South Parkway and tried to get him to Billing Hospital. As the vehicle rushed through the empty streets of the South Side, Broonzy passed away at five thirty in the morning. He was sixty-five years old.

Broonzy's funeral services were held on August 19 at Metropolitan Funeral Parlor with the Rev. Joseph Branham, pastor of the South Shore Baptist Church, presiding over the ceremony. Floral wreaths were delivered in the shape of a guitar, a bleeding heart, and a clock stopped at the time of his death. Alexis Korner sent flowers from London with a tribute to "Big Bill Broonzy—One of the greatest blues singers." Branham recited verses in Ezekiel, "And lo, thou art unto them as a lovely song of one that hath a pleasant voice, and can play well on an instrument."[11]

In attendance were members of the pantheon of the Chicago blues such as Tampa Red, Ransom Knowling, Red Nelson, Brother John Sellers, Sunnyland Slim, J. B. Lenoir, Muddy Waters, Little Walter, and Otis Spann. They shared in the celebration of his life in song and story. The coffin was closed to the music of Broonzy's final recording of "Swing Low, Sweet Chariot." Muddy Waters, Tampa Red, Sunnyland Slim, Otis Spann, Francis Clay, and Brother John Sellers were the pallbearers for their friend.[12] As Big Bill was interred, they placed white gloves on the coffin and bid him farewell. William Lee Conley Broonzy was laid to rest in Lincoln Cemetery in Worth, Illinois.

Big Bill Broonzy introduced the blues to black audiences across America. He came of age during the interwar years when the blues was part of the leisure activities of the black working class. He molded traditional folk music, ragtime, jazz, gospel, and country blues into the modern blues. The advent of mass-produced records, played on phonographs, jukeboxes, and radio, made his music part of the soundtrack of urban life. He was one of the most prolific studio musicians of his generation, producing as both a lead singer and an accompanist an astounding 744 sides for black audiences over three decades. Broonzy records were more than simply good-time music. They also helped to express the outlook of an urban industrial modernity. His blues reflected the coming-of-age of the black urban folk, confidently announcing their adjustment to life in the cities. John Szwed argues that the songsters who participated in the mass migration were critical to establishing a common voice capable of assisting migrants in the acculturation process. They converted folk songs developed for group enjoyment on the plantations to individual and small-band blues suitable for the urban masses. During the incubation process, they distilled the work songs, spirituals, dance rags, and country blues with ragtime, boogie-woogie, and swing jazz to create a new musical style relevant to the new social experience.[13]

Broonzy went on to play a role as blues ambassador to white admirers in America and around the world. He introduced them to the folk blues and to the values of black Americans, and he used the encounters to appeal to good-will and heighten awareness of the American civil rights movement. In all, he recorded 253 sides for his new audiences in the United States and Europe. At end, he was able to reconcile the conflicting paths of his career. Broonzy, in his roles as songster and urban bluesman, articulated the extraordinary journey of the ordinary black man.

In 1980, Broonzy was inducted into the Blues Foundation Hall of Fame as a performer of historic merit. The organization, founded in Memphis in 1980, selected artists based on their contributions, impact, and influence on the blues. As part of the first class of inducted artists, Broonzy was selected along with such figures as Son House, John Lee Hooker, Skip James, B. B. King, Memphis Minnie, Bessie Smith, and Muddy Waters. In 1990, the Blues Foundation inducted his autobiography, *Big Bill Blues*, into the Hall of Fame as a Classic of Blues Literature.

A fitting tribute to Broonzy's enduring influence was the adaptation of his recording of "Black, Brown and White" by advocates for racial progress. Broonzy first recorded the song in Paris in 1951 and continued to record and perform it during the formative years of the civil rights movement. Broonzy used the song to raise awareness of both racism and colorism (the practice of complexion preference born of racism) with the refrain: "They say if you're white, you're alright. If you're brown, stick around. But if you're black, oh no brother, get back, get back, get back."

The song reflected popular sentiments across the black diaspora. For example, the Trinidadian Calypso singer Lord Kitchener echoed the refrain of Broonzy in his recording "If You're Brown." The popular song expressed the cry for racial justice during West Indian independence movements of the 1950s and 1960s: "So boys if you're brown, they say you can stick around. If you're white, well everything is all right. If your skin is dark, no use to try, you've got to suffer until you die."

And on January 22, 2009, the American civil rights leader Joseph Lowery, who in 1957 cofounded the Southern Christian Leadership Conference with the Rev. Martin Luther King Jr., evoked the spirit of Broonzy's refrain when delivering the inauguration benediction of President Barack Obama:

> Lord, in the memory of all the saints who from their labors rest, and in the joy of a new beginning, we ask you to help us work for that day when black will not be asked to get back, when brown can stick around, when yellow will be mellow, when the red man can get ahead man, and when white will embrace what is right. Let all those who do justice and love mercy say amen.

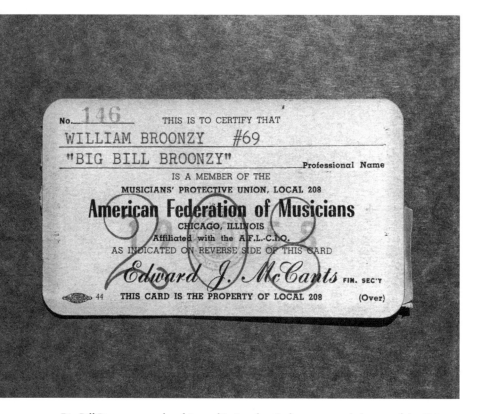

Big Bill Broonzy membership card in Local 208, the segregated chapter of the Chicago Federation of Musicians. The union card was one of the symbols of modernity for black musicians. Local 208 helped black rural musicians adjust to life in the clubs and studios of the city.

DISCOGRAPHY

Big Bill Broonzy was a leading recording artist of his generation, and the enduring value of his work is best indicated by the many reissues of his work on albums, compact discs, and videotapes released on labels both domestic and international. The most comprehensive reissue of his songs recorded from 1927 to 1947 was the 12-CD series produced by Document Records, *Big Bill Broonzy Complete Recorded Works in Chronological Order. Vols. 1–12 (1927–1947)*. Document also reissued some of his recordings as an accompanist with various bands and lead singers such as the 2-CD set of the Famous Hokum Boys and the 5-CD series with Sonny Boy Williamson. (The best way to locate his sessions as sideman is to track down the releases of the major Chicago recordings artists of the period.) In regard to his postwar rhythm-and-blues recordings, it is important to highlight the numerous sides reissued on the CD series *The Mercury Blues 'N' Rhythm Story*. In addition, four recordings from his postwar work with Chess Records can be found on *Big Bill Broonzy: House Rent Stomp*, a CD compilation on the European label Blues Encore.

An outstanding recording from the folk blues period is the three-CD reissue of *The Bill Broonzy Story* on the Verve label. In addition, *Big Bill Broonzy Sings Folk Songs*, produced by Studs Terkel, is a precious folk song album currently available on Smithsonian/Folkways. Meanwhile, the reissue of *Blues in the Mississippi Night* on Rykodisc by Alan Lomax, featuring the discussion with Broonzy, Sonny Boy Williamson, and Memphis Slim, is problematic as a social documentary exposé, but is a valuable preservation of black folk music.

In the years immediately after Broonzy's death, Muddy Waters, Memphis Slim, and Willie Dixon released three tribute albums. In 1959, Chess Records produced *Muddy Waters Sings Big Bill Broonzy*, which featured Waters; James Cotton, harmonica; Pat Hare, guitar; Otis Spann, piano; Andrew Stephenson, bass; and Francis Clay, drums. The band recorded ten standards of Broonzy's such as "Just a Dream" and "Southbound Train." While the album lacked the enthusiastic support of Waters's blues fans, it received a good review by *Billboard Magazine:* "A fortunate coupling—Broonzy's material interpreted by Muddy. Blues fans will find this hard to put down."[1] In 1961, Memphis

Slim recorded a tribute album to Broonzy and other urban bluesmen of the 1930s. *Memphis Slim's Tribute to Big Bill Broonzy, Leroy Carr, Cow Cow Davenport, Curtis Jones, Jazz Gillum* was released on Candid Records. Slim brought back harmonica player Jazz Gillum, who had fallen into poverty, and guitarist Arbee Stidham to record the album. They covered two Broonzy standard recordings: "I Feel So Good" and "Rockin' Chair Blues." In 1964, Willie Dixon produced the tribute album *Big Bill Broonzy: Remembering Big Bill* on the Mercury label. The European CD reissues were a mixed bag: One fine CD reissue of Broonzy's studio session work during the 1951 trip to Paris was *Treat Me Right: Big Bill Broonzy* on the Tradition label. A less impressive but still noteworthy CD reissue was from his London recording work, *Big Bill Broonzy: The 1955 London Sessions*, on the Sequel label. Most of the European CD reissues in circulation, however, were compilations of his 1930 and 1940 recordings.

In addition to the CDs, Big Bill was filmed when performing in Belgium and the United States, and both performances are now available on videotape. The most interesting was the thirty-minute film noir documentary *Low Lights, Blue Smoke: Big Bill Blues* by director Jean Delire. Also available is a copy of Pete Seeger's five-minute reel of Broonzy performing on a porch at the Circle Pines summer camp in Michigan in 1957. Both documentary programs were featured on the videotape *Big Bill Broonzy and Roosevelt Sykes* on the Masters of the Country Blues series by Yazoo Records. In addition, the footage shot by Seeger was on the videotape *Legends of Country Blues Guitar* by Rounder Records.

Recordings by Broonzy

Big Bill Blues. UK: Vogue VG 651 600041, 1984.
Big Bill Broonzy. Archive of Folk Music, FS-213, n.d.
Big Bill Broonzy. Austria: Story of Blues CD 3504-2, 1986.
Big Bill Broonzy. Vol. 2 (1934–1941). Blues Document BD-2096
Big Bill Broonzy. Vol. 1 (November 1927 to 9 February 1932). Austria: Document DOCD-5050, 1991.
Big Bill Broonzy. Vol. 2 (9 February 1932 to 18 October 1934). Austria: Document DOCD-5051, 1991.
Big Bill Broonzy. Vol. 3 (18 October 1934 to 3 July 1935). Austria: Document DOCD-5052, 1991.
Big Bill Broonzy. Vol. 4 (3 July 1935 to 22 April 1936). Austria: Document DOCD-5126, n.d.
Big Bill Broonzy. Vol. 5 (1 May 1936 to 31 January 1937). Austria: Document DOCD-5127, n.d.
Big Bill Broonzy. Vol. 6 (31 January 1937 to 13 October 1937). Austria: Document DOCD-5128, n.d.

Big Bill Broonzy. Vol. 7 (13 October 1937 to 15 September 1938). Austria: Document DOCD-5129, n.d.

Big Bill Broonzy. Vol. 8 (15 September 1938 to 10 February 1939). Austria: Document DOCD-5130, n.d.

Big Bill Broonzy. Vol. 9 (11 May to 8 December 1939). Austria: Document DOCD-5131, n.d.

Big Bill Broonzy. Vol. 10 (26 January to 17 December 1940). Austria: Document DOCD-5132, n.d.

Big Bill Broonzy. Vol. 11 (17 December 1940 to 6 March 1942). Austria: Document DOCD-5133, n.d.

Big Bill Broonzy. Vol. 12 (1945–1947). Austria: Document BDCD-6047, 1993.

Big Bill Broonzy: Hollerin' and Cryin' the Blues. France: Vogue LDM-30198, 1973.

Bill Broonzy: House Rent Stomp. Blues Encore CD 52007 AAD, 1990.

Big Bill Broonzy. Vol. 1: Lonesome Road Blues. France: Vogue BL. 512501, 1979.

Big Bill Broonzy—Mississippi River Blues. History 20.1935-HI.

Big Bill Broonzy 1927–1932. Matchbox MSE1004.

Big Bill Broonzy—The 1955 London Sessions. Sequel NEX CD 119.

Big Bill Broonzy Sings Folk Songs. Smithsonian/Folkways SF 40023, 1956.

Big Bill Broonzy—Trouble in Mind. Smithsonian/Folkways SFW40131, 2000.

Other Recordings Consulted

Albertson, Chris. *An Evening with Big Bill Broonzy*. Vol. 2. Denmark: Storyville CD 8017, 1994.

Arnold, Kokomo. "Chain Gang Blues." *Kokomo Arnold Vol. 1 (1930–1935)*. Document DOCD-5037, n.d.

Asch, Mose. *Big Bill Broonzy Sings Folk Songs*. Smithsonian/Folkways SFW40023, 1989.

Barefoot Bill, "Big Rock Jail." *Ed Bell (Barefoot Bill/Sluefoot Joe) Complete Recorded Works in Chronological Order, 1927–1930*. Document DOCD-5090, n.d.

Bonner, Brett J. *Big Bill Broonzy: Black, Brown & White*. USA: Evidence ECD 26062, 1995.

Calt, Stephen, and Woody Mann. *Big Bill Broonzy—Do That Guitar Rag 1928–1935*. Yazoo L-1035, 1988.

Calt, Stephen, Nick Perls, and Mike Stewart. *The Young Big Bill Broonzy 1928–1935*. Yazoo L-1011, 1990.

Charters, Samuel. *Blues Roots/Chicago – The 1930s*. Smithsonian/Folkways FWRBF16, 1967.

Clergeat, Andre. *Big Bill Broonzy. Vol 2: Feelin' Low Down*. France: Vogue BL 512510, 1980.

Cohn, Lawrence. *Big Bill Blues*. Epic EE 22017, 1969; UK: CBS 52648, n.d.

———. *Big Bill Broonzy: Good Time Tonight*. Columbia/Legacy C 46219, 1990.

Collis, John. *Big Bill Broonzy—The Southern Blues*. UK: Charly Blues Masterworks vol. 49, CDBM49, 1993.

Demetre, Jacques. *Big Bill Broonzy: Midnight Steppers*. Denmark: Bluetime BT 2001, 1986.

Dixon, Willie. *Big Bill Broonzy: Remembering Big Bill*. Mercury 20044, 1964.

Fancourt, Les. *Big Bill Broonzy: I Feel So Good*. UK: Indigo CD 2006, 1995.

Feather, Leonard. *Big Bill Broonzy*. GNP Crescendo GNPS-10004, 1973.

Fox, Charles. *An Evening with Big Bill Broonzy*. Vol. 1. Denmark: Storyville CD 8016, 1994.

Gellert, Lawrence, prod. *Cap'n, You're So Mean: Negro Songs of Protest*. Vol. 2. Rounder 4013, 1982.

Gillum, Jazz. "Reefer Head Woman." *Bill "Jazz" Gillum (1938–1949): "Roll Dem Bones."* Wolf Blues Jewels, WBJ-002, n.d.

Glovsky, Anton. *Big Bill Broonzy: Treat Me Right*. Tradition TCD 3001, 1996.

Gormick, Greg. *The Legendary Big Bill Broonzy: I Can't Be Satisfied*. Collector's Edition 6, 1996.

Green, Benny. *Big Bill Broonzy/Josh White: The Blues*. UK: Pye PEP 605, 1960.

Hall, Vera. "Boll Weevil Blues." *Alan Lomax Collection*. Archive of Folk Culture, Library of Congress, n.d.

Handcox, John. "Raggedy, Raggedy." *John Handcox Collection*. Archive of Folk Culture, Library of Congress, n.d.

Hentoff, Nat. *Big Bill Broonzy: Big Bill's Blues*. Portrait Masters J 44089, 1988.

Hermmann, Cal. *Collection of Folk Music Concert Recordings*, Archive of Folk Culture, Library of Congress, AFS 14172-14175, 1956–57.

House, Roger, prod. *Ain't Gonna Be Treated This Way: Black Life in the Great Depression*. Dancing Turtle Productions. National Public Radio. February 1992.

———, prod. *Oh, What a Time!: Black Life on the Homefront during World War II*. Dancing Turtle Productions. National Public Radio. February 1996.

Humphrey, Mark. *Big Bill Broonzy: Baby Please Don't Go*. Drive DE2-41041, 1994.

Jackson, Papa Charlie. "Shave 'Em Dry." *Too Late, Too Late. Vol. 11 (1924–1939)*. DOCD-5625, 1998.

Johnson, Merline. "Got a Man in the 'Bama Mine." *Merline Johnson: The Yas Yas Girl 1937–1947*. Wolf WBJ 006, 1998.

Josh White and Big Bill Broonzy: Folk Blues. EmArcy MG 36052, n.d.

Kinnell, Bill. *Big Bill Broonzy: Trouble in Mind*. UK: Spotlite SPJ900, 1978.

Korner, Alexis. *Big Bill Broonzy: Big Bill Blues*. UK: Vogue LAE12009, 1956.

———. *An Evening with Big Bill Broonzy Recorded in Club Montmartre Copenhagen 1956*. Denmark: Storyville SLP-114, n.d.

Lomax, Alan. *Blues in the Mississippi Night: Authentic Field Recordings of Negro Folk Music*. USA: United Artists UAL 4027, 1959; reissue on Rykodisc, RCD 90155, 1990.

Lornell, Kip. *Big Bill Broonzy, 1932–1942.* Biograph BLP C15, 1973.

The Mercury Blues 'N' Rhythm Story 1945–1955. Mercury CD 314 528 292-2, 1996.

Morgantini, J. *Big Bill Broonzy.* France: Bluebird FXMI 7275, n.d.

Oliver, Paul. *Big Bill and Sonny Boy.* UK: RCA Victor RD-7685, 1964.

———. *Big Bill Broonzy.* UK: Philips BBL 7113, 1957.

———. *Big Bill Broonzy: Trouble in Mind.* UK: Fontana 688 206 ZL, 1965.

———. *Big Bill Broonzy, 1927–32.* UK: Matchbox MSE 1004, 1985.

———. *Portraits in Blues. Vol. 2: Big Bill Broonzy.* Denmark: Storyville SLP 154, 1964.

Pittman, Sampson. "Cotton Farmer Blues." *Alan Lomax Collection.* Archive of Folk Culture, Library of Congress, n.d.

Pullum, Joe. "CWA Blues." *Vol. 1 (1934–1935).* Document DOCD-5393, n.d.

Rainey, Ma. "Blame It on the Blues." *Ma Rainey.* Milestone M-47021, 1974.

———. "Cell Bound Blues." *Immortal Ma Rainey.* Milestone MLP-2001, 1966.

———. "Chain Gang Blues." *Ma Rainey.* Milestone M-47021, 1974.

Randle, Bill. *Big Bill Broonzy's Last Session. Part Three.* UK: HMV CLP 1562, 1962.

———. *The Bill Broonzy Story.* Verve MGV3000-5, 1999. Original release 1957.

Ruyter, Michiel A. de. *Big Bill Broonzy: Big Bill's Blues.* Columbia WL 111, n.d.

Sam, Washboard. *Washboard Sam: I'm Not the Lad.* Contact BT-2012, 1989.

Schrama, Cees. *Big Bill Broonzy Amsterdam Live Concerts 1953.* Munich Records B000FVRRAA, 2006.

Slim, Bumble Bee. "Policy Dream Blues." *Bumble Bee Slim (Amos Easton) 1934–1937.* Blues Document BoB-9, n.d.

Smith, Bessie. "In House Blues." *The World's Greatest Blues Singer.* Columbia CG 33, 1972.

———. "Sam Jones Blues." *Any Woman's Blues.* Columbia G-30126, 1972.

———. "Work House Blues." *Empty Bed Blues.* Columbia G-30450, n.d.

Smith, Clara. "For Sale (Hannah Johnson's Big Jack Ass)." *Street Walkin' Blues: 25 Plaintive Paeans to the World's Oldest Profession, 1924–1956.* Jass J-CD-626.

Smith, Chris. *Blues in the Mississippi Night.* UK: Sequel NEXCD 122, 1990.

———. *Famous Hokum Boys—Vols. 1–2.* Wolf WBCD-011.

Terkel, Studs. *Blues With Big Bill Broonzy, Sonny Terry and Brownie McGhee.* Smithsonian/Folkways FW03817, 1959.

———. *Big Bill Broonzy and Pete Seeger in Concert.* USA: Verve/Folkways FVS 9008, 1965.

———. *Big Bill Broonzy and Washboard Sam.* Chess LP 1468, n.d.

———. *Big Bill Broonzy Memorial.* Mercury MG 20822, n.d.; USA: Mercury SR 60822, 1963.

———. *Big Bill Broonzy: The Blues.* EmArcy MG 36137, n.d.

———. *His Story—Big Bill Broonzy Interviewed by Studs Terkel.* Folkways FG 3586, 1957. USA: Smithsonian Folkways 03586, 1992.

———. *Studs Terkel's Weekly Almanac: Radio Programme, No. 4: Folk Music and Blues*

(Studs Terkel, Big Bill Broonzy and Pete Seeger). Smithsonian/Folkways FW03864, 1956.

———. *This Is the Blues*. Folkways FS 3817, 1959.

Van Gasteren, Louis. *Amsterdam Live Concerts 1953*. Munich CD 7229523, 2006.

Vasset, A. *Big Bill Broonzy: Unissued Test Pressing*. France: Milan CD CH 345, 1991.

Welsh, Nolan. "The Birdwell Blues." Armstrong, Louis. *The Genius of Louis Armstrong. Vol. 1, 1923–1933*. John Hammond Collection. Columbia G30416, n.d.

Wheatstraw, Peetie. "Chicago Mill Blues." *The Last Straw*. http:// music.aol.com/album/ the-last-straw.

———. "Working on the Project." *Peetie Wheatstraw Complete Recorded Works in Chronological Order*. Document vol. 5, DOCD-5245, 1994.

White, Bukka. "Parchman Farm Blues." *Aberdeen Mississippi Blues: The Vintage Recordings, 1930–1940*. Document DOCD-5679, n.d.

Wildman, Steve. *Big Bill Broonzy: The Blues*. Scepter M-529, n.d.

RECORDING SESSIONS

The sources of information for the appendix were Robert M. W. Dixon, John Godrich, and Howard Rye, *Blues and Gospel Records, 1890–1943;* and Mike Leadbitter and Neil Slaven, *Blues Records, 1943–1970.* Chris Smith has written a valuable discography as well, *Hit the Right Lick: The Recordings of Big Bill Broonzy;* however, the distribution of that publication was limited.

The appendix is divided into two sections: the first segment chronicles the recordings produced under the name Big Bill Broonzy. The second segment lists the recordings produced under the name of other musicians with Broonzy as sideman. The studio session information includes the names of musicians and the sites and dates of performances. It also describes the original release labels, the reissues on the Document label series, and the reissues on the LPs and CDs of other labels.

Location Abbreviations (international)

Au—Austria	G—Germany
B—Belgium	H—Holland
Dk—Denmark	It—Italy
E—England	J—Japan
F—France	

Label Abbreviations

This list includes the abbreviations of most of the major domestic and foreign labels that distributed Broonzy's recordings. However, it does not include all of the labels, especially those of the smaller producers.

Amadeo-Van—Amadeo-Vanguard (Germany)	Cq—Conqueror
ARC—American Record Corp.	De—Decca
Austr-Mer—Austroton-Mercury (Germany)	EmArcy
Ba—Banner	Ep—Epic
BB—Bluebird	Doc—Document
Br—Brunswick	Fkws—Folkways
Bwy—Broadway	Fon—Fontana (Holland)
Ch—Champion	Ge—Gennett
Ch—Chess	Hub
Co—Columbia	Je—Jewel

JSo—Jazz Society (France)

Lon—London (England)

Me —Melotone

Mercury

Melodisc (English)

Nixa—Pye/Nixa (England)

OK—Okeh

Or—Oriole

Pe—Perfect

Per—Period (LP)

Ph—Phillips (Holland)

Pm—Paramount

RnB—Record, Book and Film Club

Ro—Romeo

Sav—Savoy

Spr—Supertone

Stry—Storyville (Holland)

Sv—Savoy (Denmark)

Te—Tempo

TR—Top Rank (England)

UnA—United Artists

Van—Vanguard

Vg—Vogue (France)

Vi—Victor

Vo—Vocalion

Vs—Varsity

Instrument Abbreviations

acc.—accompanied

as—alto saxophone

b—bass

bj—banjo

bs – baritone sax

cl—clarinet

d—drums

eg—electric guitar

g—guitar

h—harmonica

j—jug

k—kazoo

md—mandolin

p—piano

sb—string bass

sp—speech

t—trumpet

tb—trombone

ts—tenor saxophone

v—vocals

vn—violin

Production Abbreviations

alt. tk.—alternate take

inst. —instrumental

Broonzy Recordings Issued under His Name (1927–1957)

The recordings released under Broonzy's name are listed in chronological order. The vast majority of the recordings were released under the monikers Big Bill or Big Bill Broonzy. However, some of the early releases appeared under other names such as Sammy Sampson and Big Bill Johnson, no doubt to avoid contract restrictions. The name Big Bill Broomsley on one early recording was probably a misspelling. In addition, Broonzy recorded four sides under the name Little Sam with jazz saxophonist Don Byas. Among the names selected for his sideman were Big Bill and Thomps (for guitarist John Thomas) early in his career, and the studio bands of Big Bill and the Jug Busters, Memphis Five, Chicago Five, Rhythm Band, and Fat Four during the height of his career as an urban blues musician.

Big Bill: v; acc. own g; John Thomas, g/sp
Chicago—ca. 1927

	House Rent Stomp	Pm rejected
	Big Bill Blues	Pm rejected
	Gonna Tear It Down	Pm rejected
	(Bed Slats and All)	Pm rejected
	Tod Pail Blues	Pm rejected

Big Bill and Thomps: Big Bill, g; John Thomas, g/sp
Chicago—ca. November 1927

20159-2	House Rent Stomp	Pm 12656, DocDOCD 5050

Big Bill: v; acc. own g; John Thomas, g/sp–1
Chicago—ca. February 1928

20373-1	Big Bill Blues–1	Pm 12656, DocDOCD 5050

Chicago—ca. October 1928

20922-1	Down in the Basement Blues	Pm 12707, Bwy 5072, DocDOCD 5050
20923-2	Starvation Blues	Pm12707, Bwy 5072, DocDOCD 5050

Big Bill: prob. v/g
New York City—Tuesday, 8 April 1930

JK(?)-1039	I Can't Be Satisfied	Br unissued

Sammy Sampson: v; acc. own g; Frank Brasswell, g/sp-1
New York City—Wednesday, 9 April 1930

9599-2	I Can't Be Satisfied	Pe 157, Or 8025, Ro 5025, Je 20025, DocDOCD 5050
9600-1	Grandma's Farm–1	Pe 187, Or 8086, Ro 5086, DocDOCD 5050
9601-2	Skoodle Do Do	Pe 157, Or 8026, Ro 5026, Je 20026, DocDOCD 5050

Sammy Sampson: acc. own g; prob. Georgia Tom Dorsey, p
New York City—Friday, 11 April 1930

9621-1	Tadpole Blues	Pe 179, Ba 32181, Or 8068, Ro 5068, DocDOCD 5050
9621-2	Tadpole Blues	Pe 179, DocDOCD 5050
9627-1, -2	Bow Leg Baby	Pe 163

Big Bill Johnson: Big Bill, v; acc. own g; Frank Brasswell, g–1/sp–2/v–3
Richmond, Ind.—Friday, 2 May 1930

16570	I Can't Be Satisfied–1	Ge 7230
16570-A	Bowleg Blues–1	Ge unissued
16571-A	Tadpole Blues–1	Ge unissued
16573	Skoodle Do Do–2	Ge 7210, Ch 16015, DocDOCD 5050
16581	Papa's Getting' Hot–1, 3	Ch 16015, Vs 6038, DocDOCD 5050

Sammy Sampson: Big Bill, v; acc. own g; prob. Arthur Petti(e)s, g
New York City—Tuesday, 16 September 1930.

10042-1	Police Station Blues	Ba 32391, Or 8123, Pe 199, Ro 5123, DocDOCD 5050
10043-1	They Can't Do That	Ba 32391, Or 8123, Pe 199, Ro 5123, DocDOCD 5050

Sammy Sampson: Big Bill, v; acc. own g; Georgia Tom Dorsey, p
New York City—Wednesday, 17 September 1930.

10052-1	State Street Woman	Ba 32393, Or 8125, Pe 0201, Ro 5125, DocDOCD 5050
10053-2	Meanest Kind of Blues	Pe 186, Or 8085, Ro 5085, DocDOCD 5050
10054-2	I Got the Blues for My Baby	Pe 186, Or 8085, Ro 5085, DocDOCD 050

Big Bill Johnson: Big Bill, v; acc. own g
Richmond, Ind.—Wednesday, 19 November 1930

17281	The Banker's Blues	Ch 16327, Spr 2604, DocDOCD 5050
17282-B	The Levee Blues	Ge unissued
17283	That Won't Do	Ch 16172
17284-B	How You Want It Done?	Ch 16172, Spr 2560, Sav 501, DocDOCD 5050

Big Bill Broomsley: Big Bill, v; acc. own g
Grafton, Wisc.—ca. May 1931.

	How You Want It Done?	Pm 13084
	Station Blues	Pm 13084

Big Bill Johnson: Big Bill, v; acc. own g; or **Johnson and Smith**–1; Big Bill, g; Steele Smith, bj–4; or **Steele and Johnson**–2: Big Bill, Steele Smith, v duet; acc. Big Bill, g; Steele Smith, bj; or **Steel Smith**–3: Steele Smith, v/bj–4; acc. "Big Bill Johnson" g. Both talk on 18386-A.
Richmond, Ind.—Tuesday, 9 February 1932

18382	Worried in Mind Blues	Ch 16396, Spr 2837
18383	Too Too Train Blues	Ch16400, 50069, Spr 2808, DocDOCD 5050
18384	Mistreatin' Mamma	Ch 16396, 50069, Spr 2808, DocDOCD 5050
18385	Big Bill Blues	Ch 16400, 50060, Spr 2837, DocDOCD 5050
18386-A	Brown Skin Shuffle–1	Ch 16411, 40074, Spr 2836, DocDOCD 5050
18387-A	Stove Pipe Stomp–1, 4	Ch 16411, 40074, Spr 2836, DocDOCD 5050
18388	Beedle Um Bum–2	Ch 16395, 50058, Spr 2798, Ge 5006, DocDOCD 5050
18389	Selling That Stuff–2	Ch 16395, 50058, Spr 2798, Ge 5007, DocDOCD 5050
18390	You Do It–3, 4	Ch 16426, Vs 6038, DocDOCD 5051
18391-A	Baby, If You Can't Do Better–3	Ge unissued
18392	Mr. Conductor Man	Ch 16416, 50060, DocDOCD 5051
18393	Alright Mamma Blues	Ge unissued

Big Bill: v; acc. own g
New York City—Tuesday, 29 March 1932

11605-2	Too-Too Train Blues	Ba 32653, Me M12570, Or 8190, Pe 0220, Ro 5190, DocDOCD 5051
11606-2,-3	Worrying You off My Mind No. 1	Ba 32559, Or 8168, Pe 0217, Ro 5168, DocDOCD 5051
11607-1	Worrying You off My Mind No. 2	Ba 32559, Or 8168, Pe 0217, Ro 5168, DocDOCD 5051
11608-2	Shelby County Blues	Ba 32670, Me M12599, Or 8197, Pe 0223, Ro5197, DocDOCD 5051
11609-2	Mistreatin' Mama Blues	Ba 33085, Me M13049, Or 8347, Pe 0284, Ro 5347, DocDOCD 5051
11610-2	Bull Cow Blues	Ba 32653, Me M12570, Or 8190, Pe 0220, Ro 5190, Vo 1745, JSo AA514, DocDOCD 5051
11611-2	How You Want It Done?	Ba 32436, Or 8138, Pe 0207, Ro 5138, Vo 1745, JSo AA514, DocDOCD 5051

Big Bill: v; acc. own g
New York City—Wednesday, 30 March 1932

11617-1	Long Tall Mama	Ba 33085, Me M13049, Or 8347, Pe 0284 Ro 5347, DocDOCD 5051

Big Bill and His Jug Busters: Big Bill, g/v; unknown, k; prob. Black Bob, p; unknown, sb; Jimmy Bertrand, wb
New York City—Wednesday, 30 March 1932

11624-2	M and O Blues	Ba 32436, Or 8138, Pe 0207, Ro 5138, DocDOCD 5051

Big Bill and His Jug Busters: Big Bill, g/v; unknown, t; prob. Black Bob, p; unknown, j
New York City—Thursday, 31 March 1932

11632-2	Rukus Juice Blues	Ba 32670, Me M12599, Or 8197, Pe 0223 Ro 5197, DocDOCD 5051

Big Bill: v/g; acc. unknown, p
Chicago—Friday, 23 March 1934

80388-1	Friendless Blues	BB B5535, DocDOCD 5051
80389-1	Milk Cow Blues	BB B5476, DocDOCD 5051
80390-1	Hungry Man Blues	BB B5706, DocDOCD 5051
80391-1	I'll Be Back Home Again	BB B5674, DocDOCD 5051
80392-1	Bull Cow Blues—Part 2	BB B5476, DocDOCD 5051
80393-1	Serve It to Me Right	BB B5674, DocDOCD 5051
80394-1	Starvation Blues	BB B5706, DocDOCD 5051
80395-1	Mississippi River Blues	BB B5535, DocDOCD 5051

Big Bill: v/g; acc. prob. Black Bob, p; prob. Charlie Jackson, bj
Chicago—Thursday, 14 June 1934

80613-1	At the Break of Day	BB B5571, DocDOCD 5051
80614-1	I Want to Go Home	BB B5571, DocDOCD 5051

Big Bill: v/g; prob. Black Bob, p; prob. Charlie Jackson, g–1
Chicago—Thursday, 18 October 1934

C-704-A	Hard Headed Woman	Ba 33314, Me M13281, Or 8420, Pe 0309, Ro 5420, DocDOCD 5051
C-705-A	Dying Day Blues	ARC unissued; Milan CDCH345 (CD)
C-705-B	Dying Day Blues	ARC 35-10-31, DocDOCD 5051
C-718-A	I Wanna See My Baby–1	Ba 33490, Me M13457, Or 8494, Pe 0309, Ro 5494, DocDOCD 5052
C-719-A	Serve It to Me Right	Ba 33314, Me M13281, Or 8420, Pe 0309, Ro 5420, DocDOCD 5052
C-720-B	Dirty No-Gooder	ARC 35-10-31, DocDOCD 5052

Big Bill: v/g; prob. Black Bob, p; prob. Charlie Jackson, g
Chicago—Friday, 19 October 1934

C-721-A	Let Her Go—She Don't Know	ARC 5-11-67, Cq 8577, DocDOCD 5052
C-722-A	Hobo Blues	Ba 33490, Me M13457, Or 8494, Pe 0335, Ro 5494, DocDOCD 5052
C-723-A	Prowlin' Ground Hog	Ba 33344, Me M13311, Or 8433, Pe 0313, Ro 5433, DocDOCD 5052
C-724-B	Mississippi River Blues	ARC unissued

Big Bill: acc. own vn; unknown, p

C-736-A	C-C Rider	ARC unissued, Doc DLP510 (LP); DocDOCD5052
C-736-B	C-C Rider	Ba 33344, Me M13311, Or 8433, Pe 0313, Ro 5433, DocDOCD 5052

Big Bill: v/g; acc. prob. Black Bob, p; unknown, whistle–1
Chicago—Tuesday, 26 February 1935

85517-1	The Southern Blues–1	BB B5998, B6964, MW M4836, DocDOCD 5052
85518-1	Good Jelly	BB B5998, MW M4836, DocDOCD 5052

Big Bill: v/g; acc. prob. Louis Lasky, g
Chicago—Thursday, 20 June 1935

C-1020-B	C and A Blues	ARC 5-12-65, DocDOCD 5052
C-1021-A	Something Good	ARC 5-12-65, DocDOCD 5052

Big Bill: v/g; acc. Black Bob, p
Chicago—Wednesday, 3 July 1935

C-1060-B	You May Need My Help Someday	ARC 6-04-62, Cq 8674, DocDOCD 5052
C-1061-A	Rising Sun, Shine On	ARC 5-11-67, Cq 8577, DocDOCD 5052

Big Bill: v/g; acc. Black Bob, p
Chicago—Saturday, 27 July 1935

91423-1	Mountain Blues	BB B6060, DocDOCD 5126
91424-1	Bad Luck Blues	BB B6060, DocDOCD 5126
91425-1	I Can't Make You Satisfied	BB B6111, DocDOCD 5126
91426-1	I'm Just a Bum	BB B6111, B6964, DocDOCD 5126

Big Bill: v/g; acc. Black Bob, p; Bill Settles, sb
Chicago—Thursday, 31 October 1935

96230-1	Keep Your Hands off Her	BB B6188, DocDOCD 5126
96231-1	The Sun Gonna Shine in My Door Someday	BB B6188, DocDOCD 5126
96232-1	Good Liquor Gonna Carry Me Down	BB B6230, DocDOCD 5126
96233-1	Down the Line Blues	BB B6230, DocDOCD 5126

Big Bill: v/g; acc. Black Bob, p; Bill Settles, sb
Chicago—Monday, 16 December 1935

C-1182-2	Bricks in My Pillow	ARC 6-03-55, Cq 8672, DocDOCD 5126
C-1189-2	Tell Me What You Been Doing	ARC 6-04-62, Cq 8674, DocDOCD 5126
C-1190-2	Ash Hauler	ARC 6-03-55, Cq 8672, DocDOCD 5126
C-1191-2	Evil Women Blues	ARC unissued; Doc DLP539 (LP); DocDOCD 5126; Phontastic NCD8827

Big Bill: v/g; acc. Black Bob, p; Bill Settles, sb
Chicago—Wednesday, 12 February 1936

C-1245-2	These Ants Keep Biting Me	ARC 7-01-57, Cq 8766, DocDOCD 5126
C-1246-2	Big Bill Blues (These Blues Are Doggin' Me)	ARC 6-05-56, Cq 8671, DocDOCD 5126
C-1247-1	You Know I Need Lovin'	ARC 6-06-56, Cq 8684, DocDOCD 5126
C-1248-1	Match Box Blues	ARC 6-05-56, Cq 8671, DocDOCD 5126
C-1249-1	Low Down Woman Blues	ARC 6-06-56, Cq 8684, DocDOCD 5126

Big Bill: v/g; acc. Black Bob, p; Bill Settles, sb
Chicago—Wednesday, 22 April 1936

C-1358-1	Bull Cow Blues No. 3	ARC unissued; Milan CDCH345 (CD)
C-1358-2	Bull Cow Blues No. 3	ARC 6-07-57, DocDOCD 5126
C-1359-1	Married Life's a Pain	ARC unissued; Milan CDCH345 (CD)
C-1359-2	Married Life's a Pain	ARC 7-03-68, Cq 8777, DocDOCD 5126
C-1360-1	Black Mare Blues	ARC unissued; Milan CDCH345 (CD)
C-1360-2	Black Mare Blues	ARC 7-01-57, Cq 8766, DocDOCD 5126
C-1361-1	Pneumonia Blues (I Keep on Aching)	ARC 7-03-68, Cq 8777, DocDOCD 5126

Big Bill: v/g; acc. Black Bob, p
Chicago—Friday, 1 May 1936

C-1374-2	Big Bill's Milk Cow No. 2	ARC 6-07-57, DocDOCD 5127

Big Bill: v/g; acc. Black Bob, p; Bill Settles, sb
Chicago—Wednesday, 27 May, 1936

C-1380-1	W.P.A. Blues	ARC unissued; Milan CDCH345 (CD)
C-1380-2	W.P.A. Blues	ARC 6-08-61, DocDOCD 5127
C-1381-2	I'm a Southern Man	ARC 6-08-61, DocDOCD 5127

Big Bill: v/g; acc. Black Bob, p; George Barnes, eg; Charlie McCoy, md
Chicago—Thursday, 3 September 1936

C-1455-1	Lowland Blues	ARC 6-11-72, Cq 8767, DocDOCD 5127
C-1456-1	Seven-Eleven (Dice Please Don't Fail Me)	ARC 7-03-54, DocDOCD 5127
C-1457-2	You Know I Got a Reason	ARC 6-11-72, Cq 8767, DocDOCD 5127
C-1458-1	Oh, Babe (Don't Do Me That Way)	ARC unissued; Milan CDCH345 (CD)
C-1458-2	Oh, Babe (Don't Do Me That Way)	ARC 7-02-54, Cq 8794, DocDOCD 5127

Big Bill: v/g; acc. Black Bob, p; Bill Settles, sb
Chicago—Wednesday, 16 September 1936

C-1473-1	Detroit Special	ARC 6-12-59, DocDOCD 5127
C-1474-2	Falling Rain	ARC 6-12-59, DocDOCD 5127

Big Bill: v/g; acc. Black Bob, p; Bill Settles, sb
Chicago—Wednesday, 28 October 1936

C-1634-1	Black Widow Spider	ARC 7-02-54, Cq 8794, DocDOCD 5127

Big Bill: v/g; acc. Black Bob, p; Bill Settles, sb
Chicago—Thursday, 19 November 1936

C-1688-2	Cherry Hill	ARC 7-03-54, DocDOCD 5127

Big Bill: v/g; acc. Black Bob, p; Bill Settles, sb; "Mr. Sheiks" (prob. Alfred Bell), t–1; poss. Fred Williams, d–2
Chicago—Friday, 29 January 1937

C-1799-1	Southern Flood Blues	ARC 7-04-68, Cq 8776, DocDOCD 5127
C-1800-2	My Big Money–1	ARC 7-11-67, Cq 8930, Vo 03170, DocDOCD 5127
C-1801-1	My Woman Mistreats Me	ARC 7-11-67, Cq 8930, Vo 03170, DocDOCD 5127
C-1802-2	Let's Reel and Rock–1, 2	ARC 7-06-64, Cq 8912, Vo 02944, DocDOCD 5127
C-1803-2	Come up to My House–1, 2	ARC unissued; Biograph BLPC15 (LP); DocDOCD 5127

Big Bill: v/g; acc. Black Bob, p; Bill Settles, sb; "Mr. Sheiks" (prob. Alfred Bell), t–1; unknown, 2nd g; unknown, woodblocks–2
Chicago—Sunday, 31 January 1937

C-1807-2	Get Away–1	ARC unissued; Biograph BLPC15 (LP); DocDOCD 5127, Blues Collection 15742-2 (CDs)
C-1808-1	Terrible Flood Blues–2	Me 7-04-68, DocDOCD 5127

C-1808-2	Terrible Flood Blues–2	ARC 7-04-68, Cq 8776
C-1809-1	Little Bug–1	ARC unissued; Milan CDCH345 (CD)
C-1809-2	Little Bug–1	ARC 7-05-57, Cq 8849, DocDOCD 5127
C-1810-1	Horny Frog	ARC unissued; RnB CJ46219 (LP); RnB CK46219, RnB (EU) 467247-2, RnB (J), CSCS5325, DocDOCD 5127 (CDs)
C-1810-2	Horny Frog	ARC 7-05-57, Cq 8849, DocDOCD 5128
C-1811-1	Mean Old World–1	ARC unissued; DocDOCD 5128
C-1811-2	Mean Old World–1	ARC 7-07-64, Cq 8913, DocDOCD 5128
C-1812-1	Barrel House When It Rains	ARC 7-07-64, Cq 8913, DocDOCD 5128
C-1813-1	You Do Me Any Old Way–1	ARC unissued; Ep EE22017, EpF LN24274, CBS (E) 52648, CBS (F) 21122, CBS (Cz) 11-0211-1, Por RJ44089, Por (Eu) 465020-1, Albatros VPA8188, Doc DLP539 (LPs); Por RK44089, Por (Eu) 465020-2, Blues Collection 15742-2, Doc DOCD5128 (CDs)
C-1813-2	You Do Me Any Old Way–1	ARC 7-06-64, Cq 8912, Vo 02944, DocDOCD 5128

Big Bill: v/g; acc. Black Bob, p; Alfred Bell, t–1; Fred Williams, d
Chicago—Wednesday, 9 June 1937

C-1920-1	Louise, Louise Blues	ARC 7-08-65, Cq 8914, Vo 03075, DocDOCD 5128
C-1920-2	Louise, Louise Blues	ARC unissued; DocDOCD 5128
C-1921-2	Let Me Be Your Winder–1	ARC 7-08-65, Cq 8914, Vo 03075, DocDOCD 5128

Big Bill: v/g; acc. poss. Punch Miller, t-1; Aletha Robinson, p; Fred Williams, d
Chicago—Thursday, 8 July 1937

C-1959-1	Hattie Blues	ARC unissued; DocDOCD 5128
C-1959-2	Hattie Blues	ARC unissued; DocDOCD 5128
C-1960-2	My Old Lizzie–1	ARC 7-10-57, Cq 8916, Vo 03122, DocDOCD 5128
C-1961-1	Come Home Early–1	ARC unissued; DocDOCD 5128
C-1961-2	Come Home Early–1	ARC 7-10-57, DocDOCD 5128
C-1962-1	Advice Blues	ARC unissued

Big Bill: v/g; acc. Black Bob, p; unknown, sb
Chicago—Monday, 16 August 1937

C-1961-3, -4	Come Home Early	ARC 7-10-57, Cq 8916, Vo 03122, DocDOCD 5128

Big Bill: v/g; acc. prob. Black Bob, p-1; unknown, 2nd g; unknown, sb
Chicago—Thursday, 19 August 1937

C-1988-1	My Gal Is Gone–1	ARC 7-10-66, Cq 8915, Vo 03147, DocDOCD 5128
C-1989-2	Evil Hearted Me	ARC 7-10-66, Cq 8915, Vo 03147, DocDOCD 5128

Big Bill: v/g; acc. Blind John Davis, p; Fred Williams, d
Chicago—Wednesday, 13 October 1937

C-2006-1	I Want My Hands on It	ARC 8-02-57, Cq 8999, Vo 03304, DocDOCD 5128

C-2006-2	I Want My Hands on It	ARC unissued: RnB CJ46219 (LP); RnB CK46219, RnB(Eu) 467247-2, RnB(J) CSCS5325, DocDOCD 5128 (CDs)
C-2007-1	It's Too Late Now	ARC unissued: DocDOCD 5128
C-2007-2	It's Too Late Now	ARC 8-01-58, Cq 9036, Vo 03252
C-2008-1	Made a Date with an Angel (Got No Walking Shoes)	ARC unissued: RnB CJ46219 (LP); RnB CK46219, RnB(Eu) 467247-2, RnB(J) CSCS5325, Doc DOCD 5128 (CDs)
C-2008-2	Made a Date with an Angel (Got No Walking Shoes)	ARC 8-02-57, Cq 8999, Vo 03304, DocDOCD 5129
C-2009-1	Play Your Hand	ARC 8-04-56, Vo 03400, DocDOCD 5129

Big Bill: v/g; acc. Blind John Davis, p; Bill Settles, sb
Chicago—Thursday, 21 October 1937

C-1959-3	Hattie Blues	ARC 8-01-58, Cq 9036, Vo 03252, DocDOCD 5129
C-2026-1	Somebody's Got to Go	ARC 8-04-56, Vo 03400, DocDOCD 5129
C-2027-1	Good Boy	ARC 8-03-54, Cq 9035, Vo 03337, DocDOCD 5129
C-2028-1	I Want You by My Side	Vo 04041, DocDOCD 5129
C-2029-1	Border Blues	ARC 8-03-54, Cq 9035, Vo 03337, DocDOCD 5129

Big Bill: v/g; acc. Blind John Davis, p; Bill Osborn or Austin, ts; George Barnes, eg; Oliver Hudson or Nelson, sb
Chicago—Tuesday, 1 March 1938

| C-2145-2 | Sweetheart Land | Vo 04041, DocDOCD 5129 |
| C-2146-1 | It's a Low Down Dirty Shame | ARC unissued: Doc DLP581, RnB CJ46219 (LP); RnB CK46219, RnB(Eu) 467247-2, RnB(J) CSCS5325, Doc DOCD 5129 (CDs) |

Big Bill: v/g; acc. Punch Miller, t; Joshua Altheimer, p; unknown, sb–1; poss. Fred Williams, d
Chicago—Wednesday, 30 March 1938

C-2157-1	Got to Get Ready Tonight	Vo 04095, DocDOCD 5129
C-2158-1	Trucking Little Woman	Vo 04205, Cq 9074, Co 30085, 37783, DocDOCD 5129
C-2159-1	Unemployment Stomp	Vo 04378, Cq 9148, DocDOCD 5129
C-2160-1	Why Did You Do That to Me?–1	Vo 04205, Cq 9074, Co 30085, 37783, DocDOCD 5129

Big Bill: v/g; acc. Joshua Altheimer, p; unknown, sb
Chicago—Tuesday, 5 April 1938

C-2163-1	It's Your Time Now	Vo 04280, Cq 9078, DocDOCD 5129
C-2164-1	I'll Start Cutting on You	Vo 04095, DocDOCD 5129
C-2165-1	Sad Letter Blues	Vo unissued: Doc DOCD5129
C-2166-1	The Mill Man Blues	Vo 04280, Cq 9078, DocDOCD 5129

Big Bill: v/g; acc. prob. Joshua Altheimer, p; prob. Bill Owsley, cl-1/ts–2; prob. George Barnes, eg; unknown, sb
Chicago—Thursday, 5 May 1938

C-2183-1	I'll Do Anything for You–2	Vo 04642, DocDOCD 5129
C-2184-1	Sad Pencil Blues–1, 2	Vo 04378, Cq 9148, DocDOCD 5129
C-2185-2	New Shake-Em on Down	Vo 4149, Cq 9073, Co 30084, 37782, DocDOCD 5129
C-2186-1	Night Time Is the Right Time No. 2	Vo 04149, Cq 9073, Co 30084, 37782, DocDOCD 5129

Big Bill and the Memphis Five: Big Bill, v/g; acc. "Mr. Sheiks" (prob. Alfred Bell), t; prob. Buster Bennett, as; prob. Blind John Davis, p; unknown, g; prob. Wilbur Ware, sb
Chicago—Thursday, 15 September 1938

C-2324-1	Let Me Dig It	Vo 04591, Co 30087, 37785, DocDOCD 5129
C-2325-1	WPA Rag	Vo 04429, Cq 9164, DocDOCD 5129
C-2326-1	Going Back to Arkansas	Vo unissued: RnB CJ46219 (LP); RnB CK46219, RnB(Eu) 467247-2, RnB(J) CSCS5325, DocDOCD 5130 (CDs)
C-2327-1	Rider Rider Blues	Vo 04486, Cq 9165, DocDOCD 5130

Big Bill: v/g; acc. Blind John Davis, p; unknown, sb
Chicago—Thursday, 15 September 1938

C-2329-1	Living on Easy Street	Vo 04429, Cq 9164, DocDOCD 5130
C-2330	Good Time Tonight	Vo 04532, Cq 9166, DocDOCD 5130
C-2331-1	Trouble and Lying Woman	Vo 04591, Co 30087, 37785, DocDOCD 5130
C-2332-2	I Believe I'll Go Back Home	Vo unissued: RnB CJ46219, DocDLP581 (LPs); RnB CK46219, RnB(Eu) 467247-2, RnB(J) CSCS5325, DocDOCD 5130 (CDs)

Big Bill: v/g; acc. "Mr. Sheiks" (prob. Alfred Bell), t–1; prob. Buster Bennett, as–2; Joshua Altheimer, p; unknown, d
Chicago—Tuesday, 27 September 1938

C-2345-1	Flat Foot Susie with Her Flat Yes Yes–1	Co 30135, DocDOCD 5130
C-2346-1	Trucking Little Woman No. 2–2	Vo 04486, Cq 9165, DocDOCD 5130

Big Bill: v/g; acc. Joshua Altheimer, p; Ransom Knowling, sb
Chicago—Thursday, 10 November 1938

C-2381-1	Hell Ain't but a Mile and a Quarter	Vo 04532, Cq 9166, DocDOCD 5130
C-2382-1, 4	Don't You Lay It on Me	Vo 04642, DocDOCD 5130

Big Bill: v/g; acc. Albert Ammons, p; Walter Page, sb
"From Spirituals to Swing" concert, Carnegie Hall, New York City—Friday, 23 December 1938

Done Got Wise	Van VRS8524, VSD25/26, VSD48, VanJ VY504, Fon TFL5188, FJL402, TR35065, CID SJ2,

	Am-Van AVRS9015, VgE VJD550, Gdj J1249, JtnG J1249, Vox VST26340, Amiga 850.061 (LPs); Van VCD2-48, VanJ KICJ8063, Virgin (F) 34007, DocDOCD 5130, Music Memoria 7-88048-2 (CDs)
Louise, Louise	Van VRS8524, VSD25/26, VSD48, VanJ VY504, Fon TFL5188, FJL402, TR 35065, CID SJ2, Am-Van AVRS9015, VgE VJD550, Gdj J1249, JtnG J1249, Vox VST26340, Golden Hour GH264, Amiga 850.061 (LPs); Van VCD2-48, VanJ KICJ8063, Virgin (F) 34007, DocDOCD 5130, Music Memoria 7-88048-2 (CDs)

Big Bill: v/g; acc. Joshua Altheimer, p; Fred Williams, d
Chicago—Monday, 6 February 1939

C-2461-1	Spreadin' Snake Blues	Vo unissued: RnB CJ46215 (LP); RnB CK46215, RnB(Eu) 467245-2, DocDOCD 5130 (CDs)
C-2462-1	Baby Don't You Remember?	Vo 04829, Cq 9284
C-2463 1	Whiskey and Good Time Blues	Vo unissued: Travelin' Man TM8812, Best of Blues BOB2, RnB CJ46219 (LPs); RnB CK 46219, RnB(Eu) 467247-2, RnB(J) CSCS5325, Doc DOCD 5130 (CDs)
C-2464-1	Baby I Done Got Wise	Vo 04706, Cq 9197, Co 30153, DocDOCD 5130
C-2465-1	Preachin' the Blues	Vo 05096, Cq 9343, DocDOCD 5130
C-2466-1	Just a Dream (on My Mind)	Vo 04706, Cq 9197, Co 30153, DocDOCD 5130

Big Bill and The Memphis Five–1/Big Bill–2: Big Bill, v/g; acc. unknown, t; Buster Bennett, as; Blind John Davis, p; unknown, 2nd g; unknown, sb
Chicago—Friday, 10 February 1939

C-2492-1	Fightin' Little Rooster–2	Vo 05205, Cq 9342, Co 30089, 37787, DocDOCD 5130
C-2493-1	Mary Blues–1	Vo 04760, Cq 9278, DocDOCD 5130
C-2494-1	You Can't Sell 'Em in Here–1	Vo 04829, Cq 9284, DocDOCD 5130
C-2495-1	Just Got to Hold You Tight–1	Vo unissued: DocDOCD 5130
C-2495-2	Just Got to Hold You Tight–1	Vo 04760, Cq 9278, DocDOCD 5130

Big Bill: v/g; acc. Odell Rand, cl; Joshua Altheimer, p; Ransom Knowling, sb
Chicago—Thursday, 11 May 1939

WC-2553-1	Just Wondering	Vo 05043, DocDOCD 5131
WC-2554-1	Keep on A-Smilin'	Vo 04990, DocDOCD 5131
WC-2555-1	She Never	Vo 04884, DocDOCD 5131
WC-2556-1	Woodie Woodie	Vo 04938, Cq 9309, DocDOCD 5131
WC-2557-1	Too Many Drivers	Vo 05096, Cq 9343, DocDOCD 5131
WC-2558-1	You Can't Win	Vo 04990, DocDOCD 5131
WC-2559-1	Ride, Alberta, Ride	Vo 04884, DocDOCD 5131
WC-2560-1	That's All Right, Baby	Vo 05043, DocDOCD 5131
WC-2561-1	Please Be My So and So	Vo 04938, Cq 9309, DocDOCD 5131

Big Bill: v/g; acc. Joshua Altheimer, p–1; Fred Williams, d
Chicago—Thursday, 14 September 1939

WC-2728-A	I.C. Blues–1	Vo 05601, DocDOCD 5131
WC-2729-A	Cotton Choppin' Blues–1	Vo 05149, DocDOCD 5131
WC-2730-A	Hot Dog Mama–1	Vo unissued: DocDOCD 5131
WC-2731-A	Dreamy Eyed Baby–1	Vo 05360, DocDOCD 5131
WC-2732-A	My Last Goodbye to You–1	Vo 05259, DocDOCD 5131
WC-2733-A	Don't You Want to Ride–1	Vo 05360, DocDOCD 5131
WC-2734-A	Don't You Be No Fool–1	Vo 05404, DocDOCD 5131
WC-2735-A	Just a Dream No. 2–1	Vo 05259, DocDOCD 5131
WC-2736-A	Tell Me What I Done–1	Vo 05149, Cq 9760, DocDOCD 5131
WC-2737-A	Oh Yes	Vo 05205, Cq 9342, Co 30089, 37787, DocDOCD 5131

Big Bill: v/g; acc. Joshua Altheimer, p; Fred Williams, d
Chicago—Friday, 8 December, 1939

WC-2842-A	I'm Still Your Sweetheart, Baby	Vo 05311, DocDOCD 5131
WC-2843-A	Down and Lost in Mind	OK 05641, Cq 9760, JSo AA562, DocDOCD 5131
WC-2844-A	Let's Have a Little Fun	Vo 05311, DocDOCD 5131
WC-2845-A	Messed Up in Love	OK 05641, Cq 9606, JSo AA562, DocDOCD 5131

Big Bill: v/g; acc. Joshua Altheimer, p; Fred Williams, d
Chicago—Friday, 26 January 1940

WC-2897-A	Plow Hand Blues	Vo 05452, Cq 9378, DocDOCD 5132
WC-2898-A	Jivin' Mr. Fuller Blues	Vo 05404, DocDOCD 5132
WC-2899-A	Make My Get Away	Vo 05514, Cq 9607, 9794, DocDOCD 5132
WC-2900-A	Looking for My Baby	Vo 05452, Cq 9607, 9378, DocDOCD 5132

Big Bill: v/g; acc. Joshua Altheimer, p; Fred Williams, d
Chicago—Wednesday, 17 April 1940

WC-3034-A	I've Got to Dig You	Vo 05563, Cq 9605, DocDOCD 5132
WC-3035-A	Leap Year Blues	Vo 05514, DocDOCD 5132
WC-3036-A	When I Had Money	Vo 05563, Cq 9605, 9790, DocDOCD 5132
WC-3037-A	You Got to Hit the Right Lick	Vo unissued: RnB CJ46219 (LP); RnB CK46219, RnB(Eu) 467247-2, RnB(J) CSCS5325, DocDOCD 5132 (CDs)
WC-3038-A	What Is That She Got?	Vo 05601, Cq 9606, DocDOCD 5132
WC-3039-A	Merry Go Round Blues	Vo unissued: RnB CJ46219 (LP); RnB CK46219, RnB(Eu) 467247-2, RnB(J) CSCS5325, DocDOCD 5132 (CDs)

Big Bill: v/g; acc. Joshua Altheimer, p; Washboard Sam, wb
Chicago—Monday, 10 June 1940

WC-3080-A	Medicine Man Blues	OK 05758, Cq 9762, Co 30068, 37691, DocDOCD 5132
WC-3081-A	Looking up at Down	OK 05698, Cq 9761, CoF BF384, DocDOCD 5132

| WC-3082-A | Midnight Steppers | OK 05758, Cq 9762, Co 30068, 37691, DocDOCD 5132 |
| WC-3083-A | Lone Wolf Blues | OK 05698, Cq 9761, DocDOCD 5132 |

Big Bill: v/g; acc. Blind John Davis, p; Fred Williams, d
Chicago—Friday, 20 September 1940

WC-3305-A	Hit the Right Lick	OK 05869, Cq 9608, DocDOCD 5132
WC-3306-A	You Better Cut That Out	OK 05919, Cq 9608, DocDOCD 5132
WC-3307-A	I Wonder What's Wrong with Me	OK 05919, Cq 9759, DocDOCD 5132
WC-3308-A	Bed Time Blues	OK 05983, Cq 9759, DocDOCD 5132
WC-3309-A	Merry-Go Round Blues	OK 05869, Cq 9609, DocDOCD 5132
WC-3310-A	Serenade Blues	OK 05983, Cq 9609, DocDOCD 5132

Big Bill: v/g; acc. prob. Memphis Slim, p; Ransom Knowling, sb
Chicago—Tuesday, 17 December 1940

WC-3508-1	Lonesome Road Blues	OK 06031, DocDOCD 5132
WC-3509-1	Getting Older Every Day	OK 06116, Cq 9790, DocDOCD 5132
WC-3509-2	Getting Older Every Day	OK unissued: DocDOCD 5132
WC-3510-1	That Number of Mine	OK 06080, Cq 9928, JSo AA528, DocDOCD 5132
WC-3511-1	That Gal Is Gone	OK 06031, DocDOCD 5132
WC-3512-1	I'll Never Dream Again	OK 06080, DocDOCD 5132
WC-3513-1	Rockin' Chair Blues	OK 06116, Cq 9794, 9928, JSo AA528, DocDOCD 5133

Big Bill: v/g; acc. Horace Malcolm, p–1; unknown, sb–2; Washboard Sam, wb; Jazz Gillum, h–3
Chicago—Friday, 2 May 1941

C-3740-1	Shine on, Shine On–1	OK 06303, Cq 9929, Co 30041, 37474, DocDOCD 5133
C-3741-1	Green Grass Blues–1	OK 06242, Cq 9929, DocDOCD 5133
C-3742-1	My Little Flower–1	OK 06386, DocDOCD 5133
C-3743-1	Sweet Honey Bee–1	OK 06386, DocDOCD 5133
C-3744-1	When I Been Drinking–1	OK 06303, Cq 9931, Co 30041, 37474, DocDOCD 5133
C-3745-1	Key to the Highway–2,3	OK 06242, Cq 9932, DocDOCD 5133

Big Bill: v/g; acc. Memphis Slim, p/v–1; unknown, wb
Chicago—Thursday, 17 July 1941

C-3903-1	Double Trouble	OK 06427, Cq 9930, Co 30012, 37242, DocDOCD 5133
C-3904-1	Going Back to My Plow	OK 06484, DocDOCD 5133
C-3905-1	I'm Having So Much Trouble	OK 06484, Cq 9931, DocDOCD 5133
C-3906-1	Wee Wee Hours–1	OK 06552, DocDOCD 5133
C-3907-1	Conversation with the Blues	OK 06552, Cq 9932, DocDOCD 5133
C-3908-1	All by Myself	OK 06427, Cq 9930, Co 30012, 37242, DocDOCD 5133

Big Bill: v/g; acc. Blind John Davis, p; Washboard Sam, wb; unknown, sp–1
Chicago—Tuesday, 2 December 1941

C-4082-1	Keep Your Hand on Your Heart	OK 06601, DocDOCD 5133
C-4083-1	Why Should I Spend My Money–1	OK 06630, Co 30028, 37461, DocDOCD 5133
C-4084-1	What's Wrong With Me–1	OK 6705, Co 30026, 37459, V-D 260, V-D Navy 40, DocDOCD 5133
C-4085-1	I Feel So Good–1	OK 6688, Co 30007, 37088, V-D 496, DocDOCD 5133
C-4086-1	In the Army Now	OK 06601, DocDOCD 5133
C-4087-1	Bad Acting Woman	OK 6724, Co 30023, 37456, DocDOCD 5133
C-4088-1	Night Watchman Blues	OK 6705, Co 30026, 37459, CoF BF384, V-D 260, V-D Navy 40, DocDOCD 5133
C-4089-1	She's Gone with the Wind	OK 06630, Co 30028, 37461, DocDOCD 5133

Big Bill and His Chicago Five: Big Bill, v/g; acc. Punch Miller, t; Buster Bennett, as; Memphis Slim, p; Judge Riley, d
Chicago—Friday, 6 March 1942

C-4197-1	I'm Gonna Move to the Outskirts of Town	OK6651, Co 30010, 37196, DocDOCD 5133
C-4198-1	Tell Me Baby	OK 6688, Co 30007, 37088, V-D 496, DocDOCD 5133
C-4199-1	Hard Hearted Woman	OK 6651, Co 30010, 37196, DocDOCD 5133
C-4200-1	I'm Woke up Now	OK 6724, Co 30023, 37456, DocDOCD 5133

Big Bill (as Little Sam) and the Don Byas Quartet: Big Bill, v/g; acc. Don Byas, ts; Kenny Watts, p; John Levy, b; Slick Jones, d
New York City—early 1945

HU-418-B	Please Believe Me	Hub 3003; DocBDCD 6047
HU-419-B	Why Did You Do That to Me	Hub 3003; DocBDCD 6047
HU-420	You Got to Play Your Hand	Hub 3023; DocBDCD 6047
HU-422	Just a Dream	3023; DocBDCD 6047

Big Bill: Big Bill, v/g; acc. Buster Bennett, as; Big Maceo Merriweather, p; Tyrell Dixon, d
Chicago—19 February 1945

C-4380	Doing the Best I Can	unissued; DocBDCD 6047
C-4381-1	Partnership Woman	Co 30143; DocBDCD 6047
C-4382	Where the Blues Began	unissued
C-4383-1	Humble Blues	Co 36879, 30002; DocBDCD 6047
C-4384-1	Oh Baby	OK 6739, Co 37454, 30021; DocBDCD 6047
C-4385-1	Cell No. 13 Blues	Co 37164, 30009; DocBDCD 6047
C-4386	Believe Me What I Say	unissued
C-4387	1944 Blues	unissued

Big Bill: Big Bill, v/g; acc. Buster Bennett, as; Big Maceo Merriweather, p; Tyrell Dixon, d (Omit Merriweather, Dixon–1)
Chicago—24 February 1945

C-4414-1	When I Get to Thinkin'	OK 6739, Co 37454, 30021; DocBDCD 6047
C-4415-1	Roll Them Bones	Co 36879, 30002; DocBDCD 6047
C-4414	Letter to Tojo	unissued
C-4417-1	You Got the Best Go–1	Co 37164, 30009; DocBDCD 6047

Big Bill and His Rhythm Band: Big Bill, v/g; acc. John Morton, tp; Sax Mallard, as; Bill Casimir, ts; Charles Belcher, p; Ransom Knowling, b; Judge Riley, d
Chicago—4 December 1946

CCO-4686	I Can Fix It	Co 37502, 30051; DocBDCD 6047
CCO-4687	Old Man Blues	Co 37502, 30051; DocBDCD 6047
CCO-4688	I Can't Write	Co unissued; Epic LP 37318; DocBDCD 6047
CCO-4689	What Can I Do	Co 37314, 30016; DocBDCD 6047

Big Bill: Bill Bill, v/g; acc. Memphis Slim, p; Ransom Knowling, b; Tyrell Dixon, d
Chicago—28 January 1947

CCO-4711-1A	San Antonio Blues Co	38070, 30109; DocBDCD 6047
CCO-4712-1A	Saturday Evening Blues	Co 37314, 30016; DocBDCD 6047
CCO-4713-1	Martha Blues	unissued
CCO-4714-1A	Texas Tornado Blues	unissued

Big Bill: Bill Big, v/g; acc. Sam Mallard, as; Bill Casimir, ts; Bob Call, p; unknown, b; Judge Riley, d
Chicago—29 September 1947

CCO-4848-1N	Big Bill's Boogie	Co 37965, 30101; DocBDCD 6047
CCO-4849-1	Just Rocking	Co 38070, 30109; DocBDCD 6047
CCO-4850-1	Shoo Blues	Co 37965, 30101; DocBDCD 6047
CCO-4851-1	I Feel Like Crying	unissued

Big Bill: Bill Big, v/g; acc. John Morton, tp; Sam Mallard, as; Bill Casimir, ts; Bob Call, p; Ransom Knowling, b; Judge Riley, d
Chicago—19 December 1947

CCO-4950-1	Stop Lying Woman	Co 30143; DocBDCD 6047
CCO-4951	Rambling Bill	Co 38180, 30118; DocBDCD 6047)
CCO-4952	Summer Time Blues	Co 38180, 30118; DocBDCD 6047
CCO-4953	Bad Luck Man	Co 30135; DocBDCD 6047

Big Bill Broonzy & His Fat Four: Big Bill, v/g; acc. Antonio Casey, as; Carl Sharp, p; Ransom Knowling, b; Alfred Wallace, d
Chicago—4 January 1949

2176-1	I Love My Whiskey	Merc 8122, LP 20905; Mercury 3145282922 (CD)
2177-1	You've Been Mistreating Me	Merc 8160, LP 20905; Mercury 3145282922 (CD)
2178-1	I Stay Blue All the Time	Merc 8160; Mercury 3145282922 (CD)
2179-1	Water Coast Blues	Merc 8122; Mercury 3145282922 (CD)

(The band also recorded "I'm a Wonderin' Man" at the session. This side was included on the Mercury Records 3145282922 CD, but the original discography information was not available.)

Big Bill Broonzy: Big Bill, v/g; acc. Alfred Wallace, d
Chicago—4 February 1949

2497-1	Five Feet Seven	Merc 8126, LP 20905
2498-1	I Wonder	Merc 8126, LP 20905
2499-1	Keep Your Hands off Her	Merc 8139, LP 20905
2500-1	Mindin' My Own Business	Merc 8139, LP 20905

Big Bill Broonzy with Graeme Bell and His Australian Jazz Band: Big Bill, v/g
Dusseldorf (G)—15 September 1951

John Henry	Raretone (It) LP 5006/7
In the Evening, When the Sun Goes Down	Raretone (It) LP 5006/7
Trouble in Mind	Raretone (It) LP 5006/7
Keep Your Hands off Her	Raretone (It) LP 5006/7

Add Roger Bell, tp; Don "Pixie" Roberts, cl; Derick "Kanga" Bentley, tb–1; Graeme Bell, p; Adrian "Lazy Ade" Monsbrough, as; Norman "Bud" Baker, g; Louis "Baron" Silbereisen, b; Johnny Sangster, d

I Feel So Good	Raretone (It) LP 5006/7
Who's Sorry Now	Raretone (It) LP 5006/7
Mama Don't Allow (No Music Playing in Here)	Raretone (It) LP 5006/7
When the Saints Go Marching In–1	Raretone (It) LP 5006/7

Big Bill Broonzy: v/g or g solo–1
Paris—20 September 1951

51V-4095	House Rent Stomp–1	Vg 131, 2076, LP 30037
51V-4096-1	In the Evening	Vg LP 30, 30037
51V-4096-2	In the Evening	Vg 138, LP 272
51V-4097	The Moppin' Blues	Vg 142, LP 272, 524-30
51V-4098	Hey Hey Baby	Vg 148, LP 30037
51V-4099	Willie Mae Blues	Vg 148, LP 30037
51V-4100	Black, Brown and White	Vg 134, LP 30037
51V-4101-1	Back Water Blues (Big Bill Blues)	Vg 125, LP 30037
51V-4101-2	Back Water Blues	Vg LP 605-30
51V-4102-1	Low Land Blues (Feelin' Low Down)	Vg LP 30037
51V-4102-2	Low Land Blues (Feelin' Low Down or Lonesome Road Blues)	Vg 138, LP 272
51V-4103-1	Feelin' Low Down	Vg 142, LP 30, 30037
51V-4104-2	What I Used to Do	Vg 125, 2078, LP 272, 30037
51V-4105	Make My Getaway	Vg 118, LP 605-30, 30037
	Hollerin' and Cryin' the Blues	Vg LP 605-30

Big Bill Broonzy: v/g
Paris—21 September 1951

51V-4106-1	Blues in 1890	Vg 131, LP 30, 272
51V-4106-2	Blues in 1890	Vg LP 30037

51V-4107	Big Bill Blues (I'm So Lonesome)	Vg 134, LP 272
51V-417	Big Bill Blues (Low Down Blues)	Vg LP 524-30
51V-4108-1	Lonesome Road Blues	Vg EP 7138, LP 30037
51V-4108-2	Lonesome Road Blues	Vg (E) 2068, Vg (F) LP 524-30
51V-4109	When Did You Leave Heaven	Vg EP 7138, LP 524-30, 272, 30037
51V-4110	John Henry	Vg 118, LP 30037
51V-4110	John Henry	Vg (E) 2074, Vg (F) LP 524-30

Chicago Bill or Big Bill Boonzy (*sic*): v/g
London—24 September 1951

MEL-467	Keep Your Hands Off	Melodisc (E) 1191, EP 7-65
MEL-468	Stump Blues	Melodisc (E) 1191, EP 7-65
MEL-469	Five Foot Seven	Melodisc (E) 1203, EP 7-65
MEL-470	Plough Hand Blues	Melodisc (E) 1203, EP 7-65

Big Bill Broonzy: v/g
Paris—October 1951
(There is some question that this session ever occurred. Jazz Society LP 6 was allegedly produced by King Oliver—however, he died in 1938.)

	Make Me a Pallet	Jazz Society (F) LP 6
	Take Me Back	Jazz Society (F) LP 6
	Frankie and John	Jazz Society (F) LP 6
	Hard Headed Woman	Jazz Society (F) LP 6
	St. James Infirmary	Jazz Society (F) LP 6
	Dying Day Blues	Jazz Society (F) LP 6
	Friendless Funeral Blues	Jazz Society (F) LP 6
	Crowded Graveyard	Jazz Society (F) LP 6

Big Bill Broonzy: v/g with Bob Call, p–1; Ransom Knowling, b
Chicago—8 November 1951

4521	Hey Hey	Mercury 8271, 71352, LP 20905, EmArcy LP 36157
4522	Stump Blues	Mercury LP 20822, EmArcy LP 36157
4523	Get Back	Mercury LP 20822, EmArcy LP 36157, Mercury 3145282922 (CD)
4524	Willie Mae Blues	Mercury 8261, LP 20822, EmArcy LP 36157, Mercury 3145282922 (CD)
4525	Walkin' the Lonesome Road	Mercury 8271, EmArcy LP 36157
4526	Mopper's Blues	Mercury 8284, LP 20905, EmArcy LP 36157
4527	I Know She Will	Mercury 8284, LP 20905, EmArcy LP 36157, Mercury 3145282922 (CD)
4528	Hollerin' the Blues–1	Mercury 8261, EmArcy LP 36157

Big Bill Broonzy: v/g with Sax Mallard, as; Bill Casimir, ts; Bob Call, p; Ransom Knowling, b; Judge Riley, d
Chicago—9 November 1951

| 4529 | Leavin' Day | Mercury 80039, EmArcy LP 36157 |
| 4530 | South Bound Train | Mercury 80039, LP 20822, EmArcy LP 36157 |

| 4531 | Tomorrow | Mercury 71352, LP 20822, EmArcy LP 36157 |
| 4532 | You Changed | EmArcy LP 36157 |

Big Bill Broonzy: v/g with prob. Big Crawford, b
Chicago—10 December 1951

4649	John Henry	Mercury LP 20822, EmArcy LP 26034
4650	Crawdad	Mercury LP 20905, EmArcy LP 26034
4651	Bill Bailey	Mercury LP 20822, EmArcy LP 26034
4652	Make My Get Away	Mercury LP 20905, EmArcy LP 26034
4653	Blue Tail Fly	Mercury LP 20822, EmArcy LP 26034
4654	Backwater Blues	Mercury LP 20905, EmArcy LP 26034
4655	In the Evenin'	Mercury LP 20822, EmArcy LP 26034
4656	Trouble in Mind	Mercury LP 20822 2-600, EmArcy LP 26034

(Note: All titles from above session except 4650 and 4652 are also on EmArcy LP 36052.)

Big Bill Broonzy: v/g with Blind John Davis, p–1
Paris—5 February 1952

	It's Your Time Now–1	Vg LP 605-30
	Nobody Knows the Troubles	Vg LP 605-30
	I've Seen	
	Feelin' Low Down–1	Vg LP 605-30
	How Long Blues–1	Vg LP 605-30

Paris—7 February 1952

	Black, Brown and White–1	Vg LP 272
	John Henry–1	Vg LP 272
	Get Away Blues–1	Vg LP 272

Big Bill Broonzy: v/g
Paris—19 March 1952

	Coal Black Curly Hair	Vg EP 7138, LP 524-30
	Hey! Bud Blues	Vg LP 605-30, 072
	Hey! Bud Blues (alt.tk.)	Vg LP 524-30
	Do Right Blues	Vg LP 524-30, 072
	Baby Please Don't Go	Vg LP 524-30
	Baby Please Don't Go (alt. tk.)	Vg LP 605-30, 072
	Letter to My Baby	Vg LP 524-30, 072, EP 17002
	Kind Hearted Blues	Vg LP 524-30, 072, 272
	Louise Louise Blues	Vg LP 605-30, 072
	Louise Louise Blues (alt. tk.)	Vg LP 524-30
	Down by the Riverside	Vg LP 524-30, 072
	Guitar Shuffle (inst.)	Vg EP 7138, LP 605-30, 30037

Big Bill Broonzy: v/g with Blind John Davis, p–1
Antwerp (H)—29 March 1952

	Make My Getaway	Black & Blue (F) LP 33012
	Black, Brown and White	Black & Blue (F) LP 33012
	Keep Your Hands off Her	Black & Blue (F) LP 33012

Lowland Blues–1   Black & Blue (F) LP 33012
Who's Sorry Now–1   Black & Blue (F) LP 33012
Going to Chicago–1   Black & Blue (F) LP 33012
Big Bill Blues   Black & Blue (F) LP 33012

Big Bill Broonzy: v/g with Lee Cooper, g; Big Crawford, g; Washboard Sam, wb
Chicago—April 1953
U-7507   Jacqueline   Ch LP 1468
U-7508   Little City Woman   Ch 1546, LP 1468
U-7509   Lonesome   Ch 1546, LP 1468
U-7510   Romance without Finance   Ch LP 1468

Big Bill Broonzy: v/g with Leslie Hutchinson, tp; Bruce Turner, as; Kenny Graham, ts; Benny
Green, bs; Dill Jones, p; Jack Fallon, b; Phil Seamen, d. V/g only–1
London, 26 October 1955
K565   It Feels So Good   Nixa (E) 2016, EP 1005, LP 16
           Southbound Train   Nixa (E) 2016, EP 1015, LP 16
           Trouble in Mind   rejected
           Whiskey Head Man   rejected
           Southern Saga–1   Nixa (E) EP 1047, LP 16
           When the Sun Goes Down–1   Nixa (E) 605, EP 1047, LP 16
           Going Down the Road Feeling Nixa (E) 605, EP 1047, LP 16
             Bad–1

Big Bill Broonzy: v/g
London—27 October 1955
           Saturday Evening   Nixa (E) EP 1005, LP 16
           Glory of Love   Nixa (E) EP 1005, LP 16
           St. Louis Blues   Nixa (E) EP 1005, LP 16
K-564   Mindin' My Own Business   Nixa (E) EP 1015, LP 16
           When Do I Get to Be Called Nixa (E) EP 1015, LP 16
             a Man
           Partnership Woman   Nixa (E) EP 1015, LP 16

Big Bill Broonzy: v/g
Nottingham (E)—1955
           I'm Gonna Sit Down at the   Spotlight (E) LP 900
             Feastin' Table
           Swing Low Sweet Chariot   Spotlight (E) LP 900
           Make Me a Pallet on the Floor   Spotlight (E) LP 900
           House Rent Stomp   Spotlight (E) LP 900
           Bill Bailey   Spotlight (E) LP 900
           I've Been Waiting for You   Spotlight (E) LP 900
           Goodnight Irene   Spotlight (E) LP 900

Big Bill Broonzy: v/g
Brussels (B)—11 December 1955

Nobody's Business	Black & Blue (F) LP 33012
Texas Tornado	Black & Blue (F) LP 33012
Alberta	Black & Blue (F) LP 33012
Water Coast	Black & Blue (F) LP 33012
Careless Love	Black & Blue (F) LP 33012
Pretty Little Baby	Black & Blue (F) LP 33012

Big Bill Broonzy: v/g with Kansas Fields, d
Paris—10 February 1956

Rock Me Baby	Co EP 1162, 7674, LP 1080
Careless Love	Co EP 1162, 7674, LP 1080
Somebody's Got to Go	Co EP 1162, 7674, LP 1080
Water Coast	Co EP 1121, LP 1080
Big Bill's Guitar Blues (inst.)	Co EP 1121, LP 1080
Take This Ole Hammer	Co EP 1121, LP 1080
Diggin' My Potatoes	Co LP 1080

Big Bill Broonzy: v/g
Baarn, Holland—17 February 1956

57890	Bossie Woman	Co LP 111, Philips (H) LP 08, 012
57891	Texas Tornado	Co LP 111, Philips (H) LP 08, 012
57892	Tell Me What Kind of Man	Co LP 111, Philips (H) LP 08, 012
	Jesus Is	
57893	Trouble in Mind	Co LP 111, Philips (H) LP 08, 012, 681, 555
58165	See See Rider	Co LP 111, Philips (H) LP 08, 012
58166	When I've Been Drinking	Co LP 111, Philips (H) LP 08, 012
58167	Martha	Co LP 111, Philips (H) LP 08, 012
58168	Swing Low Sweet Chariot	Co LP 111, Philips (H) LP 08, 012
58169	Key to the Highway	Co LP 111, Philips (H) LP 08, 012
58170	Goodbye Baby Blues	Co LP 111, Philips (H) LP 08, 012

(Note: Mx. nos. assigned to above session by U.S. Columbia, 58165/6, 58168 & 57892 also on Philips EP 430.714.)

Big Bill Broonzy: v/g
Copenhagen, Denmark—4 May 1956

DGF-33	Going Down the Road	Sv EP 316, LP 114
DGF-34	Ananias	unissued
DGF-35	In the Evening	Sv LP 154
DGF-36	This Train	Sv EP 316, LP 114
DGF-37	I Love You So Much	Sv LP 143
DGF-38	Diggin' My Potatoes	Sv EP 383, LP 188
DGF-39	Willie Mae Blues	Sv EP 383, LP 154
DGF-40	Bill Bailey	Sv EP 316, LP 114
DGF-41	Take This Hammer	unissued

DGF-42	John Henry	Sv EP 383
DGF-43	Glory of Love	unissued
DGF-44	The Crawdad Song	Sv LP 114
DGF-45	Blue Tail Fly	Sv LP 114
DGF-46	Black, Brown and White	Sv 454053, LP 114
DGF-46A	Guitar Blues	Sv LP 114
DGF-47	Hey Bud	Sv LP 114
DGF-48	Irene	Sv LP 114
DGF-49	Sixteen Tons	Sv EP 383, LP 143
DGF-50	Pennies from Heaven	unissued
DGF-51	Shanty in Old Shanty Town	Sv EP 316, LP 114

Big Bill Broonzy: v/g
Copenhagen (Dk)—5/6 May 1956

	Swanee River	Sv LP 154
	Swing Low Sweet Chariot	Sv LP 154
	Big Bill Talks	unissued
	Take This Hammer	Sv LP 143
	When Things Go Wrong	Sv LP 154
	Barrelhouse Shuffle (Guitar Rag)	Sv LP 154
	Down by the Riverside	Sv LP 154
	See See Rider	Sv LP 143
	John Henry	Sv LP 154
	Diggin' My Potatoes	Sv LP 143
	Bill Bailey	unissued
	Just a Dream	SV LP 154
	Careless Love	Sv LP 143
	Ananias	Sv LP 154
	Midnight Special	Sv 45053, LP 143
	Keep Your Hands off Her	Sv LP 143
	I Got a Girl	Sv LP 143
	You Better Mind	Sv LP 143
	Hey Bud	unissued
	John Henry	unissued
	Glory of Love	Sv LP 143
	I Get the Blues When It Rains	Sv LP 154
	My Name Is William Lee Conley Broonzy	Sv LP 143
	Big Bill Talks	Sv LP 154
	Louisiana Blues	Sv LP 154

(NOTE: One version of "Diggin' My Potatoes" from this session appears on Storyville SLPD 5.)

Big Bill Broonzy: v/g with Pete Seeger, v/bj–1
Chicago—1956.

	Midnight Special–1	Verve LP 9008
	Green Corn–1	Verve LP 9008
	Backwater Blues	Verve LP 9008

This Train Is Bound for Glory	Verve LP 9008
Crawdad	Verve LP 9008
Glory of Love	Verve LP 9008
Willie Mae	Verve LP 9008
Bill Bailey	Verve LP 9008
The Midnight Special–1	Fkws LP 86/4, 3864
You Got to Stand Your Test in Judgement–1	Fkws LP 86/4, 3864
That Lonesome Valley–1	Fkws LP 86/4, 3864
Alberta	Fkws LP 86/4, 3864
In the Evening	Fkws LP 86/4, 3864
I Wonder Why	Fkws LP 86/4, 3864
Makin' My Get Away	Fkws LP 86/4, 3864
Love You Baby	Fkws LP 86/4, 3864
Crawdad Hole	Fkws LP 86/4, 3864
John Henry	Fkws LP 86/4, 3864
Trouble in Mind	Fkws LP 2326
When Things Go Wrong	Fkws LP 2326
Diggin' My Potatoes	Fkws LP 2326
Poor Bill Blues	Fkws LP 2326
I Wonder When I'll Get to Be Called a Man	Fkws LP 2326
Louise Louise	Fkws LP 2326
Southbound Train	Fkws LP 2326
Joe Turner No. 2	Fkws LP 2326
Hey Hey Baby	Fkws LP 2326
Saturday Evening Blues	Fkws LP 2326
This Train–1	Fkws LP 2328
Goin' Down the Road–1	Fkws LP 2328
John Henry–1	Fkws LP 2328
Backwater Blues	Fkws LP 2328
Bill Bailey	Fkws LP 2328
I Don't Want No Woman	Fkws LP 2328
Martha	Fkws LP 2328
Tell Me Who	Fkws LP 2328
Tell Me What Kind of Man Jesus Is	Fkws LP 2328
Glory of Love	Fkws LP 2328
Alberta	Fkws LP 2328
In the Evening	Fkws LP 2328

Big Bill Broonzy: v/g
Milan (It)—June 1956

St. Louis Blues	Ricordi (It) EP 3
In the Evening	Ricordi (It) EP 3
See See Rider	Ricordi (It) EP 3
Sixteen Tons	Ricordi (It) EP 3

Big Bill Broonzy: v/g and talking with Studs Terkel
Chicago—14 November 1956

Plough Hand Blues	Fkws LP 3586
C.C. Rider	Fkws LP 3586
Bill Bailey	Fkws LP 3586
Willie Mae Blues	Fkws LP 3586
This Train	Fkws LP 3586
Mule Ridin' (Mule Ridin'–	Fkws LP 3586,
Talking Blues)	
Key to the Highway	Fkws LP 3586
Black, Brown and White	Fkws LP 3586
Joe Turner Blues No. 1	Fkws LP 3586

Big Bill Broonzy: v/g
Nottingham (E)—March 1957

Trouble in Mind	Spotlight (E) LP 900
This Train	Spotlight (E) LP 900
Willie Mae Blues	Spotlight (E) LP 900
In the Evenin'	Spotlight (E) LP 900
The Glory of Love	Spotlight (E) LP 900
The Midnight Special	Spotlight (E) LP 900
Ananias	Spotlight (E) LP 900
Keep Your Hands off Her	Spotlight (E) LP 900
Nobody's Business	Spotlight (E) LP 900
Labour Man Blues	Spotlight (E) LP 900
I'm Gonna Sit Down at The	Spotlight (E) LP 900
Feastin' Table	
C.C. Rider	Spotlight (E) LP 900

Big Bill Broonzy: v (except-1)/g
Chicago—7 May 1957.

Willie Mae	Fkws LP 3817
Shuffle Rag (Guitar Shuffle) –1	Fkws LP 3817
Hush Somebody Is Calling Me	Fkws LP 3817
(It Sounds Like the Voice of	
the Lord)	

Add Sonny Terry, v/h; Brownie McGhee, g

Keys to the Highway	Fkws LP 3817
When the Saints Go Marching	Fkws LP 3817
In (Blues Improvisation)	

(Note: For other titles from this session, see Brownie McGhee.)

Big Bill Broonzy: v/g and talking with Bill Randle
Chicago—12/13 July 1957

26961	Key to the Highway	Verve LP 3000/5, 3001
26962	Mindin' My Own Business	Verve LP 3000/5, 3001
26963	Saturday Evening Blues	Verve LP 3000/5, 3001

26964	Southbound Train	Verve LP 3000/5, 3001
26965	Tell Me What Kind of Man Jesus Is	Verve LP 3000/5, 3001
26966	Swing Low Sweet Chariot	Verve LP 3000/5, 3001
26967	Ploughhand Blues	Verve LP 3000/5, 3001
26968	Joe Turner Blues	Verve LP 3000/5, 3001
26969	Boogie Woogie	Verve LP 3000/5, 3001
26970	I Ain't Gon' Be Treated This Way	Verve LP 3000/5, 3001
26971	Makin' My Getaway	Verve LP 3000/5, 3001
26972	Hollerin' Blues	Verve LP 3000/5, 3001
26973	See See Rider	Verve LP 3000/5, 3001,
26974	Outskirts of Town	Verve LP 3000/5, 3001
26975	This Train	Verve LP 3000/5, 3002
26976	Hush Hush	Verve LP 3000/5, 3002
26977	The Flood	Verve LP 3000/5, 3002
26978	Blues	Verve LP 3000/5, 3002
26979	It Hurts Me So	Verve LP 3000/5, 3002
26980	Kansas City Blues	Verve LP 3000/5, 3002
26981	When the Sun Goes Down	Verve LP 3000/5, 3002
26982	Worried Life	Verve LP 3000/5, 3002
26983	Trouble in Mind	Verve LP 3000/5, 3002
26984	Take This Hammer	Verve LP 3000/5, 3002
26985	The Glory of Love	Verve LP 3000/5, 3002
26986	Louise Blues	Verve LP 3000/5, 3002
26987	Willie Mae Blues	Verve LP 3000/5, 3003
26988	Alberta	Verve LP 3000/5, 3003
26989	Old Folks at Home	Verve LP 3000/5, 3003
26990	Crawdad Hole	Verve LP 3000/5, 3003
26991	John Henry	Verve LP 3000/5, 3003
26992	Just a Dream	Verve LP 3000/5, 3003
26993	Frankie and Johnny	Verve LP 3000/5, 3003
26994	Bill Bailey	Verve LP 3000/5, 3003
26995	Slow Blues (Lookin' for That Woman)	Verve LP 3000/5, 3003

Broonzy Recordings as an Accompanist (1930–1942)

The recordings Broonzy made with other musicians are listed chronologically under the names of the lead singers or bands. The session information identifies the original label releases and the reissues on the Document Records series.

Frank Brasswell: v; acc. own g; Big Bill Broonzy, v–1/g–1/vn–2; Georgia Tom Dorsey, p
New York City—7 April 1930

9583-1	The Western Blues–1	Ba 32392, Or 8124, Pe 0200, Ro 5124
9584-2	Mountain Girl Blues–2	Ba 32392, Or 8124, Pe 0200, Ro 5124

Georgia Tom: acc. own p; Big Bill Broonzy, g
New York City—7 April 1930

9579-2	My Texas Blues	Or 8026
9579-3	My Texas Blues	Or 8026, Pe 163, Ro 5026, Je 20026
9580-1	Broke Man Blues	ARC unissued
9581-1	Six Shooter Blues	Or 8009, Pe 149, Ro 5009, Je 20009, Htd 16101
9581-2	Six Shooter Blues	Ba 0713
9582-2	Pig Meat Blues	Pe 149

Revs: Oriole 8026, Perfect 163, Romeo 5026, Jewel 200026 by Big Bill.

Famous Hokum Boys: Georgia Tom Dorsey, p–1/v–2/sp–3; Big Bill Broonzy, g/v–4/sp–5; Frank Brasswell, g/v–6
New York City—8 April 1930

9585-1,2	Somebody's Been Using That Thing–1, 2, 4, 6	Ba 0712, Or 8010, Pe 150, Ro 5010, Je 20010, Htd 16099
9586-1	Black Cat Rag–3	Je 20012
9586-2, 3	Black Cat Rag–3	Ba 0715, Or 8012, Pe 147, Ro 5012
9587-1	Pig Meat Strut–3	Ro 5007
9587-2	Pig Meat Strut–3	Ba 0710, Or 8007, Pe 156, Je 20007, Htd 16097

Georgia Tom Dorsey: p–1/v–2/sp–3; Big Bill Broonzy, g/v–4/sp–5; Frank Brasswell, g/v–6
New York City—9 April 1930

9594-1	Saturday Night Rub–3, 5	Ba 0715, Or 8012, Pe 147, Ro 5012
9594-2	Saturday Night Rub–3, 5	Je 20012
9595-1, 2	Eagle Riding Papa–1, 2, 4, 6	Ba 0712, Or 8010, Pe 148, Ro 5010, Je 20010, Htd 16099
9596-2	Papa's Getting Hot–1, 2, 4, 6	Ba 0711, Or 8008, Pe 150, Ro 5008, Je 20008, Htd 16098, 23009
9597-1, 2	Nancy Jane–1, 2, 4, 6	Ba 0716, Or 8013, Pe 155, Ro 5013, Je 20013
9598-2	That's the Way She Likes It–1, 2, 4, 6	Ba 0711, Or 8008, Pe 148, Ro 5008, Je 20008, Htd 16098, 23009

Georgia Tom Dorsey: p/v; Big Bill Broonzy, g/v; Frank Brasswell, v–1
New York City—10 April 1930

9610-1,2	Do That Thing–1	Pe 155
9611-2,3	You Can't Get Enough of That Stuff–1	Ba 0716, Or 8013, Pe 161, Ro 5013, Je 20013

Georgia Tom: v/train-whistle effect–1, acc. own p; Big Bill Broonzy, g–2
New York City—10 April 1930

9603-1	What Can I Do? (I Love Her So) –2	ARC unissued
9604-2	Maybe It's the Blues	ARC unissued
9605-1,-2	You Got Me in This Mess (I Ain't Gonna Do It No More) –2	Ba 0713, Or 8009, Pe 162, Ro 5009, Je 20009, Htd 16101
9606-2	Mama's Leaving Town–1, 2	Or 8025, Ro 5025, Je 20025

9607-1   The Duck's Yas Yas Yas   Or 8014, Pe 162, Ro 5014, Je 20014, Htd 16100
Revs.: Oriole 8025, Romeo 5025, Jewel 20025 by Big Bill

Famous Hokum Boys: Georgia Tom Dorsey, p/v; Big Bill Broonzy, g/v; Frank Brasswell, v–1
New York City—11 April 1930
9612-1   Rollin' Mill   Pe 161
9619-1   Somebody's Been Using That   ARC unissued
           Thing No. 2

Western Kid (Frank Brasswell): v; acc. own g–2/prob. own g–1; Big Bill Broonzy, g
Richmond, Ind.—2 May 1930
16574-B   Western Blues–2   Ge 7230
16575-B   Mountain Girl Blues–1   Ge 7210
Revs. Gennett 7210, 7230 by Big Bill.

The Hokum Boys: Big Bill Broonzy, g/v–1/sp–2; Frank Brasswell, g/sp–2
Richmond, Ind.—2 May 1930
16576-A   Nancy Jane–1   Ge unissued
16577-A   Black Cat Rag   Ge unissued
16578-   Saturday Night Rub–2   Ch 16081
16579-   Pig Meat Strut–2   Ch 16081
16580-A   Guitar Rag   Ge unissued
(This name was used by different groups recording under various labels and was different from the
Famous Hokum Boys. Broonzy was listed on five recording sessions.)

Hannah May: v; acc. Big Bill (as Sammy Sampson), g/v–1; Georgia Tom Dorsey, p/v–2
New York City—15 September 1930
10030-2   Bad Dog Blues   ARC unissued
10031-2,-3 Pussy Cat, Pussy Cat–2   Ba 32138, Or 8058, Pe 173, Re 10316, Ro 5058
10032-2   What You Call That? –1   Ba 32138, Or 8058, Pe 173, Re 10316, Ro 5058
10033-1,-2 Court House Blues –1, 2   Je 20034, Or 8034, Pe 170, Ro 5034
(Hannah May is believed to be a pseudonym for Mozelle Alderson.)

Famous Hokum Boys: Georgia Tom Dorsey, p/v; Big Bill Broonzy, g/v; poss. Arthur Petti(e)s g/v;
Mozelle Alderson (as Hannah May), v
New York City—15 September 1930
10034-2   Come on In   Or 8042, Pe 172, Ro 5042, Je 20042
10035-2   Ain't Going There No More   Ba 32310, Or 8105, Pe 192, Ro 5105

Famous Hokum Boys: Georgia Tom Dorsey, p–1/v–2; Big Bill Broonzy, g; Arthur Petti(e)s (as Bill
Williams), g–3; Mozelle Alderson (as Hannah May), v–4/sp-5
New York City—16 September 1930
10036-2   Guitar Mess Around   ARC unissued
10037-2   Barrel House Rag–3, 5   Or 8042, Pe 172, Ro 5042, Je 20042
10038-2   You Do It–1, 2, 4   Ba 32139, Or 8059, Pe 174, Ro 5059
10039-1   That Stuff I Got–1, 2, 4   Or 8059

10039-2	That Stuff I Got–1, 2, 4	Ba 32139, Or 8059, Pe 174, Ro 5059
10040-2	Pat That Bread–1, 2, 4	Or 8067, Pe 178, Ro 5067
10041-1	Come On Mama–1, 2, 4	Or 8033, Pe 169, Ro 5033, Je 20033, ARC 6-01-58, Cq 8675

Georgia Tom And Hannah May: v duet; acc. Big Bill, g; Georgia Tom Dorsey, p
New York City—16 September 1930

10041-1	Come On Mama	Je 20033, Or 8033, Pe 169, Ro 5033, ARC 6-01-58, Cq 8675
10046-2	What's That I Smell	Je 20034, Or 8034, Pe 170, Ro 5034

Perfect 169, Oriole 8033, and Romeo 5033 as by **Famous Hokum Boys**. Matrices 10042/43 are by Sammy Sampson (Big Bill Broonzy).

Bill Williams (Arthur Petties/Pettis): v; acc. prob. own g; Big Bill Broonzy, g/v–1
New York City—16 September 1930

10044-1	Mr. Conductor Man	Ba 32393, Or 8125, Pe 0201, Ro 5125
10045-1	No Good Buddy–1	Pe 179, Ro 5068
10045-2	No Good Buddy–2	Or 8068, Pe 179

(Arthur Petties/Pettis—both spellings are used on records, and the correct spelling is unknown—also used the pseudonym Bill Williams. Issues of matrix 10045 are by Bill Williams and Sammy Sampson. Revs. All issues by Big Bill.)

Famous Hokum Boys: Georgia Tom Dorsey, p/v–1/sp–2; Big Bill Broonzy, g/v–1; Mozelle Alderson (as Jane Lucas), v–1/sp–2; prob. Arthur Petti(e)s (as Bill Williams), perc.
New York City—17 September 1930

10050-1	Pie-Eating Strut–2	Ba 32310, Or 8105, Pe 192, Ro 5105
10051-2	It's All Used Up–1	Or 8067, Pe 178, Ro 5067

Georgia Tom And Hannah May, v duet; acc. Big Bill, g; Georgia Tom Dorsey, p
New York City—17 September 1930

10047-2	It's Been So Long	Je 20041, Or 8041, Pe 171, Ro 5041
10048-2	Terrible Operation Blues	Je 20033, Or 8033, Pe 169, Ro 5033, ARC 6-01-58, Cq 8675
10049-1,-2	Rent Man Blues	Je 20041, Or 8041, Pe 171, Ro 5041

Georgia Tom And Jane Lucas: Jane Lucas, Georgia Tom Dorsey, v duet-1/Jane Lucas, v–2; acc. Georgia Tom Dorsey, p; Big Bill Broonzy, g/v–3
Richmond, Ind.—19 November 1930

17275-B	What's That I Smell–1	Ch 16215, 50042, Spr 2699
17276-B	Terrible Operation Blues–1	Ch 16171, 50015, Spr 2630, De 7259, Ge 5005
17277-A	Where Did You Stay Last Night–1	Ch 16171, 50015, Spr 2730, Sav 501, De 7259, Ge 5007
17278-A	Fix It–1	Ch 16215, 50042, Spr 2630, Sav 502
17279-A	Ain't Goin' There No More No. 2–1, 3	Ch 16193, 50038, Spr 2603
17280	That's The Way She Likes It–1, 3	Ch 16193, 50038, Spr 2699
17285	Double Trouble Blues–2	Ch 16289
17286-A,B	Leave My Man Alone–1	Ch 16289

Champion 16193, 50038 as **Hokum Boys And Jane Lucas**; matrices 17281 to 17284 inclusive are by **Big Bill Johnson (Broonzy)**. (Jane Lucas is believed to be a pseudonym for Mozelle Alderson.)

Georgia Tom: acc. own p; Big Bill Broonzy, g
Richmond, Ind.—20 November 1930

17289-A	Don't Leave Me Blues	Ch 16360, Spr 2560
17290	Been Mistreated Blues	Ch 16237

Revs: Champion 16360, Superior 2560 by Big Bill

Hokum Boys and Jane Lucas: Jane Lucas, Georgia Tom Dorsey, v duet; acc. Georgia Tom Dorsey, p; Big Bill Broonzy, g; Jane Lucas, tam–1
Richmond, Ind.—20 November 1930

17287-B	Hip Shakin' Strut–1	Ch 16237, 50059, Sav 502
17288-A	Hokum Stomp	Ch 16360, 50059, Spr 2603

Harum Scarums: Mozelle Alderson, Georgia Tom Dorsey, v duet; acc. Georgia Tom Dorsey, p; Big Bill Broonzy, g
Grafton, Wisc.—January 1931

L-719-2	Come on In (Ain't Nobody Here but Me)	Pm 13104, Cr 3358, Vs 6001, 6064
L-720-2	Where Did You Stay Last Night	Pm 13104, Cr 3358, Vs 6001
L-721-1	Alabama Scratch—Part II	Pm 13054
L-722-1	Alabama Scratch—Part I	Pm 13054
L-727-1	Sittin' on Top of the World	Pm 13030, Bwy 5097, Cr 3224

Bill Gillum: v–1/h; acc. prob. Black Bob, p–1; Big Bill Broonzy, g
Chicago—14 June 1934

80611-1	Early in the Morning–1	BB B5565
80612-1	Harmonica Stomp	BB B5565

"Big Boy" Teddy Edwards: v; acc. on "tiple" g; unknown, p; poss. Big Bill Broonzy, g
Chicago—14 June 1934

80605-1	Who Did You Give My Barbecue To?—Part 1	BB B5628
80606-1	Who Did You Give My Barbecue To?—Part 2	BB B5628
80607-1	I'm Gonna Tell My Mama on You	BB B5826
80608-1	Louise	BB B5826
80609-1	Love Will Provide for Me	BB B5813
80610-1	If I Had a Girl Like You	BB B5813

Big Boy Edwards: v/prob. own bj–1/g–2; acc. Black Bob, p; Big Bill Broonzy, g/sp–3
Chicago—18 October 1934

C-706-A	Good Doing Daddy–2, 3	Vo 03079
C-706-B	Good Doing Daddy–2	Vo unissued: Ep EG37318, EpE EPC22123, LE LE300002 (LPs); Doc DOCD5440 (CD)
C-707-B	It Was No Dream–2	Vo 02884, ARC 7-07-59

C-708-A	Louise–1	Vo 02884, ARC 7-07-59
C-709-B	Dancing the Blues Away	Vo 03079
C-710-B	Hoodoo Blues	Vo 02932
C-711-A, B	Run Away Blues–2	Vo 02932

Bumble Bee Slim (Amos Easton): acc. unknown, p; prob. Big Bill Broonzy, prob. Willie Bee
James or Charlie Jackson, g–1; prob. Charlie Jackson, bj–2
Chicago—19 October 1934

C-731-A	Bad Gal–1	ARC unissued: RST BD2085 (LP); Doc DOCD5262 (CD)
C-731-B	Bad Gal–1	Vo 02885, BrG A86007
C-732-B	Black Gal, What Makes Your Head So Hard? –2	ARC unissued
C-732-C	Black Gal, What Makes Your Head So Hard?	ARC unissued
C-733-A	I Tried Everything I Could–1	ARC unissued: RST BD2085 (LP); Doc DOCD5262 (CD)
C-734-A	Sail on Little Girl No.2–1	Vo 02865
C-735-B	Good Morning–1	ARC unissued

Louisiana Johnny (prob. Johnny Wilson) and Kid Beecher: Louisiana Johnny, v; acc. prob. Kid
Beecher, ts–1/p–2; prob. own g; prob. Big Bill Broonzy, g–3
Chicago—19 October 1934

C-725-B	Charity Blues–2, 3	Vo unissued: Travelin' Man TM8812, Doc DLP578 (LPs); DOCD5331 (CD)
C-726-B	Louisiana Blues–?	Vo unissued
C-727-C	Show Me What You Got for Sale–1	Vo unissued: Doc DLP578 (LP); DOCD5331 (CD)
C-728-A	True Man Blues–2	Vo unissued: Doc DLP578 (LP); DOCD5331 (CD)
C-729-A	Hard Working Man–2, 3	Vo unissued: Travelin' Man TM8812, Doc DLP578 (LPs); DOCD5331 (CD)
C-730-A	When My Baby Leaves Home–2, 3	Vo 03497

Bumble Bee Slim: v/whistling–1; acc. unknown, p; prob. Big Bill Broonzy, g
Chicago—20 October 1934

C-737-A	Aching Pain Blues	ARC unissued: RST BD2108 (LP); Doc DOCD5262 (CD)
C-738-A	Cold-Blooded Murder	Vo 02865
C-739-A	Burned Down Mill–1	Vo 02885, BrG A86007
C-739-B	Burned Down Mill–1	Vo unissued: Doc DOCD5262 (CD)

Amos: v; acc. unknown, p–1; prob. Carl Martin, poss. Big Bill Broonzy, g
Chicago—27 October 1934

80935-1	Mean Mistreatin' Woman	BB B5780, B6586
80936-1	Worrisome Woman Blues	BB B5780, B6559
80937-1	Mean Bad Man Blues–1	BB B5862, B6612
80938-1	Muddy Water Blues–1	BB B5862, B6586

(Amos was a shortened name for Amos "Bumble Bee Slim" Easton.)

State Street Boys: Zeb Wright, vn–1; Jazz Gillum, v–2/h–3; Black Bob, p; Big Bill Broonzy, v–4/g–5/vn–6; Carl Martin, v–7/g–8; poss. Bill Settles, sb; unknown, 2nd v–9; unknown (prob. Black Bob), sp–10.

Chicago—10 January 1935

C-887-3	Mobile and Western Line–2, 3,	Vo 03131, DocDOCD 5052
	5, 9, 10	
C-888-2	Crazy about You–2, 3, 5, 8	OK 8964, Vo 03004, DocDOCD 5052
C-889-2	Sweet to Mama–3, 4, 6	OK 8965, Vo 03049, DocDOCD 5052
C-890-3	Rustlin' Man–3, 4, 6, 9	Vo 03131, DocDOCD 5052
C-891-2	She Caught the Train–3, 4, 6, 9	OK 8962, Vo 03002, DocDOCD 5052
C-892-1	Midnight Special–1, 4, 9	OK 8964, Vo 03004, DocDOCD 5052
C-893-1	The Dozen–1, 4, 5, 10	OK 8965, Vo 03049, DocDOCD 5052
C-894-2	Don't Tear My Clothes–1, 7, 8	OK 8962, Vo 03002, DocDOCD 5052

Amos: v; acc. poss. Horace Malcolm, p; Big Bill Broonzy, g

Chicago—27 February 1935

85529-1	There You Stand	BB B5880, MW M4837
85530-1	Tell Me What It's All About	BB B6008, B6635
85531-1	You Gotta Change Your Way	BB B6008, B6612
85532-1	Milk Cow Blues	BB B5880, MW M4837
85533-1	Everybody's Fishing	BB B5964, B6521
85534-1	Guilty Woman Blues	BB B5694, B6559

Charlie Jackson: v/bj; acc. Big Bill Broonzy, v–1/g–1; Teddy Edwards, v–2

Chicago—8 March 1935

C-912-B	Good Jelly–1, 2	ARC unissued
C-913-B	Who's Gonna Haul Your Ashes	ARC unissued
C-914-B	Everybody Skuddle–1	ARC unissued

(Matrix C-912 is entered as by Charlie Jackson and Big Bill; C-914 as by Big Bill and Charlie Jackson.)

Cripple Clarence Lofton: v/p; acc. Big Bill Broonzy, g–1; unknown, wb–2

Chicago—2 April 1935

C-947-B	Strut That Thing–2	Vo 02951, HJCA HC85
C-948-A	Monkey Man Blues–1	Vo 02951, HJCA HC85

Ham Gravy (Washboard Sam): v/wb; acc. Big Bill Broonzy, g; Louis Lasky, 2nd g

Chicago—20 June 1935

C-1022-B	Mama Don't Allow No. 1	Vo 03275, Cq 9168
C-1023-B	Jesse James Blues	Vo 03375

Bumble Bee Slim: acc. Big Bill Broonzy, g; Black Bob, p; prob. Washboard Sam, wb–1

Chicago—26 June 1935

C-1028-B	Can't You Trust Me No More	Vo 03209
C-1029-B	Baby Fare You Well	ARC unissued
C-1030-A	Where Was You Last Night	Vo 04661, Cq 9276
C-1031-A	I Done Lost My Baby–1	Vo 03054

C-1032-A   I'm Needing Someone (Exactly   Vo 03637, ARC 7-09-67
            Like You) –1

Ham Gravy (Washboard Sam): wb; acc. Black Bob, p; Big Bill Broonzy, g
Chicago—3 July 1935
C-1058-B   Who Pumped the Wind in My   Vo 03275, Cq 9168
            Doughnut
C-1059-A, B Mama Don't Allow No. 2   Vo 03375

Chicago Sanctified Singers—Louis Leslie: Spiritual singing (2 male and 1 female v); acc. unknown, p; prob. Big Bill Broonzy, g/poss. v
Chicago—3 July 1935
C-1062-B   Tell Me What Kind of Man   ARC 7-05-64, Cq 8876, DocDOCD5126
            Jesus Is
C-1063-B   I Ain't No Stranger Now   ARC 7-05-64, Cq 8876, DocDOCD 5126

Bumble Bee Slim: acc. Myrtle Jenkins, p; Big Bill Broonzy, g
Chicago—18 July 1935
C-1071-A   When the Sun Goes Down   Vo 03054
C-1072-B   Sail on Little Girl—No. 3   Vo 03165
C-1073-A   Cold Blooded Murder—No. 2   Vo03165

Cripple Clarence Lofton: p/whistling-1; acc. Big Bill Broonzy, g
Chicago—18 July 1935
C-1074-A   Brown Skin Girls–1   ARC 6-11-66, JCI 526, JD 003, Bm 1042
C-1075-A   You Done Tore Your Playhouse   ARC 6-11-66, Cq 8758, JCI 526, JD 003 Bm 1042
            Down

Red Nelson (Nelson Wilborn): v; acc. unknown, p; poss. Big Bill Broonzy, g
Chicago—18 July 1935
C-1076-A   Six Cold Feet in the Ground   Vo 03001
C-1077-A   When the Sun Goes Down   Vo 03001

Lil Johnson: v; acc. prob. Black Bob, p; poss. Big Bill Broonzy, g; unknown, sb
Chicago—27 July 1935
91417-1   Keep on Knocking   BB B6112, B8251, MW M4834
91418 1   I Lost My Baby   BB B6112, B8251, MW M4834

The Hokum Boys: Casey Bill Weldon, v/g; acc. Big Bill Broonzy, g; Bill Settles, sb; Teddy Edwards, sp–1
Chicago—16 December 1935
C-1187-2   Caught Us Doing It–1   Vo 03156
C-1188-1   I Ain't Going That Way   Vo 03156

Washboard Sam's Band: Washboard Sam, v/wb; Big Bill Broonzy, g; unknown, sb
Chicago—2 April 1936
100315-1   You Done Tore Your Playhouse   BB B6355, B7194, MW M7050
            Down

100316-1   Don't Low   BB B6355, MW M7050

Jazz Gillum: v/h; acc. Big Bill Broonzy, g; unknown, sb
Chicago—5 April 1936
100311-1   Sarah Jane   BB B6445, MW M7052
100312-1   I Want You by My Side   BB B6445, MW M7052
100313-1   Jockey Blues   BB B6409
100314-1   Don't You Scandalize My Name   BB B6409

The Hokum Boys: Casey Bill Weldon, g/v–1; Big Bill Broonzy, g/v–2; unknown, sb; Washboard
Sam, wb/v; unknown, 3rd v–3
Chicago—16 April 1936
C-1356-1   Keep Your Mind on It–2, 3   Vo 03232
C-1357-1   I'm Gonna Get It–1   Vo unissued: Doc DOCD5237 (CD)
C-1357-2   I'm Gonna Get It–1   Vo 03232

Lil Johnson: acc. unknown, p; Big Bill Broonzy, g
Chicago—22 April 1936
C-1365-1   My Stove's in Good Condition   Vo 03251
C-1366-2   Scuffling Woman Blues   Vo 03299
C-1367-2   Murder in the First Degree   Vo 03299

Casey Bill (Will Weldon): v/g; acc. prob. Black Bob, p; prob. Big Bill Broonzy, g
Chicago—1 May 1936
C-1368-1   You Just As Well Let Her Go   Vo 03274
C-1369-1   Keyhole Blues   Vo 03250
C-1369-2   Keyhole Blues   Vo unissued: Old Tramp OT1206 (LP); Doc
                                                  DOCD5321 (CD)
C-1370-1   Stream Line Woman   Vo 03437
C-1370-2   Stream Line Woman   Vo unissued: Old Tramp OT1206 (LP); Doc
                                                  DOCD5218 (CD)
C-1371-1   Talkin' to Myself   Vo 03407
C-1372-1   Big Katy Adam   Vo 03464
C-1373-1   Two-Timin' Woman   Vo 03250

Lil Johnson: acc. prob. Arnett Nelson, cl; prob. Black Bob, p; prob. Big Bill Broonzy, g; prob. Bill
Settles, sb
Chicago—11 June 1936
C-1397-2   Two Timin' Man   Vo 03266, Co 30059, 37682
C-1398-1   Was I?   Vo 03266, Co 30059, 37682

The Hokum Boys: Teddy Edwards, v–1; Big Bill Broonzy, g/v–2; Casey Bill Weldon, g/v chorus;
Black Bob, p; Bill Settles, sb
Chicago—11 June 1936
C-1399-1   I'm Gonna Tell Mama on You–1   Vo 03265
C-1400-1   Nancy Jane–2   Vo 03265

Washboard Sam: v/wb; acc. Arnett Nelson, cl-1; Big Bill Broonzy, g; unknown, sb
Chicago—26 June 1936

| C-1412-2 | Don't Tear My Clothes–1 | Vo 02937, ARC 6-10-55, Cq 8721, JSo AA601 |
| C-1413-2 | I'm a Prowlin' Groundhog | Vo 02937, ARC 6-10-55, Cq 8721, JSo AA601 |

Bill McKinley: v; acc. prob. own h; poss. Big Bill Broonzy, g; unknown, sb
Chicago—30 June 1936

| C-1415-1 | She Keeps On Rickin' | ARC 6-11-57 |
| C-1416-1 | I Went to the Gypsy | ARC 6-11-57 |

Washboard Sam: wb; acc. Black Bob, p; Big Bill Broonzy, g/v–1
Chicago—5 August 1936

100940-1	Give Me Lovin'	BB B6518
100941-1	Crazy about Nancy Jane–1	BB B6518
100942-1	Cherry Hill Blues	BB B6556
100943-1	Levee Blues	BB B6556

Casey Bill (Will Weldon): v/g; acc. prob. Black Bob, p; Charlie McCoy, md; prob. Big Bill Broonzy, g
Chicago—3 September 1936

C-1459-1	I Believe I'll Make a Change	Vo unissued: RnB CL46218 (LP); RnB CK46218, RnB(Eu) 467251-2, RnB(J) CSCS5327, Doc DOCD5218 (CDs)
C-1460-1	The Big Boat	Vo 03464
C-1461-1	Can't You Remember?	Vo 03407
C-1462-1, 2	Jinx Blues	Vo 03496
C-1463-2	Gonna Take My Time	Vo 03373
C-1464-1, 2	We Gonna Move (to the Outskirts of Town)	Vo 03373

Casey Bill (Will Weldon): V/g; acc. prob. Black Bob, p; prob. Big Bill Broonzy, g; poss. Bill Settles, sb
Chicago—16 September 1936

C-1471-2	Back Door Blues	Vo 03330
C-1472-1	Front Door Blues	Vo 03330
C-1472-2	Front Door Blues	Vo unissued: Old Tramp OT1206 (LP); Doc DOCD5218 (CD)

Shufflin' Sam (Washboard Sam) and His Rhythm: Black Bob, p; prob. Big Bill Broonzy, g–1; unknown, sb; Washboard Sam, wb/v
Chicago—16 September 1936

| C-1465-1 | Dirty Mother for You | Vo 03329 |
| C-1466-2 | Good Liquor | Vo 03329 |

Arnett Nelson and His Hot Four: Arnett Nelson, cl; Black Bob, p; Casey Weldon, v/g; prob. Big Bill Broonzy, g; prob. Bill Settles, sb
Chicago—8 October 1936

| C-1535-1 | Oh, Red! | ARC 6-12-69, Cq 8765 |
| C-1536-2 | You Waited Too Long | ARC 6-12-69, Cq 8765 |

Washboard Sam: wb/v; acc. Black Bob, p; Big Bill Broonzy, g; prob. John Lindsay, sb
Chicago—15 October 1936

C-1565-1	Mixed Up Blues	ARC unissued; Best of Blues BOB1 (LP); Doc DOCD5171 (CD)
C-1565-2	Mixed up Blues	Vo 03365
C-1566-1	Pains in My Heart	Vo 03365

The Hokum Boys: Prob. Bob Robinson, v; acc. Big Bill Broonzy, g/v; unknown, 2nd g; unknown, p; Bill Settles, sb; unknown, 3rd v
Chicago—28 October 1936

| C-1632-1 | Do You Catch On | Vo 03386 |
| C-1633-2 | Something Good | Vo 03406 |

Bumble Bee Slim: v; acc. unknown, cl; Black Bob, p; prob. Big Bill Broonzy, g; unknown, sb; unknown, bird-call effects–1
Chicago—4 November 1936

C-1647-2	Hobo Jungle Blues–1	Vo 03418
C-1648-1	Slave Man Blues	Vo 03418
C-1649-2	I'm Gonna Live My Life Alone	ARC unissued
C-1654-1	My Big Moments	Vo 03550, ARC 7-06-76
C-1655-1	I'll Meet You in the Bottom	Vo 03384, Cq 8867
C-1656-2	Meet Me at the Landing	Vo 03384, Cq 8867

Lil Johnson: acc. prob. Mr. Sheiks (Alfred Bell), t; prob. Black Bob, p; prob. Big Bill Broonzy, g; unknown, sb
Chicago—19 November 1936

C-1680-1	Crazy about My Rider	Vo unissued: Travelin' Man TM8811, Wolf WSE 142 (LPs), Doc DOCD5308 (CD)
C-1680-2	Crazy about My Rider	Vo 03397
C-1681-1	I'll Take You to the Cleaners	Vo unissued: Travelin' Man TM8811, Doc DLP516 (LPs); Story of Blues CD3513-2, Doc DOCD5308 (CDs)
C-1681-2	I'll Take You to the Cleaners	Vo 03397
C-1682-2	If You Don't Give Me What I Want	Vo 03455
C-1683-2	Grandpa Said "Let's Suzie-Q"	Vo 03428
C-1684-1	New Shave 'Em Dry	Vo 03428
C-1685-1	River Hip Papa	Vo 03455

Midnight Ramblers: Black Bob, p/scat v; Big Bill Broonzy, g/v; unknown, sb
Chicago—19 November 1936

| C-1689-2 | Out with the Wrong Woman | Vo 03395, DocDOCD 5127 |

Rev. Vocalion 03395 by State Street Swingers

State Street Swingers: Mary Mack, v; acc. Herb Morand, t; Arnett Nelson, cl; Myrtle Jenkins, p; poss. Big Bill Broonzy, g; unknown, sb
Chicago—19 November 1936

| C-1686-2 | Rattlesnakin' Daddy | Vo 03395 |
| C-1687-1 | You Can't Do That to Me | Vo 03572 |

Washboard Sam and His Washboard Band: wb/v; Black Bob, p; Big Bill Broonzy, g; unknown, sb
Chicago—21 December 1936

01882-1	I Love All My Women	BB B6794, B7179
01883-1	Out with the Wrong Woman	BB B6794, B7148
01884-1	Come on In	BB B6870
01885-1	Big Woman	BB B6870
01886-1	Nashville, Tennessee	BB B6765, MW M7062
01887-1	Razor Cuttin' Man	BB B6765, MW M7062

Chicago Black Swans: unknown, t; Arnett Nelson, cl; Black Bob, p; Big Bill Broonzy, g/v; unknown, 2nd g–1; unknown, sb
Chicago—26 January 1937

| C-1768-2 | Don't Tear My Clothes No. 2–1 | ARC 7-04-65, Vo 02943, Cq 8780, DocDOCD 5127 |
| C-1769-1 | You Drink Too Much | ARC 7-04-65, Vo 02943, Cq 8780, DocDOCD 5127 |

Midnight Ramblers: Black Bob, p; Big Bill Broonzy, g/v; unknown, sb; prob. Washboard Sam, v
Chicago—10 March 1937

C-1848-1	Down in the Alley	Vo 03517, DocDOCD 5128
C-1848-2	Down in the Alley	Vo unissued: Travelin' Man TM8812, Doc DLP573 (LPs), DOCD5128 (CD)
C-1849-1	Stuff They Call Money	Vo 03517, DocDOCD 5128

Black Spider Dumplin'-1/Little Bill-2: John D. Twitty, v; acc. poss. Black Bob, p; poss. Big Bill Broonzy, g; unknown, sb; prob. Washboard Sam, wb–3
Leland Hotel, Aurora, Ill.—4 May 1937

07626-	John D Blues–1	BB B6972
07627-	Sold It to the Devil–1	BB B6995
07628-	You Can't Love Me and Someone Else Too–2	BB B6972
07629-	Camp Meeting in the Air–1, 3	BB B7011
07630-	Death of the Gambler–1, 3	BB B7011

Mary Mack: v; acc. prob. Aletha Dickerson, p; poss. Big Bill Broonzy, g; unknown, sb.
Leland Hotel, Aurora, Ill.—4 May 1937

07622-1	Stingaree Man	BB B8131
07623-1	Every Night	BB B7097
07624-1	Get Going	BB B7097
07625-1	I Vouch for My Man	BB B8131

Washboard Sam and His Washboard Band: wb/v; acc. Arnett Nelson, cl–1; unknown, p; Big Bill Broonzy, g; unknown, sb
Leland Hotel, Aurora, Ill.—4 May 1937

07614-1	Easy Ridin' Mama–1	BB B6970
07615-1	The Big Boat–1	BB B6970
07616-1	Back Door–1	BB B7001, Vi20-2162
07617-1	We Gonna Move	BB B7001

07618-1	Low Down Woman	BB B7048
07619-1	I Drink Good Whiskey	BB B7048
07620-1	Lowland Blues	BB B7096
07621-1	I'm on My Way Blues	BB B7096

Bill Gillum and His Jazz Boys: Jazz Gillum, v/h–1; acc. prob. Blind John Davis, p; Big Bill Broonzy, g; unknown, d
Leland Hotel, Aurora, Ill.—11 October 1937

014334-1	My Old Lizzie–1	BB B7253
014335-1	Alberta Blues–1	BB B7341
014336-1	My Old Suitcase	BB B7253
014337-1	Birmingham Blues–1	BB B7341

Red Nelson (Nelson Wilborn): acc. poss. Blind John Davis, p; poss. Big Bill Broonzy, g–1; unknown, d; unknown, wb–2
Leland Hotel, Aurora, Ill.—11 October 1937

014342-1	Eva Mae Blues–1, 2	BB B7265
014343-1	Working Man Blues–1	BB B7960
014344-1	Relief Blues	BB B7265
014345-1	Back Home–1	BB B7960
014346-1	Jailhouse Blues–1	BB B7918
014347-1	Black Gal Stomp–1	BB B7918

Washboard Sam and His Washboard Band: wb/v; acc. Arnett Nelson, cl–1; Black Bob, p; Big Bill Broonzy, g; unknown, sb
Leland Hotel, Aurora, Ill.—11 November 1937

016500-1	Washboard's Barrel House Song–1	BB B7291
016501-1	Want to Woggie Some More–1	BB B7440, MW7499
016502-1	Ladies' Man–1	BB B7328
016503-1	You Got to Take It–1	BB B7365
016503-1	Beer Garden Blues–1	BB B7328
016505-1	Where Were You Last Night	BB B7291
016506-1	Somebody's Got to Go	BB B7403
016507-1	Looking for My Ash Hauler	BB unissued
016508-1	Gonna Be Some Walkin' Done	BB B7365
016509-1	Second Story Man	BB B7403

Lil Johnson: acc. prob. Horace Malcolm, p; Big Bill Broonzy, g; unknown, sb; unknown male, v–1
Chicago—23 December 1937

C-2064-1	Down at the Old Village Store–1	Vo 03941
C-2065-1	You Lied Your Last Time	Vo 03978
C-2066-1	Ain't That a Shame	Vo 03978
C-2067-1	Snake in the Grass	Vo 04067

The Yas Yas Girl (Merline Johnson): v; acc. Blind John Davis, p; Big Bill Broonzy, g; Ransom Knowling or Bill Settles, sb
Chicago—23 December 1937

| C-2062-1 | New Drinking My Blues Away | ARC 8-02-67, Cq 9033, Vo 03928, Co 30082, 37780 |
| C-2063-1 | Crime Don't Pay | ARC 8-02-67, Cq 9033, Vo 03928, Co 30082, 37780 |

The Red Devil (Red Nelson): v; acc. poss. Blind John Davis, p; poss. Big Bill Broonzy, g; unknown, sb
Chicago—12 January 1938

C-2076-2	Car Greasing Blues	Vo unissued
C-2007-1	Woman Friend Blues	Vo 03954
C-2078-1	Huntsman Blues	Vo 03954
C-2079-1	Chills and Fever	Vo unissued: Travelin' Man TM8812, Doc DLP545 (LPs); Old Tramp OTCD06 (CD)

Red and His Washboard Band: Red Nelson, v; Arnett Nelson, cl; unknown, p; Big Bill Broonzy, g; unknown, g; Washboard Sam, wb; unknown, k–1
Chicago—25 January 1938

| C-2082-1 | Prowling Groundhog No. 2 | Vo 03965 |
| C-2083-1 | Don't Tear My Clothes No. 3–1 | Vo 03965 |

Jazz Gillum and His Jazz Boys: Jazz Gillum, v/h; acc. Big Bill Broonzy, g; George Barnes, eg; unknown, sb; prob. Washboard Sam, wb
Leland Hotel, Aurora, Ill.—14 March 1938

020156-1	Just Like Jesse James	BB B7615
020157-1	Reefer Head Woman	BB B7615
020158-1	Gillum's Windy Blues	BB B7563
020159-1	New "Sail On, Little Girl"	BB B7524
020160-1	Sweet Sweet Woman	BB B7524
020161-1	Boar Hog Blues	BB B7563

Washboard Sam and His Washboard Band: wb/v; acc. Arnett Nelson, cl–1; Black Bob, p; Big Bill Broonzy, g; George Barnes, eg–2
Leland Hotel, Aurora, Ill.—14 March 1938

020140-1	Don't Leave Me Here–1	BB B7501, MW M7497
020141-1	My Woman's a Sender–1	BB B7552, MW M7498
020142-1	Towboat Blues–1	BB B7501, MW M7497
020143-1	Mountain Blues–1	BB B7601
020144-1	Phantom Snake Blues–1	BB B7601
020145-1	Yellow, Black and Brown	BB B7664
020146-1	It's Too Late Now–2	BB B7664
020147-1	Barbecue–3	BB B7552
020148-1	Down at the Old Village Store	BB B7526, MW M7500
020149-1	The Gal I Love–2	BB B7655

Curtis Jones: v/p; acc. prob. Punch Miller, t–1; poss. Big Bill Broonzy, g; Fred Williams, d
Chicago—30 March 1938

| C-2161-1 | Yours All Alone–1 | Vo unissued: Doc DLP592 (LP); DOCD5296 (CD) |
| C-2162-2 | Palace Blues | Vo unissued: Doc DLP592 (LP); DOCD5296 (CD) |

Jazz Gillum and His Jazz Boys: Jazz Gillum, v/h; acc. Big Bill Broonzy, g; unknown, sb; prob. Washboard Sam, wb
Leland Hotel, Aurora, Ill.—16 June 1938

020818-1	Worried and Bothered	BB B7821
020819-1	I'm That Man down in the Mine	BB B7718
020820-1	Uncertain Blues	BB B7821
020821-1	Good Old 51 Highway	BB B7718
020822-1	You're Laughing Now	BB B7769
020823-1	I'm Gonna Get It	BB B7769

Washboard Sam and His Washboard Band: wb/v; acc. Punch Miller, t–1; poss. Bill Owsley, ts–2; Black Bob, p; Big Bill Broonzy, g–3; unknown, sb
Leland Hotel, Aurora, Ill.—16 June 1938

020809-1	Bucket's Got a Hole in It–1, 3	BB B7906, MW M7759
020809-1	Save It for Me–1, 3	BB B7866, MW M7588
020810-1	Serve It Right–2, 3	BB B7732, MW M7759
020811-1	Cruel Treatment–2, 3	BB B7834, MW M7590
020812-1	Jumpin' Rooster–3	BB B7866, MW M7588
020813-1	I'm Gonna Keep My Hair Parted–3	BB B7732, MW M7760
020814-1	Sophisticated Mama	BB B7780, MW M7760
020815-1	Policy Writer's Blues–3	BB B7834, MW M7590
020816-1	I'm Gonna Pay–1, 3	BB B7780, MW M7761
020817-1	When My Love Change–1, 3	BB B7906, MW M7761

The Yas Yas Girl (Merline Johnson): Acc. Buster Bennett, ss; Blind John Davis, p; prob. Big Bill Broonzy, g–1; unknown, sb
Chicago—4 October 1938

| C-2354-1 | Don't You Make Me High | Vo 04455, Cq 9147 |
| C-2355-1, 2 | Love with a Feeling–1 | Vo 04455, Cq 9147 |

Jazz Gillum and His Jazz Boys: Jazz Gillum, v/h–1; acc. prob. Joshua Altheimer, p; prob. Big Bill Broonzy, g/v responses–2; prob. Ransom Knowling, sb
Leland Hotel, Aurora, Ill.—16 December 1938

030822-1	Mule Blues–1	BB B8027
030823-1	Let Her Go–1	BB B8027
030824-1	Get Away Old Woman–1, 2	BB B7986
030825-1	Stavin' Chain–1	BB B7986
030826-1	She Won't Treat Me Kind	BB B8106
030827-1	I'll Get Along Somehow–1	BB B8106

Washboard Sam and His Washboard Band: wb/v; acc. Herb Morand, t–1; prob. Joshua Altheimer, p; Big Bill Broonzy, g; prob. Bill Settles, sb
Leland Hotel, Aurora, Ill.—16 December 1938

030812-1	You Waited Too Long–1	BB B8018, MW M7936
030813-1	Gonna Kill My Baby–1	BB B8018, MW M7936
030814-1	Suspicious Blues–1	BB B8076, MW M7938
030815-1	Walkin' in My Sleep–1	BB B7977, MW M7934
030816-1	Washboard Swing–1	BB B7977, MW M7934
030817-1	Hand Reader Blues–1	BB B8044, MW M7937
030818-1	Rack 'Em Back	BB B8044, MW M7937
030819-1	I'll Be up Some Day	BB B8076, MW M7938
030820-1	Warehouse Blues	BB B7993, MW M7935
030821-1	CCC Blues	BB B7993, MW M7935

The Yas Yas Girl (Merline Johnson): acc. Blind John Davis, p; Big Bill Broonzy, g; unknown, sb
Chicago—10 February 1939

C-2484-1, 2	Some Day I'll Be Gone Away	Vo 04830
C-2485-1	Easy Towing Mama	Vo 04830, JSo AA598
C-2486-1	Grieving Heart Blues	Vo 04775
C-2487-1	Reckless Life Blues	Vo 04719, Cq 9205

The Yas Yas Girl and Her Rhythm Rascals: Merline Johnson, v; acc. unknown, t; Buster Bennett, as; Blind John Davis, p; Big Bill Broonzy, g; unknown, sb
Chicago—10 February 1939

C-2488-1	Breakin' 'Em Down Tonight	Vo 04719, Cq 9205
C-2489-1	Someone to Take Your Place	Vo 04885
C-2490-1	Got a Mind to Ramble	Vo 04885
C-2491-1	True Love	Vo 04775

Washboard Sam and His Washboard Band: wb/v; acc. Buster Bennett, as–1; Joshua Altheimer, p; Big Bill Broonzy, g; Ransom Knowling, sb
Chicago—15 May 1939

034792-1	This Time Is My Time	BB B8270, MW M8573
034793-1	Booker T Blues	BB B8211, MW M8571
034794-1	Good Old Easy Street	BB B8243, MW M8572
034795-1	I Believe I'll Make a Change–1	BB B8184, MW M8570
034796-1	Wasn't He Bad–1	BB B8270, MW M8573
034797-1	Diggin' My Potatoes–1	BB B8211, Vi20-2162, MW M8571
034798-1	I Love My Baby–1	BB B8243, MW M8572
034799-1	That Will Get It–1	BB B8184, MW M8570

Jazz Gillum: v/h–1; acc. John Cameron, ts; Joshua Altheimer, p; Big Bill Broonzy, g
Chicago—17 May 1939

034810-1	Got to Reap What You Sow–1	BB B8287, MW M8542
034811-1	Big Katy Adams–1	BB B8189, MW M8539
034812-1	Against My Will–1	BB B8189, MW M8539
034813-1	Keyhole Blues–1	BB B8221, MW M8540

034814-1	Talking to Myself–1	BB B8221, MW M8540
034815-1	Hard Drivin' Woman	BB B8287, MW M8542
034816-1	Somebody Been Talking to You–1	BB B8257, MW M8541
034817-1	One Time Blues–1	BB B8257, MW M8541

Alfred Fields: v; acc. prob. Joshua Altheimer, p; Big Bill Broonzy, g; Washboard Sam, wb/sp–1
Chicago—7 July 1939

WC-2644-A	Money Green	OK 06129
WC-2645-A	Mighty Blue	OK 06129
WC-2646-A	'29 Blues	OK 06020
WC-2647-A	Hug and Kiss Me	Co unissued
WC-2648-A	I've Retired	Vo 05018
WC-2649-A	Single Woman	Co unissued
WC-2650-A	In My Prime–1	Vo 05018
WC-2651-A	Quit Your Jivin'	OK 06020
WC-2652-A	Spongy Baby–1	OK 05727
WC-2653-A	Step Pepper Stepper–1	OK 05727

Sonny Boy Williamson (John Lee Williamson): v/h; acc. Walter Davis, p–1; Big Bill Broonzy, eg
Chicago—21 July 1939

040525-1	Bad Luck Blues–1	BB B8265, MW M8575
040526-1	My Little Baby–1	BB B8265, MW M8575
040527-1	Doggin' My Love Around–1	BB B8307, MW M8576
040528-1	Little Low Woman Blues–1	BB B8307, MW M8576
040529-1	Good for Nothing Blues–1	BB B8237, MW M8574
040530-1	Sugar Mama Blues No. 2–1	BB B8237, MW M8574
040531-1	Good Gravy	BB B8333, MW M8577
040532-1	T.B. Blues–1	BB B8333, MW M8577
040533-1	Something Going on Wrong–1	BB B8357, MW M8578
040534-1	Good Gal Blues–1	BB B8357, MW M8578
040535-1	Joe Louis and John Henry Blues–1	BB B8403, MW M8579
040536-1	Thinking My Blues Away–1	BB B8403, MW M8579
040537-1	I'm Not Pleasing You–1	BB B8383, MW M8580
040538-1	New "Jailhouse Blues" –1	BB B8383, MW M8580
040539-1	Life Time Blues–1	BB B8439, MW M8581
040540-1	Miss Ida Lee–1	BB B8439, MW M8581
040541-1	Tell Me, Baby–1	BB B8474, MW M8582
040542-1	Honey Bee Blues–1	BB B8474, MW M8582

Monkey Joe and His Music Grinders: Jesse "Monkey Joe" Coleman, v/p; Buster Bennett, as; Big Bill Broonzy, g; Alfred Elkins, v bass
Chicago—13 September 1939

WC-2702-A	You Don't Have to Tell Me	Vo 05274
WC-2703-A	Carry My Business On	Vo 05166
WC-2704-A	Mountain Baby Blues	Vo 05348
WC-2705-A	Just Give Some Away	Vo 05166
WC-2706-A	Bad Luck Man Blues	OK 05685

WC-2707-A	Bitin' on Me	Vo 05348
WC-2708-A	Old Man Blues	OK 06153
WC-2709-A	McComb City Blues	OK 06153
WC-2710-A	That Same Cat	Vo 05274
WC-2711-A	We Can't Get Along	OK 05685

Roosevelt Scott: v; acc. prob. Jesse Coleman, p; Big Bill Broonzy, g; prob. Alfred Elkins, v bass
Chicago—13 September 1939

WC-2712-A	Black Gal Blues	Vo 05206
WC-2713-A	Send Me an Angel Down	Vo 05137
WC-2714-A	Do You Call That Right?	Vo 05137
WC-2715-A	Brown Skin Woman Swing	Vo 05206

Washboard Sam and His Washboard Band: wb/v; acc. Buster Bennett, as/v interjections–1; prob. Horace Malcolm, p; Big Bill Broonzy, g
Chicago—7 November 1939

044068-1	Has My Gal Been by Here?	BB B8323, MW M8798
044069-1	Somebody Changed That Lock on My Door	BB B8323, MW M8798
044070-1	Don't Fool with Me	BB B8342, MW M8799
044071-1	Jersey Cow Blues	BB B8342, MW M8799
044072-1	So Early in the Morning	BB B8358, MW M8800
044073-1	Beauty Spot	BB B8377, MW M8801
044074-1	We Gonna Do Some Rug Cuttin'–1	BB B8377, MW M8801

Washboard Sam and Buster Bennett: sp; acc. Buster Bennett, p; Big Bill Broonzy, g.
Chicago—7 November 1939

044075-1	Block and Tackle	BB B8358, MW M8800

Washboard Sam and His Washboard Band: wb/v; prob. Buster Bennett, as–1; prob. Horace Malcolm, p; Big Bill Broonzy, g
Chicago—22 March 1940

049035-1	Going Back to Arkansas–1	BB B8424, MW M8802
049036-1	Louise–1	BB B8469, MW M8804
049037-1	I Won't Be Sober Long–1	BB B8424, MW M8802
049038-1	Oh Babe–1	BB B8469, MW M8804
049039-1	How Can I Play Fair?	BB B8450, MW M8803
049040-1	She Fooled Me	BB B8450, MW M8803
049041-1	Sun Gonna Shine in My Door	BB B8500, MW M8805
049042-1	Beale Street Sheik	BB B8500, MW M8805

Jazz Gillum: Acc. own h; Big Bill Broonzy, g; prob. Alfred Elkins or Al Collins, b
Chicago—9 May 1940

044969-1	It Sure Had a Kick	BB B8505
044970-1	She Belongs to Me	BB B8529
044971-1	Longest Train Blues	BB B8505
044972-1	Key to the Highway	BB B8529, Vi20-2160, Groove G5002

Lil Green: v; acc. Simeon Henry, p; Big Bill Broonzy, g; Ransom Knowling, sb; group v–1
Chicago—9 May 1940

044973-1	Cherry Tree Blues	BB B8464
044974-1	Romance in the Dark	BB B8524, Vi 20-2161, Groove G5004
044975-1	Just Rockin'	BB B8464
044976-1	What Have I Done?	BB B8524, V-D 191

Washboard Sam and His Washboard Band: wb/v; prob. Buster Bennett, as–1; prob. Joshua Altheimer, p; Big Bill Broonzy, g; unknown, b
Chicago—29 July 1940

049340-1	Why Did You Do That to Me? –1	BB B8525, MW M8928
049341-1	Digging My Potatoes—No.2 –1	BB B8554, MW M8930
049342-1	Chiselin' Blues–1	BB B8525, MW M8928
049343-1	Morning Dove Blues–1	BB B8554, MW M8930
049344-1	Good Time Tonight	BB B8644, MW M8933
049345-1	Dissatisfied Blues	BB B8644, MW M8933

Washboard Sam and His Washboard Band: wb/v; prob. Buster Bennett, as–1; prob. Blind John Davis, p; Big Bill Broonzy, g; unknown, b
Chicago—5 August 1940

049370-1	I'm Going to St. Louis–1	BB B8569, MW M8931
049371-1	Greyhound Bus–1	BB B8540, MW M8929
049372-1	Oh Joe–1	BB B8540, MW M8929
049373-1	Just Got to Hold You–1	BB B8599, MW M8932
049374-1	Yes I Got Your Woman	BB B8599, MW M8932
049375-1	Good Luck Blues	BB B8569, MW M8931

Washboard Sam and His Washboard Band: wb/v; acc. Horace Malcolm, p; Big Bill Broonzy, g; Leroy Bachelor, b; Josephine Kyles, sp–1
Chicago—16 January 1941

059127-1	Ain't You Comin' Out Tonight–1	BB B8675
059128-1	Come on Back	BB B8699
059129-1	Just to Prove I Love You	BB B8699
059130-1	Every Tub Stands on Its Own Bottom	BB B8727
059131-1	She's Makin' a Fool Out of Me	BB B8727
059132-1	She's a Bad Luck Woman	BB B8675

Lil Green: v; acc. Simeon Henry, p; Big Bill Broonzy, g; Ransom Knowling, sb; group v–1
Chicago—21 January 1941

059150-1	Give Your Mama One Smile	BB B8640
059151-1	My Mellow Man	BB B8640, Vi 20-2161
059152-1	Knockin' Myself Out	BB B8659, Vi 20-3283
059153-1	I Won't Sell My Love–1	BB B8659

Washboard Sam and His Washboard Band: wb/v; acc. Simeon Henry, p; Big Bill Broonzy, g;
William Mitchell, b

Chicago—31 January 1941

059186-	Little Leg Woman	BB B8792
059187-	She's All in My Life	BB B8815
059188-	He's a Creepin' Man	BB B8815
059189-1	I Can Beat You Playing That Hand	BB B8761
059190-	Down at the Bad Man's Hall	BB B8792
059191-1	Traveling Man	BB B8761

Jazz Gillum: v/h; acc. Big Bill Broonzy, g; prob. Alfred Elkins, bass cano [*sic*, per Bluebird files];
Washboard Sam, wb

Chicago—20 March 1941

059433-1	I'm Still Walking the Hi-Way	BB B8778
059434-1	Get Your Business Straight	BB B8739
059435-1	Muddy Pond Blues	BB B8739
059436-2	Little Woman	BB B8778

Sonny Boy Williamson (John Lee Williamson): v/h; acc. Blind John Davis, p; Big Bill Broonzy, g;
prob. William Mitchell, b

Chicago—4 April 1941

064019-1	Western Union Man	BB B8731
064020-1	Big Apple Blues	BB B8766
064021-1	Springtime Blues	BB B8955
064022-1	My Baby Made a Change	BB B8766
064023-1	Shotgun Blues	BB B8731
064024-1	Coal and Iceman Blues	BB B8797
064025-1	Drink on, Little Girl	BB B8955
064026-1	Mattie Mae Blues	BB B8797

Lil Green: v; acc. Simeon Henry, p; Big Bill Broonzy, g; Ransom Knowling, sb; group v–1

Chicago—23 April 1941

064130-1	Why Don't You Do Right?	BB B8714, Vi 20-3283, Groove G5004
064131-1	Love Me	BB B8714
064132-	I'm Going to Copyright Your Kisses	BB B8790
064133-1	What's the Matter with Love?	BB B8754
064134-1	Country Boy Blues	BB B8754
064135-1	How Can I Go On	BB B8790

Jean Brady, v; acc. Blind John Davis, p; Big Bill Broonzy, g; unknown, sb

Chicago—24 April 1941

C-3696-1	My Mellow Man	OK 06254
C-3697-1	Just to Prove That I Love You	OK unissued
C-3698-1	Knockin' Myself Out	OK 06254
C-3699-1	Monday Morning Blues	OK unissued

Bill McKinley: v/h; acc. prob. Big Bill Broonzy, g; unknown, sb; Washboard Sam, wb
Chicago—2 May 1941

| C-3746-1 | Poor Boy Blues | Vo unissued: RnB CK47914, RnB (Eu) 471832-2, RnB (J) SRCS5965, Doc DOCD5198 (CDs) |
| C-3747-1 | Is That a Monkey You Got | Vo unissued: RnB CK47467, RnB (Eu) 468770-2, RnB (J) SRCS5678, Doc DOCD5198 (CDs) |

Washboard Sam and His Washboard Band: wb/v; acc. Memphis Slim, p; Big Bill Broonzy, g; William Mitchell, b
Chicago—26 June 1941

064477-1	Life Is Just a Book	BB B8909
064478-1	I'm Not the Lad	BB B8878
064479-1	My Feet Jumped Sally	BB B8844
064480-1	Flying Crow Blues	BB B8844
064481-1	Levee Camp Blues	BB B8909
064482-1	I'm Feeling Low Down	BB B8878
064483-1	Brown and Yellow Woman Blues	BB B8937
064484-1	She Belongs to the Devil	BB B8937

Lil Green: v; acc. Simeon Henry, p; Big Bill Broonzy, g; Ransom Knowling, sb; group v–1
Chicago—23 July 1941

064727-	Hello Babe	BB B8865
064728-1	If I Didn't Love You	BB B8865
064729-	Let's Be Friends	BB B8895
064730-	Because I Love My Daddy So	BB B8826
064731-	I'm Going to Start a Racket	BB B8895
064732-	You're Just Full of Jive	BB B8826

Jazz Gillum: v/h; acc. Big Bill Broonzy, g; Alfred Elkins, imb; Amanda Sorter, wb
Chicago—24 July 1941

064737-1	Riley Springs Blues	BB B8846
064738-1	That's What Worries Me	BB B8872
064739-1	I Got Somebody Else	BB B8816
064740-1	Maybe You'll Love Me Too	BB B8846
064741-1	It Looks Bad for You	BB B8816
064742-1	Me and My Buddy	BB B8872

Clara Morris: v; acc. prob. Blind John Davis, p; prob. Big Bill Broonzy, g; unknown, sb
Chicago—19 August 1941

| C-3974-1 | Working for My Man | OK unissued |
| C-3975-1 | Moan Man Blues | OK unissued |

Washboard Sam and His Washboard Band: wb/v; acc. Memphis Slim, p; Big Bill Broonzy, g; Alfred Elkins, b
Chicago—4 November 1941

| 070375-1 | Let Me Play Your Vendor | BB B8967 |
| 070376-1 | Broadcast Blues | BB B8967 |

070377-1	Gonna Hit the Highway	BB B8967, Vi20-2789
070378-1	I've Been Treated Wrong	BB B9007
070379-1	Evil Blues	BB B8997
070380-1	Get Down Brother	BB B9018
070381-1	Lover's Lane Blues	BB B9007
070382-1	You Stole My Love	BB B9018

Jazz Gillum: Acc. own h; Horace Malcolm, p; Big Bill Broonzy, g; Alfred Elkins, sb or imb
Chicago—5 December 1941

070440-1	It's All Over Now	BB B8975
070441-1	War Time Blues	BB B8943
070442-1	You Are Doing Me Wrong	BB B8975
070443-1	One Letter Home	BB B8943
070444-1	Down South Blues	BB B9004
070445-1	You Drink Too Much Whiskey	BB B9004
070446-1	No Friend Blues	BB B9034
070447-1	From Now On	BB B9034

Kansas Katie (Ethel King): v; acc. Memphis Slim (Peter Chatman), p; Big Bill Broonzy, g
Chicago—8 December 1941

070458-1	Don't You Know Me	BB B8999
070459-1	I Can't Let You Go	BB B8944
070460-1	Deep Sea Diver	BB B8944
070461-1	He's My Man	BB B8999

Lil Green: v; acc. Simeon Henry, p; Big Bill Broonzy, g; Ransom Knowling, sb; group v–1.
Chicago—21 January 1942

070196-1	99 Blues	BB B9030
07197-1A	Don't Know What I Will Do	BB B8949
070198-1A	You Got Me to the Place	BB B9010
070199-1	Keep Your Hand on Your Heart	BB B8949
070800-	I Have a Place to Go	BB B8985
070801-1A	If You Want to Share Your Love	BB B9030
070802-1	If I'm a Fool	BB B8985
070803-1	I'm Wasting My Time on You	BB B9010

Washboard Sam and His Washboard Band: wb/v; acc. Frank Owens, as–1; Roosevelt Sykes, p;
Big Bill Broonzy, g
Chicago—10 February 1942

074058-1	Rockin' My Blues Away–1	BB unissued: BB 61042-2, Doc DOCD5176 (CDs)
074059-1	Good Old Cabbage Greens–1	BB 34-0705
074060-1	River Hip Mama–1	BB B9039, Vi20-2789
074061-1	Do That Shake Dance–1	BB unissued: BB 61042-2, Doc DOCD5176 (CDs)
074062-1	How Can You Love Me	BB B9039
074063-1	Cry on Baby	BB unissued
074064-1	Dark Road Blues	BB unissued
074065-1	Stop and Fix It	BB 34-0705

St. Louis Jimmy: v; acc. Roosevelt Sykes, p; Big Bill Broonzy, g; Alfred Elkins, b
Chicago—25 March 1942

074160-1	St. Louis Woman Blues	BB B9040
074161-1	Poor Boy Blues	BB B9040
074162-1	Back on My Feet Again	BB 34-0718
074163-1	Nothing but Blues	BB 34-0718
074164-1	Soon Forget You	BB B9016
074165-1	Can't Stand Your Evil Ways	BB B9016

Jazz Gillum: acc. own h–1; Blind John Davis, p; Big Bill Broonzy, g; Alfred Elkins, b
Chicago—30 July 1942

074648-1	I'm Gonna Leave You on the Outskirts of Town–1	BB B9042
074649-1	I Couldn't Help It Blues–1	BB 34-0709
074650-1	My Big Money–1	BB 34-0707
074651-1	Woke Up Cold in Hand–1	BB B9042
074652-1	Water Pipe Blues–1	BB unissued: RCA (E) RD7816, Travelin' Man TM808 (LPs); Doc DOCD6199 (CD)
074653-1	Tell Me, Mama	BB 34-0707, Groove G5002
074654-1	Deep Water Blues	BB 34-0709
074655-1	You're Tearing Your Playhouse Down–1	BB unissued: RCA (E) RD7816, Travelin' Man TM808 (LPs); Doc DOCD6199 (CD)

Sonny Boy Williamson (John Lee Williamson): v/h; acc. Blind John Davis, p; Big Bill Broonzy, g; Alfred Elkins, b
Chicago—30 July 1942

074656-1	Love Me, Baby	BB 34-0713
074657-1	What's Getting' Wrong with You?	BB unissued: BB(F) PM42049 (LP); Doc DOCD5058 (CD)
074658-1	Blues That Made Me Drunk	BB unissued: RCA(J) RA5707, RCA(F) NL90027(2) (LPs); Doc DOCD5058 (CD)
074659-1	Come on Baby and Take a Walk	BB unissued: BB(F) PM42049, RCA(J) RA5707 (LPs); Doc DOCD5058 (CD)

Washboard Sam and His Washboard Band: wb/v; acc. Memphis Slim, p; Big Bill Broonzy, g; Ransom Knowling, sb
Chicago—31 July 1942

074682-1	Don't Have to Sing the Blues	BB unissued: Travelin' Man TM8812, Document DLP507 (LPs); Doc DOCD5176 (CD)
074683-1	Red River Dam Blues	BB unissued: BB 61042-2, Doc DOCD5176 (CDs)
074684-1	Down South Woman Blues	BB unissued: BB 61042-2, Doc DOCD5176 (CDs)
074685-1	Ain't That a Shame?	BB unissued: BB 61042-2, Doc DOCD5176 (CDs)
074686-1	I Laid My Cards on the Table	BB 34-0710
074687-1	I Get the Blues at Bedtime	BB 34-0710

NOTES

Introduction

1. Angela Davis, *Blues Legacies and Black Feminism* (New York: Vintage Books, 1999), 91.

2. Paul Oliver, "Blues," in *The New Grove Gospel, Blues and Jazz* (New York: Norton, 1986), 155; William Barlow, *Looking up at Down* (Philadelphia: Temple University Press, 1989), 301, 310.

1. Born in the "Age of Blues"

1. William Broonzy and Yannick Bruynoghe, *Big Bill Blues: William Broonzy's Story as Told to Yannick Bruynoghe* (New York: Da Capo Press, 1992), 31.

2. Big Bill Broonzy, interview by Bill Randle, *The Bill Broonzy Story*, USA: Verve MGV3000-5, 1999.

3. Broonzy and Bruynoghe, *Big Bill*, 31–32.

4. Leon Litwack, *Been in the Storm So Long: The Aftermath of Slavery* (New York: Knopf, 1979), 179–83.

5. Booker T. Washington, *Up from Slavery* (Oxford: Oxford University Press, 1995), 12.

6. "Oh Freedom!" in *The Norton Anthology of African American Literature*, ed. Henry Louis Gates Jr. and Nellie Y. McKay (New York: Norton, 1997), 15–16.

7. Eric Foner, *A Short History of Reconstruction* (New York: Harper and Row, 1990), 26–27, 276–81.

8. Litwack, *Been in the Storm*, 247–51.

9. Washington, *Up from Slavery*, 20–21.

10. Litwack, *Been in the Storm*, 240–41.

11. Herbert Gutman, *The Black Family in Slavery and Freedom, 1750–1925* (New York: Vintage Books, 1977), 425–31, 443–44.

12. Alan Lomax, *The Land Where the Blues Began* (New York: Pantheon Books, 1993), 424–25.

13. Big Bill Broonzy, *Big Bill Broonzy. Vol. 4 (3 July 1935 to 22 April 1936)*, Austria: Document DOCD-5126, n.d.

14. Ibid.

15. Big Bill Broonzy, *Big Bill Broonzy. Vol. 9 (11 May to 8 December 1939)*, Austria: Document DOCD-5131, n.d.

16. Litwack, *Been in the Storm*, 305–9; Lomax, *Land*, 425.

17. Washington, *Up from Slavery*, 65–67.

18. Broonzy and Bruynoghe, *Big Bill*, 32.

19. Gutman, *Black Family*, 449–50.

20. Broonzy, interview by Randle, *Broonzy Story*.

21. Paul Oliver, album notes, *Big Bill Broonzy 1927–1932*, Matchbox MSE 1004, 1985.

22. Lomax, *Land*, 423–24.

23. Charles Edward Smith, "Big Bill and the Country Blues," *Jazz Monthly* 3, no.11 (January 1958): 10.

24. Robert Heilbroner and Aaron Singer, *The Economic Transformation of America, 1600 to the Present*, 3rd ed. (Fort Worth, Tex.: Harcourt Brace, 1994), 200.

25. Ibid., 251.

26. Ibid., 145–46.

27. Broonzy and Bruynoghe, *Big Bill*, 53.

28. Tristram Potter Coffin and Hennig Cohen, eds., *Folklore: From the Working Folk of America* (New York: Anchor Books, 1974), 365–66, 390–92; Howard W. Odum and Guy B. Johnson, *The Negro and His Songs* (Chapel Hill: University of North Carolina Press, 1925), 206.Tristram Potter Coffin suggests that the heroes of folklore are embodiments of group ideals and values. The telling of their exploits created standards for the common people to respect, encourage, or avoid. In history, the heroes were selected to exhibit exceptional qualities. Howard Odum, for example, wrote that the Joe Turner character embodied the dual values of admiration and fear of notorious figures in black folklore. His research of Negro ballads depicted Joe Turner as a convict who ran away from a chain gang dragging along "fohty links o' chain."

29. Broonzy and Bruynoghe, *Big Bill*, 53–54.

30. Lomax, *Land*, 427.

31. Big Bill Broonzy, "It Was Born in Us to Sing the Blues," *Melody Maker*, August 27, 1955, 3.

32. Lomax, *Land*, 429; Arnold Van Gennep, *The Rites of Passage* (Chicago: University of Chicago Press, 1960), 65–67.

33. Broonzy, interview by Randle, *Broonzy Story*.

34. Broonzy and Bruynoghe, *Big Bill*, 60–61.

35. Jerry Pytak, "The Economics of Cotton Farming," *New International* 5, no. 4 (April 1939): 120–23; and *New International* 5, no. 5 (May 1939): 144–48.

36. Broonzy and Bruynoghe, *Big Bill*, 80.

37. Big Bill Broonzy, *Big Bill Broonzy. Vol. 10 (26 January to 17 December 1940)*, Austria: Document DOCD-5132, n.d.

38. Merline Johnson, "Got a Man in the 'Bama Mine," *Merline Johnson: The Yas Yas Girl 1937–1947*, Wolf WBJ 006, 1998.

39. Bill Broonzy, interview by Alan Lomax, *Blues in the Mississippi Night: Authentic Field Recordings of Negro Folk Music*, USA: Rykodisc, RCD 90155, 1990.

40. Washboard Sam, "Levee Camp Blues," *Washboard Sam, I'm Not the Lad*, Contact BT-2012, 1989.

41. Broonzy, interview by Lomax, *Blues in the Mississippi Night*.

42. Lomax, *Land*, 427.

43. Paul Laurence Dunbar, "The Corn-Stalk Fiddle," in *Lyrics of Lowly Life* (New York: Dodd, Mead, 1896).

44. Broonzy and Bruynoghe, *Big Bill*, 54.

45. Ibid., 55.

46. Paul Oliver, *The Story of the Blues* (Boston: Northeastern University Press, 1997), 52–56.

47. Broonzy, interview by Randle, *Broonzy Story*.

48. Big Bill Broonzy, "Mule Ridin'-Talkin' Blues," *Big Bill Broonzy— Story*, Folkways FG 3586, 1957.

49. Alan Lomax, *Folksongs of North America* (New York: Doubleday, 1960), 506–7.

50. Broonzy, "Crawdad Blues," Randle, *Broonzy Story*.

51. Broonzy, interview by Randle, *Broonzy Story*.

52. Paul Oliver, *Songster and Saints* (Cambridge: Cambridge University Press, 1984), 20–22.

53. Broonzy, interview by Terkel, *Big Bill—Story*.

54. Broonzy, "See See Rider," *Broonzy Story*.

55. Margaret McKee and Fred Chisenhall, *Beale Black & Blue* (Baton Rouge: Louisiana State University Press, 1981), 132.

56. Broonzy, interview by Terkel, *Big Bill—Story*.

57. Lomax, *Land*, 428.

58. Oliver, *Story of the Blues*, 57.

59. McKee and Chisenhall, *Beale*, 105.

60. Samuel A. Floyd Jr., *The Power of Black Music* (New York: Oxford University Press, 1995), 66–70.

61. Stephen Calt, Nick Perls, and Mike Stewart, liner notes, *The Young Big Bill Broonzy 1928–1935*, USA: Yazoo Records L-1011, 1990.

62. Giles Oakley, *The Devil's Music* (New York: Da Capo Press, 1997), 40–43.

63. McKee, *Beale*, 25, 34–35.

64. William Barlow, *Looking up at Down* (Philadelphia: Temple University Press, 1989), 120–21.

65. Big Bill Broonzy, interview by Alan Lomax, The Alan Lomax Collection, The Association for Cultural Equity, Hunter College, New York.

66. Edgar Lee Masters, "Fiddler Jones," in *Spoon River Anthology* (New York: Collier Books, 1962), 83.

67. Paul Laurence Dunbar, "The Party," in *Dark Symphony: Negro Literature in America*, ed. James A. Emanuel and Theodore L. Gross (New York: Free Press, 1968), 40.

68. Lomax, *Land*, 429.

69. Broonzy and Bruynoghe, *Big Bill*, 34; Lomax, *Land*, 429.

70. Broonzy, interview by Lomax.

71. Broonzy and Bruynoghe, *Big Bill*, 36.

72. Ibid., 34.

73. McKee, *Beale*, 213.

74. Benjamin Filene, *Romancing the Folk: Public Memory & American Roots Music* (Chapel Hill: University of North Carolina Press, 2000), 27–32.

75. Lomax, *Land*, 432–33.

76. Ibid., 432.

2. "Makin' My Get Away"

1. Arthur E. Barbeau and Florette Henri, *Unknown Soldiers: Black American Troops in World War I* (Philadelphia: Temple University Press, 1974), 17–19, 33; "Negro Conscription," in *Black Protest and the Great Migration*, ed. Eric Arnesen (Boston: Bedford/St. Martin's, 2003), 90.

2. Neil Wynn, *From Progressivism to Prosperity: World War I and American Society* (New York: Holmes and Meier, 1986), 46, 177; Barbeau and Henri, *Unknown Soldiers*, 35.

3. William Broonzy and Yannick Bruynoghe, *Big Bill Blues: William Broonzy's Story as Told to Yannick Bruynoghe* (New York: Da Capo Press, 1992), 34; Alan Lomax, *The Land Where the Blues Began* (New York: Pantheon Books, 1993), 433.

4. Big Bill Broonzy, *Big Bill Broonzy. Vol. 10 (26 January to 17 December 1940)*, Austria: Document DOCD-5132.

5. Barbeau and Henri, *Unknown Soldiers*, 42–44.

6. Lomax, *Land*, 433.

7. Emmett Scott, *The American Negro in the World War* (Chicago: Homewood, 1919), 67–69, 73–74, 104; Foy Lisenby, *Charles Hillman Brough* (Fayetteville: University of Arkansas Press, 1996), 45; Broonzy and Bruynoghe, *Big Bill*, 37.

8. Barbeau and Henri, *Unknown Soldiers*, 38–39.

9. Lomax, *Land*, 434.

10. Broonzy and Bruynoghe, *Big Bill*, 37–38.

11. Lomax, *Land*, 433.

12. Wynn, *From Progressivism*, 122–23.

13. Barbeau and Henri, *Unknown Soldiers*, 48–52.

14. Broonzy and Bruynoghe, *Big Bill*, 33–34.

15. Lisenby, *Charles Hillman Brough*, 25.

16. Lomax, *Land*, 434.

17. Scott, *American Negro*, 79–80.

18. Lomax, *Land*, 433.

19. Barbeau, *Unknown Soldier*, 89; Wynn, *From Progressivism*, 178.

20. Scott, *American Negro*, 316.

21. Barbeau and Henri, *Unknown Soldiers*, 102–4; Scott, *American Negro*, unnumbered photo plate.

22. Barbeau and Henri, *Unknown Soldiers*, 104–5; Lomax, *Land*, 434.

23. Lomax, *Land*, 434.

24. Wynn, *From Progressivism*, 178.

25. Lomax, *Land*, 435.

26. Big Bill Broonzy, *Big Bill Broonzy. Vol. 4 (3 July 1935 to 22 April 1936)*, Austria: Document DOCD-5126.

27. Barbeau and Henri, *Unknown Soldiers*, 166–69; Lomax, *Land*, 434–35.

28. Lomax, *Land*, 435–36.

29. Ibid., 436.

30. Broonzy and Bruynoghe, *Big Bill*, 83.

31. Ibid., 62.

32. Ibid., 62–63, 103–4; Sheldon Harris, *Blues Who's Who*, 5th ed. (New Rochelle, N.Y.: Arlington House, 1979), 69.

33. Broonzy and Bruynoghe, *Big Bill*, 35.

34. Ibid., 103–4.

35. Lomax, *Land*, 436–38.

36. Allan H. Spear, *Black Chicago: The Making of a Ghetto, 1890–1920* (Chicago: University of Chicago Press. 1967), 130.

37. Charles S. Johnson, Edwin R. Embree, and W. W. Alexander, *The Collapse of Cotton Tenancy* (Chapel Hill: University of North Carolina Press, 1935), 34–35; Florette Henri, *Black Migration: Movement North, 1900–1920* (Garden City, N.Y.: Anchor Press/Doubleday, 1976), 26–29; Spear, *Black Chicago*, 130–33.

38. George Stith (organizer Southern Tenant Farmers Union), interview by the author, June 5, 1991.

39. "White Folks Ain't Jesus (How Long)," unidentified singer, Lawrence Gellert, prod., *Cap'n, You're So Mean: Negro Songs of Protest*, vol. 2, Rounder Records 4013, 1982.

40. John Handcox, "Raggedy, Raggedy," *John Handcox Collection*, Archive of Folk Culture, Library of Congress.

41. Spear, *Black Chicago*, 130–33.

42. Vera Hall, "Boll Weevil Blues," *Alan Lomax Collection*, Archive of Folk Culture, Library of Congress.

43. Sampson Pittman, "Cotton Farmer Blues," *Alan Lomax Collection*, Archive of Folk Culture, Library of Congress.

44. Spear, *Black Chicago*, 130–33.

45. John Handcox, *John Handcox Collection*.

46. Paul Oliver, *Bessie Smith*, Kings of Jazz series (New York: A. S. Barnes, 1961), 47.

47. Big Bill Broonzy, "Southern Flood Blues," *Big Bill Broonzy. Vol. 5 (1 May 1936 to 31 January 1937)*, Austria: Document DOCD-5127.

48. Johnson, Embree, and Alexander, *Collapse of Cotton Tenancy*, 35–45.

49. "Standing on the Street in Birmingham," unidentified singer, Gellert, prod., *Cap'n, You're So Mean*.

50. Lomax, *Land*, 436.

51. Henri, *Black Migration*, 56–58.

52. Ibid., 12–21.

53. "Negro Conscription," 92.

54. Wynn, *From Progressivism*, 190; Barbeau and Henri, *Unknown Soldiers*, 187–88.

55. Walter White, "The Race Conflict in Arkansas," in *Black Protest and the Great Migration*, ed. Eric Arnesen (Boston: Bedford/St. Martin's, 2003), 175.

56. Ibid.

57. "How the Arkansas Peons Were Freed," in *Black Protest and the Great Migration*, ed. Eric Arnesen (Boston: Bedford/St. Martin's, 2003), 177–79; Lisenby, *Charles Hillman Brough*, 47–48.

58. Broonzy, interview by Alan Lomax, *Blues in the Mississippi Night: Authentic Field Recordings of Negro Folk Music*, USA: Rykodisc, RCD 90155, 1990.

59. Henri, *Black Migration*, 39–40.

60. Broonzy, interview by Alan Lomax, *Blues in Mississippi Night*.

61. Kokomo Arnold, "Chain Gang Blues," *Kokomo Arnold vol. 1, 1930–1935*, Document DOCD 5037, n.d.

62. Ma Rainey, "Chain Gang Blues," *Ma Rainey*, Milestone M-47021, 1974.

63. Big Bill Broonzy, "Midnight Special," *Big Bill Broonzy. Vol. 3 (18 October 1934 to 3 July 1935)*, Austria: Document DOCD-5052, 1991. The Midnight Special was a train line that passed by a prison farm in Sugarland, Texas. It was the chief means of transportation for people visiting convicted friends and relatives.

64. Barefoot Bill, "Big Rock Jail," *Ed Bell (Barefoot Bill/Sluefoot Joe) Complete Recorded Works in Chronological Order, 1927–1930*, Document DOCD 5090, n.d.

65. Bessie Smith, "Work House Blues," *Empty Bed Blues*, Columbia G-30450, n.d.

66. Bukka White, "Parchman Farm Blues," *Aberdeen Mississippi Blues: The Vintage Recordings, 1930–1940*, Document DOCD 5679, n.d.

67. Henri, *Black Migration*, 43–46.

68. Ibid., 54–55; Spear, *Black Chicago*, 157.

69. Henri, *Black Migration*, 54–55; Spear, *Black Chicago*, 157.

70. Henri, *Black Migration*, 52.

71. James Grossman, *Land of Hope: Chicago, Black Southerners, and the Great Migration* (Chicago: University of Chicago Press, 1989), 89–97.

72. Henri, *Black Migration*, 60–62.

73. Ibid., 60; Tristram Potter Coffin and Hennig Cohen, eds., *Folklore: From the Working Folk of America* (New York: Anchor Books, 1974), 31.

74. Lomax, *Blues in the Mississippi Night*.

75. Barlow, *Looking Up*, 288; Henri, *Black Migration*, 62–66.

3. "House Rent Stomp"

1. Florette Henri, *Black Migration: Movement North, 1900–1920* (Garden City, N.Y.: Anchor Press/Doubleday, 1976), 51, 66.

2. Paul Oliver, *Blues Fell This Morning*, Canto ed. (Cambridge: Cambridge University Press, 1994), 45–46.

3. Ibid., 58.

4. Big Bill Broonzy, "I'm a Southern Man," *Big Bill Broonzy. Vol. 5 (1 May 1936 to 31 January 1937)*, Austria: Document DOCD-5127, n.d.

5. Oliver, *Blues Fell*, 67.

6. Big Bill Broonzy, "The Southern Blues," *Big Bill Broonzy. Vol. 3 (18 October 1934 to 2 July 1935)*, Document DOCD-5052, 1991.

7. T. Arnold Hill, "Why Southern Negroes Don't Go South," in *Black Protest and the Great Migration*, ed. Eric Arnesen (Boston: Bedford/St. Martin's, 2003), 186.

8. Henri, *Black Migration*, 66–70.

9. St. Clair Drake and Horace Cayton, *Black Metropolis: A Study of Negro Life in a Northern City* (New York: Harcourt, Brace, 1945), 581–82; E. Franklin Frazier, *The Negro Church in America* (New York: Schocken Books, 1974), 53–53.

10. Tristram Potter Coffin and Hennig Cohen, eds., *Folklore: From the Working Folk of America* (New York: Anchor Books, 1974), 351–57.

11. Big Bill Broonzy, "You May Need My Help Someday," *Big Bill Broonzy. Vol. 3*.

12. Big Bill Broonzy, "I Don't Want No Woman," *Big Bill Broonzy Sings Folk Songs*, Smithsonian/Folkways SF 40023, 1956.

13. Frazier, *Negro Church*, 52–53; Drake and Cayton, *Black Metropolis*, 584–87; Hazel Carby, "It Jus Be's Dat Way Sometime": The Sexual Politics of Women's Blues," in *Unequal Sisters, A Multicultural Reader in U.S. Women's History*, ed. Ellen Carol DuBois and Vicki Ruiz (New York: Routledge, 1990), 244.

14. Bessie Smith, "In House Blues," *The World's Greatest Blues Singer*, Columbia CG 33, 1972.

15. Ma Rainey, "Blame It on the Blues," *Ma Rainey*, Milestone M-47021, 1974.

16. Big Bill Broonzy, "She Caught the Train," *Big Bill Broonzy. Vol. 3*.

17. Bessie Smith, "Sam Jones Blues," *Any Woman's Blues*, Columbia G 30126, 1972.

18. Big Bill Broonzy, "Baby Don't You Remember?" *Big Bill Broonzy. Vol. 8 (15 September 1938 to 10 February 1939)*, Austria: Document DOCD-5130, n.d.

19. Drake and Cayton, *Black Metropolis*, 584–87.

20. Rainey, "Blame It on the Blues."

21. Big Bill Broonzy, "Tell Me What You Been Doing," *Big Bill Broonzy. Vol. 4 (3 July 1935 to 22 April 1936)*, Austria: Document DOCD-5126, n.d.

22. Big Bill Broonzy, "When I Been Drinking," *Big Bill Broonzy. Vol. 11 (17 December 1940 to 6 March 1942)*, Austria: Document DOCD-5133, n.d.

23. Broonzy, "Low Down Woman Blues," *Big Bill Broonzy. Vol. 4.*

24. Carby, "It Jus Be's," 244–45; Angela Davis, *Blues Legacies and Black Feminism* (New York: Vintage Books, 1999), 25–33.

25. Ma Rainey, "Cell Bound Blues," *Immortal Ma Rainey,* Milestone MLP-2001, 1966.

26. Big Bill Broonzy, interview by Alan Lomax, The Alan Lomax Collection, The Association for Cultural Equity, Hunter College, New York.

27. James Grossman, *Land of Hope: Chicago, Black Southerners, and the Great Migration* (Chicago: University of Chicago Press, 1989), 99; Allan H. Spear, *Black Chicago: The Making of a Ghetto, 1890–1920* (Chicago: University of Chicago Press. 1967), 129–30.

28. Grossman, *Land of Hope,* 115–16.

29. Ibid., 4.

30. Drake and Cayton, *Black Metropolis,* 174–76.

31. Alan Lomax, *The Land Where the Blues Began* (New York: Pantheon Books, 1993), 442.

32. Mark R. Wilson, Stephen R. Porter, and Janice L. Reiff, "American Car & Foundry Corporation," www.enyclopedia.chicagohistory.org.

33. "Business in Bronzeville," in *The Black Urban Condition: A Documentary History, 1866–1971,* ed. Hollis Lynch (New York: Thomas Y. Crowell, 1973), 267–68; Drake and Cayton, *Black Metropolis,* 348–50.

34. Chicago Commission on Race Relations, "The Truth about the North," in *Black Protest and the Great Migration,* ed. Eric Arnesen (Boston: Bedford/St. Martin's, 2003), 68; Drake and Cayton, *Black Metropolis,* 58–64, 202.

35. "Black Housing," in *The Black Urban Condition: A Documentary History, 1866–1971,* ed. Hollis Lynch (New York: Thomas Y. Crowell, 1973), 127.

36. Grossman, *Land of Hope,* 171–75.

37. Drake and Cayton, *Black Metropolis,* 65–72.

38. Ibid., 73–76.

39. Grossman, *Land of Hope,* 144–46.

40. Drake and Cayton, *Black Metropolis,* 75; Frazier, *Negro Church,* 53–59; Morton Leeds, "The Process of Cultural Stripping and Reintegration: The Rural Migrant in the City," in *The Urban Experience and Folk Tradition,* ed. Americo Paredes and Ellen Stekert (Austin: University of Texas Press, 1971), 167–70.

41. Frazier, *Negro Church,* 77–79; LeRoi Jones, *Blues People* (New York: William Morrow, 1963), 105–12.

42. William Barlow, *Looking up at Down* (Philadelphia: Temple University Press, 1989), 292; Giles Oakley, *The Devil's Music* (New York: Da Capo Press, 1997), 101, 112.

43. Drake and Cayton, *Black Metropolis,* 77–81.

44. John Steiner, "Chicago," in *Jazz,* ed. Nat Hentoff and Albert J. McCarthy (New York: Da Capo Press, 1974), 139–45.

45. William Russell, "Three Boogie-Woogie Blues Pianists," in *The Art of Jazz,* ed. Martin Williams (New York: Oxford University Press, 1959), 101; Max Harrison, "Boogie-Woogie," in *Jazz,* ed. Nat Hentoff and Albert J. McCarthy (New York: Da Capo Press, 1974), 109; George Lines, liner notes, *Boogie-Woogie Trio,* Storyville SLP 4006, 1976.

46. Donald Spivey, *Union and the Black Musicians: The Narrative of William Everett Samuels and Chicago Local 208* (Lanham, Md.: University Press of America, 1984), 30.

47. Don DeMichael, liner notes, *The Genuis of Louis Armstrong, vol. 1: 1923–1933,* Columbia G30416, n.d.

48. Big Bill Broonzy, "Baby, I Done Got Wise," in *Selections from the Gutter: Jazz Portraits from "The Jazz Record*," ed. Art Hodes and Chadwick Hanson. (Berkeley and Los Angeles: University of California Press, 1977), 58.

49. Elijah Wald, *Josh White: Society Blues* (Amherst: University of Massachusetts, 2000), 18; Lomax, *Land*, 443.

50. Mike Rowe, *Chicago Breakdown* (New York: Da Capo Press, 1975), 41.

51. Rowe, *Chicago Breakdown*, 47–48; Barry Lee Pearson, *Sounds So Good to Me: The Bluesman's Story* (Philadelphia: University of Pennsylvania Press, 1984), 27.

52. Paul Oliver, *The Story of the Blues* (Boston: Northeastern University Press, 1997), 91–92.

53. Big Bill Broonzy and Yannick Bruynoghe, *Big Bill Blues: William Broonzy's Story as Told to Yannick Bruynoghe* (New York: Da Capo Press, 1992), 68.

54. Ibid., 68.

55. Big Bill Broonzy, "House Rent Stomp," *Big Bill Broonzy. Vol. 1 (November 1927 to 9 February 1932)*, Austria: Document DOCD-5050, 1991.

56. Big Bill Broonzy, "Pig Meat Strut," *Big Bill Broonzy. Vol. 1*.

57. Nat Hentoff and Nathan Shapiro, eds., *Hear Me Talkin' to Ya* (1955; rpt., New York: Dover, 1966), 129; Barlow, *Looking Up*, 290; Ronald L. Morris, *Wait until Dark: Jazz and the Underworld, 1880–1940* (Bowling Green, Ky.: Bowling Green University Popular Press, 1980), 19–26.

58. Steiner, "Chicago," 143 48; Hentoff and Shapiro, *Hear Me*, 103–12; Morris, *Wait Until*, 22–26.

59. Rowe, *Chicago Breakdown*, 40–45.

60. William Howland Kenney, "African American Blues and the Phonograph," in *Recorded Music in American Life: The Phonograph and Popular Memory, 1890–1945* (New York: Oxford University Press, 1999), 110–11, 130.

61. John F. Szwed, "Negro Music: Urban Renewal," in *Our Living Traditions: An Introduction to American Folklore*, ed. Tristram Potter Coffin (New York: Basic Books, 1968), 273–75.

62. David Jasen, *Spreadin' Rhythm Around: Black Popular Songwriters, 1880–1930* (New York: Schirmer Books, 1998), 312; Kenney, "African American Blues," 126–27.

63. Jasen, *Spreadin' Rhythm*, 312–14; Kenney, "African American Blues," 126–28.

64. Jasen, *Spreadin' Rhythm*, 318–20.

65. Kenney, "African American Blues," 127–28; Jasen, *Spreadin' Rhythm*, 314–17.

66. Broonzy, "Baby, I Done," 58.

67. Ibid.; Lomax, *Land*, 443.

68. Samuel Charters, *The Bluesmakers* (New York: Da Capo Press. 1991), 143–47.

69. Lomax, *Land*, 443.

70. Ibid.

71. Guido van Rijn, liner notes, *Too Late, Too Late, vol. 11 (1924–1939)*, DOCD-5625, 1998.

72. Papa Charlie Jackson, "Shave 'Em Dry," *Too Late, Too Late, vol. 11 (1924–1939)*.

73. Big Bill Broonzy, *Big Bill Broonzy. Vol. 2 (9 February 1932 to 18 October 1934)*, Austria: Document DOCD-5051, 1991.

74. Hentoff and Shapiro, *Hear Me*, 109–10, 177–80, 244–45.

75. Andre Millard, *America on Record: A History of Recorded Sound* (Cambridge: Cambridge University Press, 1995), 262; Jasen, *Spreadin' Rhythm*, 319.

76. Broonzy and Bruynoghe, *Big Bill*, 46–47.

77. Jasen, Spreadin' Rhythm, 319.

78. Lomax, *Land*, 444.

79. Broonzy and Bruynoghe, *Big Bill*, 154–55.

"Stuff They Call Money"

1. St. Clair Drake and Horace Cayton, *Black Metropolis: A Study of Negro Life in a Northern City* (New York: Harcourt, Brace, 1945), 716–22; James H. Cone, "The Blues: A Secular Spiritual," in *Write Me a Few of Your Lines: A Blues Reader,* ed. Steven C. Tracey (Amherst: University of Massachusetts Press, 1999), 231–33.

2. Robert McElvaine, *The Great Depression* (New York: Times Books, 1984), 170–74; T. H. Watkins, *The Great Depression: America in the 1930s* (Boston: Little Brown, 1993), 53–54.

3. John Steiner, "Chicago," in *Jazz,* ed. Nat Hentoff and Albert J. McCarthy (New York: Da Capo Press, 1974), 142.

4. Big Bill Broonzy, "Unemployment Stomp," *Big Bill Broonzy. Vol. 7 (13 October 1937 to 15 September 1938),* Austria: Document DOCD-5129, n.d.

5. Broonzy, "Unemployment Stomp," *Big Bill Broonzy. Vol. 7.*

6. William Jones, *The Tribe of Black Ulysses: African American Lumber Workers in the Jim Crow South* (Urbana: University of Illinois Press, 2005), 63.

7. Big Bill Broonzy, "Starvation Blues," *Big Bill Broonzy. Vol. 2 (9 February 1932 to 18 October 1934),* Austria: Document DOCD-5051, 1991.

8. Paul Oliver, "Big Maceo," in *The Art of Jazz,* ed. Martin Williams (New York: Oxford Press, 1959), 110.

9. Nat Hentoff and Nathan Shapiro, eds. *Hear Me Talkin' to Ya* (New York: Dover, 1966), 196–98.

10. Ibid., 198–99.

11. Broadus Mitchell, *Depression Decade: From New Era through New Deal, 1929–1941,* vol. 9, *The Economic History of the United States* (New York: Rinehart, 1947), 211–12.

12. Broonzy, "Hungry Man Blues," *Big Bill Broonzy. Vol. 2.*

13. Big Bill Broonzy, "Plow Hand Blues," *Big Bill Broonzy. Vol. 10 (26 January to 17 December 1940),* Austria: Document DOCD-5132, n.d.

14. Big Bill Broonzy, "Mean Old World," *Big Bill Broonzy. Vol. 6 (31 January 1937 to 13 October 1937),* Austria: Document DOCD-5128, n.d.

15. Drake and Cayton, *Black Metropolis,* 218; T. Arnold Hill, "Why Southern Negroes Don't Go South," in *Black Protest and the Great Migration,* ed. Eric Arnesen (Boston: Bedford/St. Martin's, 2003), 184.

16. Mitchell, *Depression Decade,* 99, 104–7; Harvard Sitkoff, *A New Deal for Blacks* (Oxford: Oxford University Press, 1978), 34–35; John Kirby, *Black Americans in the Roosevelt Era: Liberalism and Race* (Knoxville: University of Tennessee Press, 1980), 97–98.

17. McElvaine, *Great Depression,* 187.

18. William Broonzy and Yannick Bruynoghe, *Big Bill Blues: William Broonzy's Story as Told to Yannick Bruynoghe* (New York: Da Capo Press, 1992), 85.

19. Big Bill Broonzy, "Black, Brown and White," *The Mercury Blues 'N' Rhythm Story 1945–1955,* Mercury CD 314-528-294-2, 1996.

20. Ibid.

21. Drake and Cayton, *Black Metropolis,* 84; E. Franklin Frazier, "Some Effects of the Depression on the Negro in Northern Cities," *Science and Society* 2, no. 4 (Fall 1938): 489–99.

22. McElvaine, *Great Depression,* 188; Sitkoff, *New Deal,* 37.

23. Broonzy, "Stuff They Call Money," *Big Bill Broonzy. Vol. 6.*

24. Big Bill Broonzy, "Made a Date with an Angel," *Big Bill Broonzy. Vol. 7 (13 October 1937 to 15 September 1938),* Austria: Document DOCD-5129, n.d.

25. Drake and Cayton, *Black Metropolis*, 75; Paul Oliver, *Blues Fell This Morning*, Canto ed. (Cambridge: Cambridge University Press, 1994), 119–20; Wayland D. Hand, "'The Fear of Gods': Superstition and Popular Belief," in *Our Living Traditions: An Introduction to American Folklore*, ed. Tristram Potter Coffin (New York: Basic Books, 1968), 216–19.

26. Broonzy, "I Wonder What's Wrong with Me," *Big Bill Broonzy. Vol. 10*.

27. St. Clair Drake and Horace Cayton, "The Churches of Bronzeville," in *Afro-American Religious History*, ed. Milton Sernett (Durham: Duke University Press, 1985), 351–57; E. Franklin Frazier, "The Negro Church and Assimilation," in *Afro-American Religious History*, 367–68; Cone, "Blues: Secular," 126–27.

28. Broonzy, "Dying Day Blues," *Big Bill Broonzy. Vol. 2*.

29. Cone, "Blues: Secular," 116.

30. Oliver, *Blues Fell*, 158–61.

31. Big Bill Broonzy, "Good Liquor Gonna Carry Me Down," *Big Bill Broonzy. Vol. 4 (3 July 1935 to 22 April 1936)*, Austria: Document DOCD-5126, n.d.

32. Drake and Cayton, *Black Metropolis*, 595–99.

33. Ibid.; Oliver, *Blues Fell*, 174–75.

34. Big Bill Broonzy, "You Can't Sell 'Em in Here," *Big Bill Broonzy. Vol. 8 (15 September 1938 to 10 February 1939)*, Austria: Document DOCD-5130, n.d.

35. McElvaine, *Great Depression*, 174; Robert McElvaine, *Down and Out in the Great Depression: Letters from the "Forgotten Man"* (Chapel Hill: University of North Carolina Press, 1983), 89.

36. Sitkoff, *New Deal*, 37–38.

37. Big Bill Broonzy, "Police Station Blues," *Big Bill Broonzy. Vol. 1 (November 1927 to 9 February 1932)*, Austria: Document DOCD-5050, 1991.

38. Nolan Welsh, "The Birdwell Blues," Louis Armstrong, *The Genuis of Louis Armstrong, vol. 1: 1923–1933*, John Hammond Collection, Columbia G30416, n.d.

39. Broonzy, "They Can't Do That," *Big Bill Broonzy, vol. 1*.

40. Drake and Cayton, *Black Metropolis*, 202–9.

41. Ibid., 576–77; Richard Wright, *12 Million Black Voices* (New York: Thunder's Mouth Press, 1944), 106–8.

42. McElvaine, *Great Depression*, 170–74.

43. Broonzy, "Pneumonia Blues," *Big Bill Broonzy. Vol. 4*.

44. Broonzy, "Sad Letter Blues," *Big Bill Broonzy. Vol. 7*.

45. Big Bill Broonzy, "Going Back to My Plow," *Big Bill Broonzy. Vol. 11 (17 December 1940 to 6 March 1942)*, Austria: Document DOCD-5133, n.d.

46. Drake and Cayton, *Black Metropolis*, 743–44.

47. McElvaine, *Great Depression*, 138–55.

48. Ibid., 188–89; Kirby, *Black Americans*, 101–3.

49. Watkins, *Great Depression: America*, 14–17.

50. Mitchell, *Great Depression*, 200–201.

51. Ibid., 316–18.

52. Guido van Rijn, *Roosevelt's Blues* (Jackson: University Press of Mississippi, 1997), 69–72.

53. Joe Pullum, "CWA Blues," *Vol. 1 (1935–1935)*, Document DOCD-5393, n.d.

54. Mitchell, *Great Depression*, 319–24; van Rijn, *Roosevelt's Blues*, 80–81.

55. Broonzy and Bruynoghe, *Big Bill*, 93.

56. Ibid.

57. Ibid., 94–95.

58. Broonzy, Bill. "W.P.A. Rag," *Big Bill Broonzy. Vol. 7*.

59. McElvaine, *Great Depression*, 193–94.

60. Drake and Cayton, *Black Metropolis*, 214–21.

61. Mitchell, *Great Depression*, 322.

62. Peetie Wheatstraw, "Working on the Project," *Peetie Wheatstraw Complete Recorded Works in Chronological Order*, Document vol. 5, DOCD-5245, n.d.

63. Mitchell, *Great Depression*, 328–30.

64. Donald Spivey, *Union and the Black Musicians: The Narrative of William Everett Samuels and Chicago Local 208* (Lanham, Md.: University Press of America, 1984), 52–56.

65. Ibid., 52–56, 102; Robert D. Leiter, *The Musicians and Petrillo* (New York: Bookman, 1953), 43, 51.

66. Leiter, *Musicians and Petrillo*, 61–64; Mitchell, *Great Depression*, 327–28.

67. Spivey, *Union*, 58–60.

68. Peetie Wheatstraw, "Chicago Mill Blues," *The Last Straw*, http://music.aol.com/album/the-last-straw.

"Done Got Wise"

1. Raymond Williams, *The Sociology of Culture* (Chicago: University of Chicago Press, 1981), 228.

2. Michael W. Harris, *The Rise of Gospel Blues: The Music of Thomas Andrew Dorsey in the Urban Church* (Oxford: Oxford University Press, 1992), 48–51; Paul Oliver, "Blues," *The New Grove Gospel, Blues and Jazz* (New York: Norton, 1986), 79; Paul Oliver, "Gospel," ibid., 199–200.

3. Michael Harris, *Rise of Gospel*, 148–49; David Jasen, *Spreadin' Rhythm Around: Black Popular Songwriters, 1880–1930* (New York: Schirmer Books, 1998), 324.

4. Giles Oakley, *The Devil's Music* (New York: Da Capo Press, 1997), 162.

5. Lester Melrose, "My Life in Recording," *American Folk Music Occasional* 2 (1970): 59.

6. Melrose, "My Life," 59–61; Mike Rowe, *Chicago Breakdown* (New York: Da Capo Press, 1975), 17–20.

7. Robert M. W. Dixon et al., *Blues and Gospel Records, 1890–1943* (Oxford: Clarendon Press, 1997), xxxii; Robert M. W. Dixon and John Godrich, *Recording the Blues* (New York: Stein and Day, 1970), 67.

8. Big Bill Broonzy, "Baby, I Done Got Wise," in *Selections from the Gutter: Jazz Portraits from "The Jazz Record,"* ed. Art Hodes and Chadwick Hanson (Berkeley and Los Angeles: University of California Press, 1977), 58.

9. Dixon and Godrich, *Recording*, 64–67; Arnold Shaw, *Honkers and Shakers: The Golden Years of Rhythm & Blues* (New York: Collier Books, 1978), 11–12.

10. Paul Oliver, "Sales Tax on It: Race Records in the New Deal Years," in *Nothing Else to Fear: New Perspectives on America in the Thirties*, ed. Stephen W. Baskerville and Ralph Willett (Dover: Manchester University Press, 1985), 199–200.

11. Rowe, *Chicago Breakdown*, 43; Robert Gordon, *Can't Be Satisfied: The Life and Times of Muddy Waters* (New York: Little, Brown, 2002), 95.

12. Broonzy, "Baby, I Done," 59.

13. Dixon, *Recording*, 70–71, 78.

14. Ibid., 80.

15. Elijah Wald, *Escaping the Delta: Robert Johnson and the Invention of the Blues* (New York: Amistad, 2005), 41.

16. William Howland Kenney, "African American Blues and the Phonograph," in *Recorded Music*

in American Life: The Phonograph and Popular Memory, 1890–1945 (New York: Oxford University Press, 1999), 112–20; 131–32.

17. Melrose, "My Life," 60.

18. Bob Koester, "Lester Melrose: An Appreciation," *American Folk Music Occasional* 2 (1970): 58.

19. Shaw, *Honkers*, 23–24.

20. Broonzy, "Baby, I Done," 59; Bob Hall and Richard Noblett, liner notes, *Leroy Carr 1930–1935, The Piano Blues,* Magpie PYCD 07.

21. Paul Oliver, *The Story of the Blues* (Boston: Northeastern University Press, 1997), 128; Rowe, *Chicago Breakdown,* 21.

22. Wald, *Escaping,* xiii–xxiv.

23. Koester, "Lester Melrose," 58.

24. Bumble Bee Slim, "Policy Dream Blues," *Bumble Bee Slim (Amos Easton) 1934–1937,* Blues Document BoB-9, n.d.

25. Jazz Gillum, "Reefer Head Woman," *Bill "Jazz" Gillum (1938–1949): "Roll Dem Bones,"* Wolf Blues Jewels, WBJ-002, n.d.

26. Big Bill Broonzy and Yannick Bruynoghe, *Big Bill Blues: William Broonzy's Story as Told to Yannick Bruynoghe* (New York: Da Capo Press, 1992), 145–49.

27. Alan Lomax, *The Land Where the Blues Began* (New York: Pantheon Books, 1993), 446.

28. Donald Spivey, *Union and the Black Musicians: The Narrative of William Everett Samuels and Chicago Local 208* (Lanham, Md.: University Press of America, 1984), 92–93.

29. Kenney, "African American Blues," 133–34.

30. Big Bill Broonzy and Yannick Bruynoghe, "Who Got the Money?" *Living Blues,* no. 55 (November/December 1982): 21; Rowe, *Chicago,* 17.

31. Broonzy and Bruynoghe, "The Money," 21.

32. Oliver, *Story,* 128; Rowe, *Chicago,* 23.

33. Dixon, *Recording,* 77–78.

34. Broonzy, "Baby I Done," 60.

35. Ibid.

36. Broonzy and Bruynoghe, *Big Bill,* 124–26, 136.

37. Broonzy, *Big Bill,* 112–15; Paul Oliver, "Big Maceo," in *The Art of Jazz,* ed. Martin Williams (New York: Oxford Press, 1959), 117.

38. Paul Oliver, *Blues Off the Record: Thirty Years of Blues Commentary* (New York: Da Capo Press, 1988), 113.

39. Roger D. Abrahams, "Trickster, the Outrageous Hero," in *Our Living Traditions: An Introduction to American Folklore,* ed. Tristram Potter Coffin (New York: Basic Books, 1968), 174–76.

40. John Hammond, *On Record* (New York: Summit Books, 1977), 199–200; Elijah Wald, *Josh White: Society Blues* (Amherst: University of Massachusetts Press, 2000), 58.

41. Harold Cruse, *The Crisis of the Negro Intellectual* (New York: William Morrow, 1967), 83–85.

42. Robert Cantwell, *When We Were Good: The Folk Revival* (Cambridge: Harvard University Press, 1996), 68; Wald, *Josh,* 58.

43. Hammond, *On Record,* 202.

44. Cantwell, *When We,* 65–66.

45. Wald, *Josh,* 59.

46. Big Bill Broonzy, "Truth about the Blues," *Living Blues,* no. 55 (November/December 1982): 19; Stanley Dance, "The Perennial Blues," *Saturday Review,* May 11, 1957, 35.

47. Broonzy and Bruynoghe, *Big Bill,* 97.

48. Hammond, *On Record*, 206.

49. Broonzy, "Truth About," 19.

50. Paytress, *I Was There*, 14.

51. Robert D. Leiter, *The Musicians and Petrillo* (New York: Bookman, 1953), 68–71, 132.

52. Broonzy and Bruynoghe, *Big Bill*, 112.

53. Gordon, *Can't Be*, 71, 315.

6. Blacks, Whites, and Blues

1. Paul Oliver, "Blues to Drive the Blues Away, in *Jazz*, ed. Nat Hentoff and Albert J. McCarthy (New York: Da Capo Press, 1974), 101–2.

2. Big Bill Broonzy, *Big Bill Broonzy. Vol. 12 (1945–1947)*, Austria: Document BDCD-6047, 1993.

3. Dick Shurman et al., introduction to CD booklet, *The Mercury Blues 'N' Rhythm Story: 1945–1955*, Mercury 3145282932, 1996, 4–7.

4. Jim O'Neal, "It's Just the Blues," in CD booklet, *The Mercury Blues 'N' Rhythm Story: 1945–1955*, Mercury 3145282932, 1996, 19–20.

5. Robert March (Chicago acquaintance of Big Bill Broonzy) to author, e-mail, June 1, 2009.

6. Ibid.

7. Robert Gordon, *Can't Be Satisfied: The Life and Times of Muddy Waters* (New York: Little, Brown, 2002), 110.

8. Benjamin Filene, *Romancing the Folk: Public Memory & American Roots Music* (Chapel Hill: University of North Carolina Press, 2000), 39–40, 49.

9. Elijah Wald, *Josh White: Society Blues* (Amherst: University of Massachusetts, 2000), 56, 65, 74; Filene, *Romancing*, 113.

10. Alan Lomax, *Blues in the Mississippi Night—The Story of the Recording*, CD booklet, *Blues in the Mississippi Night: Authentic Field Recordings of Negro Folk Music*, USA: Rykodisc, RCD 90155, 1990.

11. Filene, *Romancing*, 92.

12. Lomax, *Blues*.

13. Wald, *Josh*, 74.

14. Lomax, *Blues*.

15. Over the next fifty years, Lomax drew upon the interviews for articles, radio programs, a book, and a CD release. He used material from the interview at the New York Folklore Society in 1947; in a 1948 article entitled "I Got the Blues" for *Common Ground*; and in radio programs for the BBC in 1950. In 1959, he released the session on the album *Blues in the Mississippi Night*. In the 1990, the album was reissued on CD, Lomax revealed the identity of the participants. In 1993, he used information from his interviews with Broonzy in *Land Where the Blues Began*.

16. Big Bill Broonzy and Yannick Bruynoghe, *Big Bill Blues: William Broonzy's Story as Told to Yannick Bruynoghe* (New York: Da Capo Press, 1992), 34.

17. Broonzy and Bruynoghe, *Big Bill*, 34; Robert March (Chicago acquaintance of Big Bill Broonzy and labor historian) to author, e-mail, June 1, 2009.

18. "Do You Remember . . . Big Bill Broonzy?" *Negro Digest* 9, August 1951, 25; "Meet Bill Broonzy," *Melody Maker*, August 11, 1951, 9.

19. Wald, *Josh*, 75; Filene, *Romancing*, 69, 163, 190; Pete Seeger (folk musician and acquaintance of Big Bill Broonzy), interview by the author, March 13, 2000.

20. Wald, *Josh*, 75.

21. Seeger interview.

22. Broonzy and Bruynoghe, *Big Bill*, 83.

23. Broonzy continued to perform "Black, Brown and White" in folk and blues concerts, using it to raise the consciousness of white audiences. However, it was not recorded until 1951, when the French label Vogue released it for European audiences. Broonzy recorded it again for Vogue in 1952; for the Dutch label Black & Blues in 1952; and for the Danish label Savoy in 1956. Meanwhile, in the United States, Mercury Records would record "Black, Brown and White" in 1951 (but withhold it for several years before releasing it on an LP). Folkways recorded it in 1956 in the aftermath of the U.S. Supreme Court decision in *Brown v. Board of Education* in 1954 and the bus boycott led by the Rev. Martin Luther King and the Montgomery Improvement Association in Montgomery, Alabama, in 1955.

24. Studs Terkel (Chicago radio host, historian, and acquaintance of Big Bill Broonzy), interview by the author, May 30, 2002.

25. Ibid.

26. Broonzy and Bruynoghe, *Big Bill*, 87–88.

27. Ibid., 82.

28. LeRoi Jones, *Blues People* (New York: William Morrow, 1963), 121.

29. Terkel interview, May 30, 2002.

30. "Meet Bill Broonzy," *Melody Maker*, August 11, 1951, 9.

31. March to the author, e-mail, June 1, 2009.

32. Filene, *Romancing*, 118.

33. Bill Randle, liner notes, *The Bill Broonzy Story*, USA: Verve MGV3000-5, 1999; Hugues Panassié, "Big Bill Doesn't Sell His Music—He Gives It Away," *Melody Maker*, September 15, 1951, 9; Seeger interview.

34. "Meet Big Bill," *Melody Maker*.

35. Scott Hreha, "Certain Blacks Dig They Freedom" (Ph.D. dissertation, University of Minnesota, June 1997).

36. "Big Bill Sings Farewell to London," *Melody Maker*, September 29, 1951, 12.

37. Ernest Borneman, "Big Bill Talkin'," *Melody Maker*, September 29, 1951, 11.

38. Don Gold, "Big Bill Broonzy," *Down Beat*, February 6, 1958, 15–16.

39. Derrick Stewart-Baxter, "Preachin' the Blues," *Jazz Journal* 4, no.10 (October 1951): 3.

40. Humphrey Lyttelton (British jazz musician and acquaintance of Big Bill Broonzy), interviewed in *Red, White, and Blues*, dir. Mike Figgis, *Martin Scorsese Presents the Blues: A Musical Journey*, Sony Music, 2003.

41. Panassié, "Big Bill Doesn't Sell His Music," 9.

42. Ibid.

43. Max Jones, "Big Bill Broonzy: Kingsway Hall, London, Recital," untitled notes for London Jazz Club Program, September 22, 1951, 2.

44. Borneman, "Big Bill Talkin'," 11; M. Jones, "Big Bill Broonzy: Kingsway," 3.

45. Derrick Stewart-Baxter, "Preachin' the Blues," *Jazz Journal* 4, no.11 (November 1951): 13.

46. Paul Oliver (blues historian and acquaintance of Big Bill Broonzy), interview by the author, February 8, 2007.

47. Stewart-Baxter, "Preachin'," 13.

48. Borneman, "Big Bill Talkin'," 11.

49. Stewart-Baxter, "Preachin'," 13; Borneman, "Big Bill Talkin'," 11.

50. Lyttelton, interview in *Red, White, and Blues*.

51. Humphrey Lyttleton, "I'm Sorry," BBC News, www.bbc.co.uk.

52. George Melly (British jazz writer and acquaintance of Big Bill Broonzy), interview in *Red, White, and Blues.*

53. Gold, "Big Bill," 15–16; "Big Bill Sings," *Melody Maker,* 12.

54. Oliver interview.

55. Big Bill Broonzy to Win Stracke, letter titled "THIS IS WHAT MR HERBERT WILCOX DON TO BIG BILL," January 24, 1953.

56. Big Bill Broonzy to Win Stracke, undated postcard from Algeria, 1953.

57. Eric Clapton and John Mayall (British blues musicians), interviews in *Red, White, and Blues.*

58. Alexis Korner, "Big Bill Broonzy: Some Personal Memories," *Jazz Journal* 11, no.3 (March 1958): 1; Gordon, *Can't,* 157–58.

59. Broonzy to Stracke.

60. Big Bill Broonzy, "Jacqueline," *Big Bill Broonzy: House Rent Stomp,* Blues Encore CD 52007 AAD, 1990.

61. Steve James, "Big Bill Broonzy—A Life in Europe," www.broonzy.com.

62. Broonzy and Bruynoghe, *Big Bill,* 70.

63. Broonzy, *Big Bill,* 9; Jim O'Neal, "Big Bill: Opening the Door to the Blues," *Living Blues,* no.55 (November/December 1982): 4.

64. Broonzy and Bruynoghe, *Big Bill,* 9.

65. Yannick Bruynoghe, "In Chicago with Big Bill and Friends: Chicago Scrapbook Excerpts," *Living Blues,* no. 55 (November/December 1982): 9–10.

66. *Big Bill Broonzy and Roosevelt Sykes,* dir. Jean De Lire, *Masters of the Country Blues,* Yazoo 518, 1995; Bruynoghe, "In Chicago," 9–10; Jean De Lire, www.imdb.com/name/nm0217209.

67. Max Jones, "The Last of a Line," *Melody Maker,* August 23, 1958, 12.

7. Final Days

1. Big Bill Broonzy and Yannick Bruynoghe, *Big Bill Blues: William Broonzy's Story as Told to Yannick Bruynoghe* (New York: Da Capo Press, 1992), 131; "500 Pounds 'Blues' for Broonzy," *Melody Maker,* August 23, 1958, 1.

2. Bill Randle, liner notes, *The Bill Broonzy Story,* USA: Verve MGV3000-5, 1999; Cal Herrmann, *Collection of Folk Music Concert Recordings,* Library of Congress Archive of Folk Culture, 1956–57.

3. Robert March (Chicago acquaintance of Big Bill Broonzy and labor historian) to author, e-mail, June 1, 2009; Cal Hermmann, *Collection of Folk Music Concert Recordings,* Library of Congress Archive of Folk Culture, 1956–57 .

4. Don Gold, "Big Bill Benefit Concert," *Down Beat,* January 9, 1958, 37–38; March to the author, e-mail message.

5. Gold, "Big Bill Benefit," 37–38.

6. *Biography of a Hunch,* booklet, Old Town School of Folk Music, Chicago, n.d., 8.

7. Yannick Bruynoghe, "Chicago," *Blues News,* www.blues.co.nz.

8. Gold, "Big Bill Benefit," 18; B. Asbell, "The Whisper of Big Bill Broonzy," *Melody Maker,* February 6, 1958, 13.

9. Tony Brown, "Well Done!" *Melody Maker,* March 15, 1958, 3.

10. "500 Pounds," 1.

11. Randle, *Bill Broonzy Story.*

12. Don Gold, "Tangents," *Down Beat,* October 2, 1958, 42; Sandra Tooze, *Muddy Waters: The Mojo Man* (Toronto: ECW Press, 1997), photo plate, n.p.; Robert Gordon, *Can't Be Satisfied: The Life and Times of Muddy Waters* (New York: Little, Brown), 338.

13. John F. Szwed, "Negro Music: Urban Renewal," *Our Living Traditions: An Introduction to American Folklore,* ed. Tristram Potter Coffin (New York: Basic Books, 1968), 275–82.

Discography

1. Robert Gordon, *Can't Be Satisfied,* 164–65.

BIBLIOGRAPHY

Books, Periodicals, Online Sources

Abrahams, Roger D. "Trickster, the Outrageous Hero." In *Our Living Traditions: An Intro-duction to American Folklore*, edited by Tristram Potter Coffin, 170–78. New York: Basic Books, 1968.

Arnaudon, Jean-Claude. *Dictionnaire du blues.* Paris: Filipacchi, 1977.

Asbell, B. "The Whisper of Big Bill Broonzy." *Melody Maker*, February 6, 1958, 13.

Astbury, Ray. "Big Bill Broonzy on Archive of Folk Music." *Matrix*, December 1969, 11.

Baggelaar, Kristin, and Donald Milton. *Folk Music: More Than a Song.* New York: Crom-well, 1976.

Balliett, Whitney. "Billie, Big Bill, and Jelly Roll." *Saturday Review*, July 14, 1956, 32–33.

Barbeau, Arthur E, and Florette Henri. *Unknown Soldiers: Black American Troops in World War I.* Philadelphia: Temple University Press, 1974.

Barlow, William. *Looking up at Down.* Philadelphia: Temple University Press, 1989.

"Best of the Blues." *Time*, September 1, 1958, 39.

"Big Bill Blues." *Sing Out!* 7, no. 1 (Spring 1957): 22–23.

"Big Bill Broonzy." *Down Beat*, September 18, 1958, 11.

"Big Bill Broonzy." *Sing Out!* 8, no. 3 (Winter 1959): 31.

"Big Bill Broonzy." *Variety*, August 29, 1958, 79.

"Big Bill Broonzy Benefit Concert." *Down Beat*, January 9, 1958, 37–38.

"Big Bill Sings Farewell to London." *Melody Maker*, September 29, 1951, 12.

"'Bill Broonzy Story Set a Standout Contribution to History of the Blues." *Variety*, June 21, 1961, 51.

Biography of a Hunch. Old Town School of Folk Music. Pamphlet. Chicago, n.d.

"Black Housing." In *The Black Urban Condition: A Documentary History, 1866–1971*, ed-ited by Hollis Lynch, 127–28. New York: Thomas Y. Crowell, 1973. Originally pub-lished as Sophonisba P. Breckinridge, "The Color Line in the Housing Problem," *Survey*, February 1, 1913, 575.

Bogaert, Karel. *Blues Lexicon.* Antwerpen: Standaard Uitgeverig, 1971.

Borneman, Ernest. "Big Bill Talkin.'" *Melody Maker,* September 29, 1951, 11.

Botto, Silvia. "Blues Memories: I primi concerti di blues in Italia: II soggiorno italiano di Big Bill Broonzy." *Feelin' Good,* no. 11 (1987): 20–26.

Bourgoin, Suzanne M., ed. *Contemporary Musicians: Profiles of the People in Music.* Detroit: Gale Research, 1995.

Briggs, Keith. Liner notes. *Sonny Boy Williamson.* Document vol. 4, DOCD 5058. 1991.

"Broonzy." *Jazz Journal* 5, no.3 (March 1952): 8–9.

Broonzy, Big Bill. "Baby, I Done Got Wise." In *Selections from the Gutter: Jazz Portraits from "The Jazz Record,"* edited by Art Hodes and Chadwick Hanson, 58. Berkeley and Los Angeles: University of California Press, 1977. Originally published in *Jazz Record,* March 1946, 9–12.

———. Interview by Alan Lomax. 1942. Chicago. (Transcript courtesy of The Alan Lomax Collection. The Association for Cultural Equity at Hunter College, New York)

———. "It Was Born in Us to Sing the Blues." *Melody Maker,* August 27, 1955, 3, 13.

———. "Ménage à trois." *Jazz Magazine,* no.8, 1955, 24.

———. "A 19th Century Blues Session." *Melody Maker,* September 3, 1955, 5.

———. "'No Drinking Here,' Said the Club Boss." *Melody Maker,* September 17, 1955, 7.

———, to Alan Lomax. April, 11, 1953. (Courtesy of Alan Lomax Archive, Hunter College, New York)

———, to Win Stracke. Letter titled "THIS IS WHAT MR HERBERT WILCOX DON TO BIG BILL." January 24, 1953. (Courtesy Old Town School of Folk Music, Chicago)

———. "Truth about the Blues." *Living Blues,* no. 55 (November/December 1982): 17–20.

———. "Work Songs on the Yellow Dog." *Melody Maker,* September 24, 1955, 5.

Broonzy, Big Bill, and Yannick Bruynoghe. *Big Bill Blues: William Broonzy's Story as Told to Yannick Bruynoghe.* 1955. New York: Da Capo Press, 1992.

———. "Who Got the Money?" *Living Blues,* no. 55 (November/December 1982): 21.

"Broonzy and Sellers Welcomed by Barber." *Melody Maker,* February 23, 1957, 14.

Brown, Sterling. "Negro Folk Expression: Spirituals, Seculars, Ballads and Work Songs." In *A Son's Return,* edited by Mark Sanders. Boston: Northeastern University Press, 1996.

Brown, Tony. "Well Done!" *Melody Maker,* March 15, 1958, 3.

Bruin, Leo. "Big Bill Broonzy in Nederland." *Block,* no. 76 (1990): 25–27.

Bruynoghe, Yannick. "Big Bill." In *This Is Jazz,* edited by Ken Williamson. London: Newnes, 1960.

———. "Chicago." *Blues News.* www.blues.co.nz.

———. "Chicago, Home of the Blues." In *Just Jazz 2,* edited by Sinclair Traill and Gerald Lascelles. London: Peter Davis, 1958.

———. "In Chicago with Big Bill and Friends: Chicago Scrapbook Excerpts." *Living Blues,* no. 55 (November/December 1982): 6–16.

———. "Mes blues, ma guitare et moi: Les souvenirs de Big Bill Broonzy." Part 1. *Jazz Magazine*, January 1959, 37–39; Part 2. *Jazz Magazine*, February 1959, 32–34; Part 3. *Jazz Magazine*, March 1959, 22–25; Part 4. *Jazz Magazine*, May 1959, 27.

Bruynoghe,Yannick, and Stanley Dance. "The Perennial Blues." *Saturday Review*, May 11, 1957, 35.

"Business in Bronzeville." In *The Black Urban Condition: A Documentary History, 1866–1971*, edited by Hollis Lynch, 267–68. New York: Thomas Y. Crowell, 1973. Originally published in *Time*, April 18, 1938, 70, 72.

Calt, Stephen, Nick Perls, and Mike Stewart. Liner notes. *The Young Big Bill Broonzy 1928–1935*. Yazoo L-1011. 1990.

Cantwell, Robert. *When We Were Good: The Folk Revival*. Cambridge: Harvard University Press, 1996.

Carby, Hazel. ""It Jus Be's Dat Way Sometime": The Sexual Politics of Women's Blues." In *Unequal Sisters: A Multicultural Reader in U.S. Women's History*, edited by Ellen Carol DuBois and Vicki Ruiz. New York: Routledge, 1990. Originally published in *Radical America* 20, no. 4 (1986).

Case, Brian, et al. *The Illustrated Encyclopedia of Jazz*. New York: Harmony Books, 1978.

"Charity Concert in March." *Melody Maker*, August 23, 1958, 2.

Charters, Samuel. "Big Bill Broomsley." *Country Blues*. New York: Rinehart, 1959.

———. *The Bluesmakers*. 1967. New York: Da Capo Press. 1991.

———. *Country Blues*. With a new introduction by the author. New York: Da Capo Press. 1975.

Chicago Commission on Race Relations. "The Truth about the North." In *Black Protest and the Great Migration*, edited by Eric Arnesen, 67–72. Boston: Bedford/St. Martin's, 2003. Originally published in *The Negro in Chicago: A Study of Race Relations and a Riot*, 93–97 (Chicago: University of Chicago Press, 1922).

"Chronique des disques: Portrait in Blues." *Jazz Hot* 38, no. 282 (April 1972): 24.

Clarke, Donald. *The Penguin Encyclopedia of Popular Music*. London and New York: Penguin Books, 1998.

Coffin, Tristram Potter, and Hennig Cohen, eds. *Folklore: From the Working Folk of America*. New York: Anchor Books, 1974.

Cohen, Lizabeth. *Making a New Deal: Industrial Workers in Chicago, 1919–1939*. Cambridge: Cambridge University Press, 1990.

Coller, Derek. "Big Bill Broonzy." *Matrix*, March 1961, 3–6.

Cone, James H. "The Blues: A Secular Spiritual." In *Write Me a Few of Your Lines: A Blues Reader*, edited by Steven C. Tracey, 231–51. Amherst: University of Massachusetts Press, 1999. Originally published in James H. Cone, *The Spirituals and the Blues* (New York: Seabury Press, 1972).

Courlander, Harold. *Negro Folk Music USA*. New York: Columbia University Press, 1963.

Cressant, Pierre. "Big Bill Broonzy." *Jazz Hot*, no. 59 (1951): 17.

Cruse, Harold. *The Crisis of the Negro Intellectual*. New York: William Morrow, 1967.

Dalton, James. "Big Bill and the Blues." *Blues Revue Quarterly*, no. 13 (Summer 1994): 52–54.

Dance, Stanley, ed. *Jazz Era: The Forties*. New York: Da Capo Press, 1988.

———. *The World of Swing: An Oral History of Big Band Jazz*. New York: Da Capo Press, 1974.

Daniel, Peter. *The Shadow of Slavery: Peonage in the South, 1901–1969*. Urbana: University of Illinois Press, 1972.

Dauer, Alfons M., and Stephen Longstreet. *Knaurs Jazz Lexikon*. Munich: Th. Knaur Nachfolger, 1957.

Davis, Angela. *Blues Legacies and Black Feminism*. New York: Vintage Books, 1999.

DeMichael, Don. Liner notes. *The Genius of Louis Armstrong, Vol. 1: 1923–1933*. Columbia G30416, n.d.

Dicaire, David. "Big Bill Broonzy: Keys to the Highway." In *Blues Singers: Biographies of 50 Legendary Artists of the 20th Century*, 64–68. Jefferson, N.C.: McFarland, 1999.

Dick, Bruce. "Richard Wright and the Blues Connection." *Mississippi Quarterly* 42 (Fall 1989): 393–408.

Dixon, Robert M. W., and John Godrich. *Recording the Blues*. New York: Stein and Day, 1970.

Dixon, Robert M.W., et al. *Blues and Gospel Records, 1890–1943*. Oxford: Clarendon Press, 1997.

"Do You Remember . . . Big Bill Broonzy?" *Negro Digest*, August 1951, 25–26.

Douglass, Frederick. *Narrative of the Life of Frederick Douglass*. Boston: Bedford Books, 1993.

Drake, St. Clair, and Horace Cayton. *Black Metropolis: A Study of Negro Life in a Northern City*. New York: Harcourt, Brace, 1945.

———. "The Churches of Bronzeville." In *Afro-American Religious History*. edited by Milton Sernett, 349–63. Durham: Duke University Press, 1985. Originally published in Drake and Cayton, *Black Metropolis: A Study of Negro Life in a Northern City*, 412–29 (New York: Harcourt, Brace, 1945).

———. "Life in Bronzeville." In *The Black Urban Condition: A Documentary History, 1866–1971*, edited by Hollis Lynch, 348–50. New York: Thomas Y. Crowell, 1973. Originally published as "Black Metropolis." *Negro Digest*, December 1945, 74–82.

Du Bois, W. E. B. "Of the Faith of the Fathers." In *Afro-American Religious History: A Documentary Witness*, edited by Milton Sernett, 309–19. Durham: Duke University Press, 1985. Originally published in Du Bois, *The Souls of Black Folk*, 189–206 (New York: Kraus-Thomson Organization, 1973).

———. *The Souls of Black Folk*. New York: Dover, 1994.

Dunbar, Ernest. *The Black Expatriates*. New York: Dutton, 1968.

Dunbar, Paul Laurence. "The Corn-Stalk Fiddle." In *Lyrics of Lowly Life*. New York: Dodd, Mead, 1896. Paul Laurence Dunbar Digital Text Collection of Wright College. www.libraries.wright.edu/dunbar.

———. "The Party." In *Dark Symphony, Negro Literature in America*, edited by James A. Emanuel and Theodore L. Gross. New York: Free Press, 1968.

Eagle, Bob. "Blues Forum." *Talking Blues*, July–September 1976.

Edwards, David "Honeyboy." *The World Don't Owe Me Nothing: The Life and Times of Delta Bluesman Honeyboy Edwards.* As told to Janis Martinson and Michael Robert Frank. Chicago: Chicago Review Press, 1997.

Epstein, Dena J. *Sinful Tunes and Spirituals: Black Folk Music to the Civil War.* Urbana: University of Illinois Press, 1977.

Evans, David. *Big Road Blues.* Berkeley and Los Angeles: University of California Press, 1982.

"Excerpts from Big Bill's Letters to Yannick Bruynoghe." *Living Blues*, no. 55 (November/December 1982): 22–23.

Fantasia, Rick. *Cultures of Solidarity: Consciousness, Action, and Contemporary American Workers.* Berkeley and Los Angeles: University of California Press, 1988.

Fassio, Edoardo. "Big Bill Broonzy." *Il Blues*, no. 53 (1995): 14–20.

Feather, Leonard, ed. *The New Edition of the Encyclopedia of Jazz.* New York: Horizon Press, 1960.

Federighi, Luciano. "I due volti di un grande bluesman: Big Bill Broonzy." *Feelin' Good*, no. 30 (1990): 26–37.

Ferris, William. *Blues from the Delta.* New York: Da Capo Press, 1978.

Filene, Benjamin. *Romancing the Folk: Public Memory & American Roots Music.* Chapel Hill: University of North Carolina Press, 2000.

"Five Feet Seven." *Bulletin Du Hot Club De France*, March 1966, 11–12.

"500 Pounds 'Blues' for Broonzy." *Melody Maker*, August 23, 1958, 1.

Floyd, Samuel A., Jr. *The Power of Black Music.* New York: Oxford University Press, 1995.

Foner, Eric. *A Short History of Reconstruction.* New York: Harper and Row, 1990.

Frazier, E. Franklin. "The Negro Church and Assimiliation." In *Afro-American Religious History*, edited by Milton Sernett, 364–78. Durham: Duke University Press, 1985. Originally published in Frazier, *The Negro Church in America*.

———. *The Negro Church in America.* New York: Schocken Books, 1974.

———. "Some Effects of the Depression on the Negro in Northern Cities." *Science and Society* 2, no. 4 (Fall 1938): 489–99.

Fulmer, Douglas. "String Band Traditions." *American Visions*, April/May 1995, 46.

"A Gallery of the Greats." *B.M.I.: The Many Worlds Of Music*, no. 1 (1973): 3–13.

Garon, Paul. *Blues & the Poetic Spirit.* New York: Da Capo Press, 1978.

Gold, Don. "Big Bill Benefit Concert." *Down Beat*, January 9, 1958, 37–38.

———. "Big Bill Broonzy." *Down Beat*, February 6, 1958, 15–16, 38–39.

———. "Tangents." *Down Beat*, October 2, 1958, 42.

Goldmann, Lucien. *Cultural Creation.* St. Louis: Telos Press, 1976.

Gordon, Robert. *Can't Be Satisfied: The Life and Times of Muddy Waters.* New York: Little, Brown, 2002.

Gosnell, Harold. *Negro Politicians: The Rise of Negro Politics in Chicago.* Chicago: University of Chicago Press, 1967.

Green, Adam. *Selling the Race: Culture, Community, and Black Chicago, 1940-1955.* Chicago: University of Chicago Press, 2009.

Griffin, Farah Jasmine. *"Who Set You Flowin'?": The African-American Migration Narrative.* New York: Oxford University Press, 1995.

Groom, Bob. "Big Bill Broonzy." *Blues World,* no. 33 (Autumn 1970): 7–9.

Grossman, James. *Land of Hope: Chicago, Black Southerners, and the Great Migration.* Chicago: University of Chicago Press, 1989.

Grubbs, Donald H. *Cry from the Cotton: The Southern Tenant Farmers' Union and the New Deal.* Chapel Hill: University of North Carolina Press, 1971.

Gutman, Herbert. *The Black Family in Slavery and Freedom, 1750–1925.* New York: Vintage Books, 1977.

Hall, Bob, and Richard Noblett. Liner notes. *Leroy Carr 1930–1935, The Piano Blues.* Magpie PYCD 07, n.d.

Hammond, John. *On Record.* New York: Summit Books, 1977.

Hand, Wayland D. "'The Fear of Gods": Superstition and Popular Belief." In *Our Living Traditions: An Introduction to American Folklore,* edited by Tristram Potter Coffin, 215–27. New York: Basic Books, 1968.

Hardy, Phil, and Dave Laing, eds. *The Encyclopedia of Rock.* New York: Schirmer Books, 1988.

Harris, Michael W. *The Rise of Gospel Blues: The Music of Thomas Andrew Dorsey in the Urban Church.* Oxford: Oxford University Press, 1992.

Harris, Sheldon. *Blues Who's Who.* 5th ed. New Rochelle, N.Y.: Arlington House, 1979.

Harrison, Max. "Boogie-Woogie." In *Jazz,* edited by Nat Hentoff and Albert J. McCarthy, 105–36. New York: Da Capo Press, 1974.

Heckman, Don. "A Gallery of the Greats." *B.M.I.: The Many Worlds Of Music* (Summer 1969): 25.

Heilbroner, Robert, and Aaron Singer. *The Economic Transformation of America, 1600 to the Present* 3rd ed. Fort Worth, Tex.: Harcourt Brace, 1994.

Henderson, Donald. "The Negro Migration, 1916–1918." *Journal of Negro History* 6 (October 1921).

Henri, Florette. *Black Migration: Movement North, 1900–1920,* Garden City, N.Y.: Anchor Press/Doubleday, 1976.

Hentoff, Nat. "A Life in the Blues." *HiFi/Stereo Review* 7 (August 1961): 73.

———. "Wild Bill's Last Date: Bill Broonzy Story." *Reporter* 24 (April 13, 1961): 43–44.

Hentoff, Nat, and Nathan Shapiro, eds. *Hear Me Talkin' to Ya.* 1955. Reprint, New York: Dover, 1966.

Hermans, Sjef, and Erik van Keirsbilck. "Additions and Corrections." *Block,* no. 80 (1991): 23–25.

———. "Big Bill Broonzy: Een blues fundament blootgelegd." *Block,* no.76 (1990): 21–24.

———. "Big Bill Broonzy Discography." *Block,* no. 76 (1990): 1–12.

Herzhaft, Gerard. *Encyclopedia of the Blues.* Fayetteville: University of Arkansas Press, 1992.

Hill, T. Arnold. "Why Southern Negroes Don't Go South." In *Black Protest and the Great Migration,* edited by Eric Arnesen, 184–88. Boston: Bedford/St. Martin's, 2003. Originally published in *Survey* 43, no. 6 (29 November 1919): 183–85.

Hobsbawm, Eric. *The Age of Extremes.* New York: Vintage Books, 1996.

———. *The Age of Revolution.* New York: Mentor Books, 1962.

Hodes, Art. "Big Bill." In *Selections from the Gutter: Jazz Portraits from "The Jazz Record,"* edited by Art Hodes and Chadwick Hanson, 57. Berkeley and Los Angeles: University of California Press, 1977.

———. "Sittin' In." *Down Beat,* April 13, 1961, 44.

Holland, Ted. *This Day in African-American Music.* San Francisco: Pomegranate, 1993.

"How the Arkansas Peons Were Freed." In *Black Protest and the Great Migration,* edited by Eric Arnesen, 177–79. Boston: Bedford/St. Martin's, 2003. Originally published in *Pittsburgh Courier,* July 28, 1923.

Hreha, Scott. "Certain Blacks Dig They Freedom," Ph.D diss., University of Minnesota, June 1997. www.onefinalnote.com/archive/thesis.

Hudtwalcker, Olaf. "Erinnerungen an Big Bill Broonzy." *German Blues Circle Info,* no. 34 (July 1979): 20–22.

Hunton, Addie W., and Katherine M. Johnson. *Two Colored Women with the American Expeditionary Forces.* Brooklyn: Brooklyn Eagle Press, 1920.

Hutton, Jack. "Bill Broonzy Took a Back Seat." *Melody Maker,* November 12, 1955, 3.

———. "Broonzy Farewell." *Melody Maker,* March 16, 1957, 10.

Huyton, Trevor. "Big Bill's Blues." *Matrix,* February 1965, 18–19.

Iseton, Bill. "Big Bill Broonzy: Selected Discography." *Jazzology* 2 (January 1947): 7.

Jackson, Bruce. "The Glory Days of the Lord." In *Our Living Traditions: An Introduction to American Folklore,* edited by Tristram Coffin, 108–19. New York: Basic Books, 1968.

James, Steve. "Big Bill Broonzy—A Life in Europe." www.broonzy.com.

———. "Big Bill's Blues: The Life and Times of Blues Pioneer Big Bill Broonzy." *Acoustic Guitar,* September 2001, n.p.

Jasen, David. *Spreadin' Rhythm Around: Black Popular Songwriters, 1880–1930.* New York: Schirmer Books, 1998.

Johnson, Charles. *Shadow of the Plantation.* Chicago: University of Chicago Press, 1934.

Johnson, Charles S, Edwin R. Embree, and W. W. Alexander. *The Collapse of Cotton Tenancy.* Chapel Hill: University of North Carolina Press, 1935.

Jones, LeRoi. *Blues People.* New York: William Morrow, 1963.

Jones, Max. "Big Bill Broonzy: Kingsway Hall, London, Recital." Notes for London Jazz Club Program. September 22, 1951.

———. "The Last of a Line." *Melody Maker,* August 23, 1958, 12.

———. "Magnificent Seven Blues Singers." *Melody Maker,* January 13, 1968, 8.

————. "Memories of Broonzy." *Melody Maker,* December 6, 1975, 38.

————. "Not Enough of Big Bill." *Melody Maker,* February 23, 1957, 14.

Jones, Max, and Sinclair Traill, eds. "Rosy View of Skiffle." *Melody Maker,* April 6, 1957, 5.

Jones, William. *The Tribe of Black Ulysses: African American Lumber Workers in the Jim Crow South.* Urbana: University of Illinois Press, 2005.

Kahn, H. "They Don't Appreciate Real Blues in France." *Melody Maker,* February 2, 1952, 9.

Karlsson, Ingemar. "Big Bill Broonzy." *Jefferson,* no. 105 (1994): 6–10.

Keil, Charles. *Urban Blues.* Chicago: University of Chicago Press, 1991.

Kelley, Robin D. G. *Hammer and Hoe: Alabama Communists during the Great Depression.* Chapel Hill: University of North Carolina, 1991.

————. "Without a Song: New York Musicians Strike Out against Technology." In *Three Strikes: Miners, Musicians, Salesgirls, and the Fighting Spirit of Labor's Last Century,* edited by Howard Zinn et al., 123–56. Boston: Beacon Press, 2001.

Kenney, William Howland. "African American Blues and the Phonograph." In *Recorded Music in American Life: The Phonograph and Popular Memory, 1890–1945,* 109–34. New York: Oxford University Press, 1999.

————. *Chicago Jazz: A Cultural History, 1904–1930.* New York: Oxford University Press, 1993.

Kinkle, Roger D. *The Complete Encyclopedia of Popular Music and Jazz, 1900–1950.* New Rochelle, N.Y.: Arlington House, 1974.

Kirby, John. *Black Americans in the Roosevelt Era: Liberalism and Race.* Knoxville: University of Tennessee Press, 1980.

Koester, Bob. "Lester Melrose: An Appreciation." *American Folk Music Occasional* 2 (1970): 58.

Korner, Alexis. "Big Bill Broonzy: Some Personal Memories." *Jazz Journal* 11, no. 3 (March 1958): 1.

————. "Guitar Groove: A Guide to Blues Guitar." *Melody Maker,* February 17, 1968, 17.

Larkin, Colin, ed. *The Guinness Encyclopedia of Popular Music.* Enfield, Middlesex, UK: Guinness; New York: Stockton Press, 1995.

Leadbitter, Mike, and Neil Slaven. *Blues Records, 1943–1970.* London: Record Information Service, 1987.

Leeds, Morton. "The Process of Cultural Stripping and Reintegration: The Rural Migrant in the City." In *The Urban Experience and Folk Tradition,* edited by Americo Paredes and Ellen Stekert, 165–73. Austin: University of Texas Press, 1971.

Leiter, Robert D. *The Musicians and Petrillo.* New York: Bookman, 1953.

Levine, Lawrence. *Black Culture and Black Consciousness: Afro-American Thought from Slavery to Freedom.* New York: Oxford University Press, 1977.

Lines, George. Liner notes. *Boogie-Woogie Trio.* Storyville SLP 4006. 1976.

Lisenby, Foy. *Charles Hillman Brough.* Fayetteville: University of Arkansas Press, 1996.

Litwack, Leon. *Been in the Storm So Long: The Aftermath of Slavery.* New York: Knopf, 1979.

Lomax, Alan. *Blues in the Mississippi Night—The Story of the Recording.* CD booklet. *Blues in the Mississippi Night: Authentic Field Recordings of Negro Folk Music.* USA: Ryko-disc, RCD 90155, 1990. Original release was United Artists UAL 4027, 1959.

———. *Folksongs of North America.* New York: Doubleday, 1960.

———. "I Got the Blues." In *Mother Wit from the Laughing Barrel: Readings in the Inter-pretation of Afro-American Folklore,* edited by Alan Dundes. Englewood Cliffs: Pren-tice-Hall, 1972. Originally published in *Common Ground* 8, no. 4 (1948): 38–52.

———. *The Land Where the Blues Began.* New York: Pantheon Books, 1993.

Lott, Eric. *Love and Theft: Blackface Minstrelsy and the American Working Class.* Oxford: Oxford University Press, 1993.

Lyttelton, Humphrey. *I'm Sorry I Haven't a Clue's Humphrey Lyttelton in Conversation: Play as I Please.* BBC Audiobooks, 2009.

———. "There's No Argument—The Money Is Big Bill's." *Melody Maker,* September 6, 1958, 11.

MacLeod, R. R., transcriber. *Document Blues–2.* Edinburgh, Scotland: PAT, 1995; *Docu-ment Blues–4.* PAT, 1996. MacLeod transcribed the hundreds of recorded songs of prewar blues artists reissued on the Document, Blues Document, and Yazoo labels.

———. *Blues Document.* Edinburgh, Scotland: PAT, 1997.

———. *Yazoo 1–20.* Edinburgh, Scotland: PAT; *Yazoo 21–83.* PAT.

Mann, Woody. *Six Black Blues Guitarists.* New York: Oak, 1973.

Masters, Edgar Lee. *Spoon River Anthology.* New York: Collier Books, 1962.

"Maybe I'll Sing Again, Says Big Bill." *Melody Maker,* March 15, 1958, 1.

McCarthy, Albert J. "Discography of Big Bill Broonzy." *Jazz Forum* 4 (April 1947): 25–30.

McDevitt, Sean, and Jeffrey L. Perlah, "100 Years of the Blues: Prewar Vets." *Guitar* 15, no. 10 (August 1998): 34, 39, 43, 112.

McElvaine, Robert. *Down and Out in the Great Depression: Letters from the "Forgotten Man."* Chapel Hill: University of North Carolina Press, 1983.

———. *The Great Depression.* New York: Times Books, 1984.

McKee, Margaret, and Fred Chisenhall. *Beale Black & Blue.* Baton Rouge: Louisiana State University Press, 1981.

"Meet Bill Broonzy." *Melody Maker,* August 11, 1951, 9.

Melrose, Lester. "My Life in Recording." *American Folk Music Occasional* 2 (1970): 59–61.

Millard, Andre. *America on Record: A History of Recorded Sound.* Cambridge: Cambridge University Press, 1995.

Mitchell, Broadus. *Depression Decade: From New Era through New Deal, 1929–1941.* Vol. 9 of *The Economic History of the United States.* New York: Rinehart, 1947.

Morris, Ronald L. *Wait until Dark: Jazz and the Underworld, 1880–1940.* Bowling Green, Ky.: Bowling Green University Popular Press, 1980.

Murray, Albert. *The Omni-Americans.* New York: Outerbridge and Dienstfrey, 1970.

———. *Stomping the Blues.* New York: Da Capo Press, 1976.

———. *Train Whistle Guitar.* New York: Vintage Books, 1974.

Myrdal, Gunnar. *An American Dilemma.* Vols. 1 and 2. New York: Pantheon Books. 1944.

"Negro Conscription." In *Black Protest and the Great Migration.* edited by Eric Arnesen, 90–92. Boston: Bedford/St. Martin's, 2003. Originally published in *New Republic* 12, no. 155 (October 20, 1917): 317–18.

Oakley, Giles. *The Devil's Music.* New York: Da Capo Press, 1997.

Obrecht, Jas., ed. *Blues Guitarists from the Pages of "Guitar Player" Magazine.* Saratoga: Guitar Player Productions, 1975.

———. "The Legend of Big Bill Broonzy." *Guitar Player* 20, no. 8 (August 1986): 68–74.

Olaussen, Rune. "Big Bill Blues." *Orkester Journalen* 26 (January 1958): 13.

———. "Big Bill Broonzy dod." *Orkester Journalen* 26, no. 9 (September 1958): 4.

Odum, Howard W. *Rainbow round My Shoulder.* Indianapolis: Bobbs-Merrill, 1928.

Odum, Howard W., and Guy B. Johnson. *The Negro and His Songs.* Chapel Hill: University of North Carolina Press. 1925.

"Oh Freedom!" In *The Norton Anthology of African American Literature,* edited by Henry Louis Gates Jr. and Nellie Y. McKay. New York: Norton, 1997. ·

Oliver, Paul. *Bessie Smith.* Kings of Jazz series. New York: A. S. Barnes, 1961.

———. "Big Bill Broonzy and John Sellers." *Music Mirror* 4, no. 4 (May 1957). Reprinted as "Blues Backstage: With Big Bill and John Sellers," in *Blues off the Record* (Tunbridge Wells: Baton, 1984), 211–13.

———. "Big Maceo." In *The Art of Jazz,* edited by Martin Williams, 109–22. New York: Oxford University Press, 1959,

———. "Blues." In *The New Grove Gospel, Blues and Jazz,* 36–188. New York: Norton, 1986.

———. *Blues Fell This Morning.* Canto ed. Cambridge: Cambridge University Press, 1994.

———. *Blues off the Record: Thirty Years of Blues Commentary.* 1984. Reprint, New York: Da Capo Press, 1988.

———. "Blues to Drive the Blues Away." In *Jazz,* edited by Nat Hentoff and Albert J. McCarthy, 83–104. New York: Da Capo Press, 1974.

———."Gospel." In *The New Grove Gospel, Blues and Jazz,* 189–222. New York: Norton, 1986.

———. "Just a Dream: Big Bill Broonzy." In Oliver, *Blues off the Record,* 111–15. Tunbridge Wells: Baton Press, 1984.

———. "Sales Tax on It: Race Records in the New Deal Years." In *Nothing Else to Fear: New Perspectives on America in the Thirties,* edited by Stephen W. Baskerville and Ralph Willett, 198–211. Dover: Manchester University Press, 1985.

———. *Songster and Saints.* Cambridge: Cambridge University Press, 1984.

——. *The Story of the Blues.* Boston: Northeastern University Press, 1997.

——. Album notes. *Big Bill Broonzy 1927–1932.* Matchbox MSE 1004. 1985.

O'Neal, Jim. "Big Bill: Opening the Door to the Blues." *Living Blues,* no. 55 (November/ December 1982): 4–5.

——. "It's Just the Blues." CD booklet. *The Mercury Blues "N' Rhythm Story: 1945–1955,* 8–21. Mercury 3145282932. 1996.

Oster, Harry. *Living Country Blues.* Detroit: Folklore Associates, 1969.

Ottley, Roi. *The Lonely Warrior: The Life and Times of Robert S. Abbott.* Chicago: Regnery, 1955.

Panassié, Hugues. "Big Bill Doesn't Sell His Music—He Gives It Away." *Melody Maker,* September 15, 1951, 9.

——. "The Blues Singers." *Melody Maker,* May 10, 1952, 9.

Panassié, Hugues, and Madeleine Gautier. *Guide to Jazz.* Boston: Houghton Mifflin, 1956.

Panassié, Madeleine Gautier. "A propos de Big Bill Broonzy a Yannick et Margo Buynoghe." *Bulletin De Hot Club De France,* no. 283 (November 1980): 12–13.

Papo, Alfredo. "Big Bill en Barcelona." *Solo Blues* 1, no. 2 (Fall 1985): 18–19.

Parrish, Lydia. *Slave Songs of the Georgia Sea Islands.* New York: Creative Age Press, 1942.

Pastonesi, Marco. "Un blues del Mississippi: Big Bill Broonzy." *Musica Jazz* 37, no. 2 (February 1981): 11–14.

Paytress, Mark. *I Was There: Gigs That Changed the World.* London: Cassell Illustrated Books, 2005.

Pearson, Barry Lee. *Sounds So Good to Me: The Bluesman's Story.* Philadelphia: University of Pennsylvania Press, 1984.

Peretti, Burton W. *The Creation of Jazz: Music, Race, and Culture in Urban America.* Urbana: University of Illinois Press, 1992.

Peterson, Paul. "Big Bill Broonzy." *Jazz Report* 5, no. 5 (1966/67): 1.

Pytak, Jerry. "The Economics of Cotton Farming." *New International* 5, no. 4 (April 1939): 120–23; pt. 2, *New International* 5, no. 5. (May 1939): 144–48.

Randle, Bill. "Big Bill Broonzy: Last Session." *ABC TV Hootenanny* 1, no. 2 (April 1964): 24–25, 68–69.

——. Liner notes. *The Bill Broonzy Story.* USA: Verve MGV3000-5. 1999. Original release 1957.

Richardson, Herbert. "Black Workers and Their Responses to Work through the Songs They Sang." Ph.D diss., Rutgers University, 1987.

"Roosevelt Sykes par Big Bill Broonzy." *Bulletin Du Hot Club De France,* October 1966, 31–32.

Rosengarten, Theodore. *All God's Dangers: The Life of Nate Shaw.* New York: Vintage Books, 1989.

Rourke, Constance. "Traditions for a Negro Literature." In *The Roots of American Culture.* New York: Kennikat Press, 1965.

Rowe, Mike. *Chicago Breakdown*. New York: Da Capo Press, 1975.

Roxon, Lillian. *Lillian Roxon's Rock Encyclopedia*. New York: Grosset and Dunlap, 1969.

Russell, Tony, ed. "Big Bill Broonzy." *The Blues Collection*, no. 27 (1992).

Russell, William. "Three Boogie-Woogie Blues Pianists." In *The Art of Jazz*, edited by Martin Williams, 95–108. New York: Oxford University Press, 1959.

Rye, Howard. "Big Bill 1927 to 1947." *Collector's Item*, no.11 (April 1982): 9–12.

———. "Big Bill 1927 to 1947." *Collector's Item*, no. 57 (April 1991): 9–13.

Santelli, Robert. *The Big Book of Blues*. New York: Penguin, 1993.

Scanlon, Ann. "Story of the Blues." *Vox*, no. 28 (January 1993): 18.

Scott, Emmett. *The American Negro in the World War*. Chicago: Homewood, 1919.

Shaw, Arnold. *Honkers and Shakers: The Golden Years of Rhythm & Blues*. New York: Collier Books, 1978.

Shurman, Dick, et al. Introduction to CD booklet. *The Mercury Blues 'N' Rhythm Story: 1945–1955*, 4–7. Mercury 3145282932. 1996.

Sitkoff, Harvard. *A New Deal for Blacks*. Oxford: Oxford University Press, 1978.

Smith, Charles Edward. "Big Bill and the Country Blues." *Jazz Monthly* 3, no. 11 (January 1958): 7 10, 32.

———. "Big Bill Broonzy." *Jazz Monthly* 4, no. 9 (November 1958): 3.

Smith, Chris. *Hit the Right Lick: The Recordings of Big Bill Broonzy*. Bromham, UK: Blues & Rhythm Magazine, 1996.

———. "100 Years of Big Bill Broonzy." *Juke Blues*, no. 41 (1998): 41–44.

———. "State Street Boys, Alabama Rascals, See See Riders and Big Bill Broonzy." *Blues & Rhythm*, no. 77 (March 1993): 4–5.

Southern, Eileen. *Biographical Dictionary of Afro-American and African Musicians*. Westport, Ct.: Greenwood Press, 1982.

———. *The Music of Black Americans*. New York: Norton, 1983.

Spear, Allan H. *Black Chicago: The Making of a Ghetto, 1890–1920*. Chicago: University of Chicago Press, 1967.

Spivey, Donald. *Union and the Black Musicians: The Narrative of William Everett Samuels and Chicago Local 208*. Lanham, Md.: University Press of America, 1984.

Springer, Robert. "Le blue moderne." In *Le blues authentique: Son histoire et ses themes*, 161–212. Paris: Filipacchi, 1985.

Stambler, Irwin, and Grelun Landon. *Encyclopedia of Folk, Country, and Western Music*. New York: St. Martin's Press, 1969.

Stewart-Baxter, Derrick. "Blues in the Country." *Jazz Journal* 12, no. 4 (April 1959): 3–4.

———. "Lightly and Politely: About Big Bill Broonzy." *Jazz Journal* 4, no. 11 (November 1951): 2.

———. "Preachin' the Blues." *Jazz Journal* 4, no. 10 (October 1951): 3.

——— "Preachin' the Blues." *Jazz Journal* 4, no. 11 (November 1951): 13–14.

———. "Preachin' the Blues." *Jazz Journal* 5, no. 2 (February 1952): 8–9.

Steiner, John. "Chicago." In *Jazz*, edited by Nat Hentoff and Albert J. McCarthy, 137–70. New York: Da Capo Press, 1974.

Summerfield, Maurice J. *The Jazz Guitar.* Gateshead: Ashley Mark, 1978.

Surge, Frank. *Singers of the Blues.* Minneapolis: Lerner, 1969.

Szwed, John F. "Negro Music: Urban Renewal." In *Our Living Traditions: An Introduction to American Folklore,* edited by Tristram Potter Coffin, 272–82. New York: Basic Books, 1968.

Taft, Michael. *Blues Lyric Poetry.* New York: Garland, 1983.

Terkel, Studs. "Big Bill Broonzy." *Jazz Journal* 11, no. 5 (May 1958): 33–36.

———. "Big Bill's Last Session." *Jazz Journal* 11, no. 11 (October 1958): 9–18. Reprinted in *Guitar Player* 7, no. 3 (April 1973): 20, 41–44.

———. "On Big Bill and the Blues." *Jazz Review,* no. 1 (December 1958): 28–29.

Testoni, Giancarlo. "Il mondo del blues." *Musica Jazz* 21, no. 6 (June 1965): 24–26; *Musica Jazz* 21, no. 11 (November 1965): 14–16.

Titon, Jeff Todd. *Downhome Blues Lyrics.* Urbana: University of Illinois Press, 1990.

Toll, Robert. *Blacking Up: The Minstrel Show in Nineteenth Century America.* Oxford: Oxford University Press, 1974.

Tooze, Sandra. *Muddy Waters: The Mojo Man.* Toronto: ECW Press, 1997.

Tracy, Steven. *Write Me a Few of Your Lines: A Blues Reader.* Amherst: University of Massachusetts Press, 1999.

Tuttle, William M. *Race Riot: Chicago in the Red Summer of 1919.* Urbana: University of Illinois Press, 1996.

Van Gennep, Arnold. *The Rites of Passage.* Chicago: University of Chicago Press, 1960.

van Rijn, Guido. *Roosevelt's Blues.* Jackson: University Press of Mississippi Press, 1997.

———. Liner notes. *Too Late, Too Late: More Newly Discovered Titles & Alternate Takes.* Document vol. 11, DOCD 5625. 1998.

Vasset, Andre. *Black Brother: La vie & l'oeuvre de Big Bill Broonzy, chanteur, guitariste et personnalite capitale du monde du blues.* France: Decombat, 1996.

Vincent, Ted. "The Social Context of Black Swan Records." In *Write Me a Few of Your Lines,* edited by Steven C. Tracey. Amherst: University of Massachusetts Press, 1999.

Voce, Steve. "Big Bill in Concert." *Jazz Journal* 15, no. 3 (March 1962): 8–10.

Wald, Elijah. *Escaping the Delta: Robert Johnson and the Invention of the Blues.* New York: Amistad, 2005.

———. *Josh White: Society Blues.* Amherst: University of Massachusetts, 2000.

Washington, Booker T. *Up from Slavery.* Oxford: Oxford University Press, 1995.

Watkins, T. H. *The Great Depression: America in the 1930s.* Boston: Little, Brown, 1993.

"Weep No More: Photo-Editorial." *Ebony,* November 1958, 54.

Weisbrot, Robert. *Father Divine: The Utopian Evangelist of the Depression Era Who Became an American Legend.* Boston: Beacon Press, 1983.

Welding, Pete. "Big Bill Reconsidered." *Saturday Review,* February 14, 1970, 62–63.

Wharton, Vernon Lane. *The Negro in Mississippi, 1865–1890.* New York: Harper Torchbooks, 1947.

White, Joseph L. *The Psychology of Blacks: An Afro-American Perspective.* Englewood Cliffs: Prentice Hall, 1984.

White, Walter. "The Race Conflict in Arkansas." In *Black Protest and the Great Migration*, edited by Eric Arnesen, 173–177. Boston: Bedford/St. Martin's, 2003. Originally published in *Survey* 43, no. 7 (13 December 1919): 233–34.

Whiteis, David. "The Blues as Real Life." *Down Beat*, October 1990, 44.

Whitman, Walt. *Leaves of Grass: The "Death-Bed" Edition*. New York: Modern Library, 1993.

Williams, Raymond. *The Sociology of Culture*. Chicago: University of Chicago Press, 1981.

Wilson, Mark R., Stephen R. Porter, and Janice L. Reiff. "American Car & Foundry Co." www.encyclopedia.chicagohistory.org.

Wolfe, Charles, and Kip Lornell. *Life and Legend of Leadbelly*. New York: Harper Collins, 1993.

Wolters, Raymond. *Negroes and the Great Depression*. Westport, Ct.: Greenwood, 1970.

Wright, Richard. *American Hunger*. New York: Perennial Library, 1977.

———. *12 Million Black Voices*. New York: Thunder's Mouth Press, 1944.

Wynn, Neil. *From Progressivism to Prosperity: World War I and American Society*. New York: Holmes and Meier, 1986.

Yurchenco, Henrietta. "Three Giants of Folk Music." *Sing Out!* 12, no. 3 (1962): 57.

Films Consulted

Big Bill Broonzy and Roosevelt Sykes. 1956. Directed by Jean Delire. VHS Masters of the Country Blues. Yazoo 518. 1995.

Chicago Blues. Directed by Harley Corkliss. Vest-DVD 13095. 1995.

Goin' to Chicago. Directed by George King. VHS. University of Mississippi, 1994.

Legends of Country Blues Guitar (episode on Bill Broonzy). Directed by Pete Seeger. VHS. Vestapol Productions, 1994.

Red, White, and Blues. Directed by Mike Figgis. DVD. *Martin Scorsese Presents the Blues: A Musical Journey*, vol. 7. Sony Music, 2003.

Interviews by the Author

Armstrong, Howard (1930s blues musician). Telephone, Fall 2002.

Black, Timuel (Chicago historian). Chicago, June 22, 1994.

Bourne, St. Clair (New York City journalist). New York City, June 28, 1995, and by telephone, November 11, 1995.

Hancock, John (organizer Southern Tenant Farmers Union). Telephone, June 1991.

Hayes, Charles (Chicago congressman and meatpacker organizer). Chicago, June 21, 1994.

March, Robert (Chicago acquaintance of Bill Broonzy and labor historian). Chicago, May 29, 2009, and by email, June 1–2, 2009.

Murray, Albert Murray (jazz writer and historian). New York City, February 3, 2000.

Oliver, Paul (blues historian and acquaintance of Bill Broonzy). Cambridge, Mass., February 8, 2007.

Seeger, Pete (folk musician and acquaintance of Bill Broonzy). Telephone, March 13, 2000.

Stith, George (organizer Southern Tenant Farmers Union). Gould, Ark., June 5, 1991.

Terkel, Studs (Chicago radio host, historian, and acquaintance of Bill Broonzy). Telephone, June 24, 1997 and August 23, 2000, and in Chicago on May 30, 2002.

Travis, Dempsey (Chicago historian and businessman). Chicago, June 16, 1994.

INDEX

Carr, Leroy, 108
Carter, Louis, 38
Casey, Antonio, 124
Casimir, Bill, 123
"CCC Blues," 110
"Cell Bound Blues" (Rainey), 59
Cermak, Anton, 82
"Chain Gang Blues" (Arnold), 46
"Chain Gang Blues" (Rainey), 46
Chatman, Peter (Memphis Slim), 50, 107, 116, 125, 128–29, 147, 151
cheating, 56, 57–58
Chess, Leonard, 124
Chess, Phil, 124
Chess Records, 124–25
Chicago: aid agencies for migrants, 63; bars and speakeasies, 68–69; black musicians attracted to, 64–66; black population of, 60; Broonzy debut as band leader in, 104; Broonzy's arrival in, 59–60; final performances for black audiences in, 125–26; housing segregation, 61–62; KAM Temple benefit, 150–51; Maxwell Street, 66–67; Old Town School of Folk Music, 151; population density, South Side, 89; prostitution in, 86–87; race riot (1919), 62; reaction of white and black natives to migrants, 61–63; rent-party circuit, 67–68; residential segregation, 88–89; road shows in, 64–65; Roosevelt College folk concert (1957), 149; South Side entertainment district, 64, 69–70, 79–80; South Side ghetto community, 60; "Spend Your Money Where You Can Work" campaign, 90; studio sessions dominated by, 107; Studs Terkel in, 133; unemployment in, 82; white audiences in, 135–36; work in, 60
Chicago Black Swans, 108–9
"Chicago Breakdown," 115
Chicago Commission on Race Relations, 62
Chicago Defender, 50–51
Chicago Federation of Musicians (CFM), 66, 69, 95–96, 156
"Chicago Mill Blues" (Wheatstraw), 96–97
Chicago Music Company, 71
"Chicken Reel, The," 24
childhood of Broonzy: birth story, 10–11; farm-

ing jobs, 13–14; move from Louisiana to Mississippi Delta, 9–10; siblings, 10; transition to adulthood, 13–14; youth in Arkansas, 12–15
child performers during Depression, 80
chord structures, 147
Chris Barber Band, 152
churches. See religion and the church
cigar-box fiddle, 20–21, 24
cigarettes, 149
Circle Pines camp (Michigan), 150
Civilian Conservation Corps (CCC), 94–95
civil rights activism, 124, 145
Civil Works Administration (CWA), 92
Clapton, Eric, 143, 145, 152
Clay, Francis, 153
coal mining, 14–15
Cobb, E. C., 100
cocaine, 110
Coffin, Tristram Potter, 212n28
colorism, 8–9, 154
Columbia, 103
Columbia Broadcasting System (CBS), 114, 127
Colyer, Ken, 152
"Come On In," 101
complexion, 8–9, 154
Compton, Glover, 64
Consolidated Film Industries, 104, 114
convict lease system, 45–46
Cooper, Jack, 125
Cooper, Lee, 125
Copeland, Aaron, 131, 136
"Corn-Stalk Fiddle, The" (Dunbar), 16
cornstalk instruments, 16
corporations: industrial capitalism, rise of, 11–12; WWI and, 28–29. See also recording industry
correspondence with Bruynoghe, 145–46
cotton agriculture: black draft, opposition to, 29–30; boll weevil infestation, 41–42; economic changes and, 12, 14; Great Depression and, 80–81; tenancy system and, 40. See also sharecropping, tenancy, and post-Bellum plantations
Cotton Belt, 12
"Cotton Chopping' Blues," 115